Collins New Primary Maths

Homework Pack 3

Series Editor: Peter Clarke

Authors: Jeanette Mumford, Sandra Roberts, Andrew Edmondson

William Collins' dream of knowledge for all began with the publication of his first book in 1819. A self-educated mill worker, he not only enriched millions of lives, but also founded a flourishing publishing house. Today, staying true to this spirit, Collins books are packed with inspiration, innovation and practical expertise. They place you at the centre of a world of possibility and give you exactly what you need to explore it.

Collins. Freedom to teach.

Published by Collins
An imprint of HarperCollinsPublishers
77 – 85 Fulham Palace Road
Hammersmith
London
W6 8JB

Browse the complete Collins catalogue at
www.collinseducation.com

10 9

ISBN-978-0-00-722024-3

The authors assert their moral rights to be identified as the authors of this work

British Library Cataloguing in Publication Data
A Catalogue record for this publication is available from the British Library

Cover design by Laing&Carroll
Cover artwork by Jonatronix Ltd
Internal design by Steve Evans and Mark Walker Design
Illustrations by Steve Evans and Mark Walker
Edited by Jean Rustean
Proofread by Ros Davies

Printed and bound by Martins the Printers, Berwick-upon-Tweed

Mixed Sources
Product group from well-managed
forests and other controlled sources
www.fsc.org Cert no. SW-COC-1806
© 1996 Forest Stewardship Council

FSC is a non-profit international organisation established to promote the responsible management of the world's forests. Products carrying the FSC label are independently certified to assure consumers that they come from forests that are managed to meet the social, economic and ecological needs of present and future generations.

Find out more about HarperCollins and the environment at
www.harpercollins.co.uk/green

Contents

Unit D2

Unit E2

Unit A3

Unit B3

Contents

Name _____ Date _____

Lunch queue order

- **Read, write and order numbers**

Martin (1st)   Joe   Dem   Sam   Paul   Deb   Harry   Mei   Pip   Liam   Ann   Hannah

Write the name of the person in these positions:

a _____ second   **b** _____ 10th   **c** _____ fifth

d _____ 8th   **e** _____ eleventh   **f** _____ 3rd

g _____ 12th   **h** _____ sixth   **i** _____ 4th

1 Write the positions of the girls, using numbers, for example, 9th.

2 Write the positions of the boys, using words, for example, second.

3 Write the first twenty positions, using numbers and words, for example first (1st), second (2nd) …

Collins New Primary Maths

Name _____ Date _____

Find the multiple

- **Count on in steps of 3, 4 or 5 from any small number**

■

	2			
	7			
11				
16				
	32			
			39	
				50

a Fill in the missing numbers to complete the grid. Colour all the multiples of 5.

b Look at each of the numbers below. Write the multiple of 5 that is closest to, but not more than each number.

10 → 10   47 → ☐   16 → ☐

26 → ☐   33 → ☐   52 → ☐

41 → ☐   28 → ☐   38 → ☐

1

1	2	3
4		
		30

a Fill in the missing numbers to complete the grid. Colour all the multiples of 3.

b Look at each of the numbers below. Write the multiple of 3 that is closest to, but not more than each number.

16 → 15   13 → ☐   11 → ☐

5 → ☐   28 → ☐   8 → ☐

24 → ☐   31 → ☐   19 → ☐

2

1			
5		7	
9			
13			16
17			
21			
		27	
		31	
			40

a Fill in the missing numbers to complete the grid. Colour all the multiples of 4.

b Look at each of the numbers below. Write the multiple of 4 that is closest to, but not more than each number.

7 → 4   43 → ☐   30 → ☐

35 → ☐   16 → ☐   19 → ☐

21 → ☐   27 → ☐   14 → ☐

Collins
New
Primary
Maths

Name _____ Date _____

Pick up 10s

- **Recall pairs of 10 that total 100**

 A game for 2 players.

How to play:

- Shuffle the cards and spread them out on the table.
- Take turns to turn over two cards.
- If they add up to 100, the player keeps them.
- If the cards do not add up to 100, place them face down again in the same place.
- Continue until all the cards have been won. The player with the most pairs is the winner.

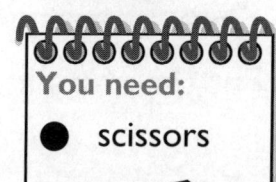

You need:
- scissors

30	50	80	100
20	50	70	0
20	40	70	90
10	40	60	90
10	30	60	80

Make another set of cards with multiples of 5 that add up to 100 then play again.

Collins New Primary Maths

Name _____ Date _____

Catching stars

- **Add mentally combinations of one-digit and two-digit numbers**

■ Put the stars in the pot and make a new star number.

▲ On the back of this sheet, complete the following calculation in five different ways:

☐ 6 + 7 = ☐ ☐

Collins
New
Primary
Maths

Name _____ Date _____

Face the facts

- **Recall all addition and subtraction facts for each number to 20**

Write out the addition and subtraction facts for three other numbers from 13 to 20. Draw a ☺ next to the ones you know by heart. Draw a * next to about ten that you need to learn. Ask someone at home to test you.

12	
12 + 0 = 12	12 – 0 = 12
11 + 1 = 12	12 – 1 = 11
10 + 2 = 12	12 – 2 = 10
9 + 3 = 12	12 – 3 = 9
8 + 4 = 12	12 – 4 = 8
7 + 5 = 12	12 – 5 = 7
6 + 6 = 12	12 – 6 = 6

Ask someone at home to test you on your facts. Can you say each answer in less than 3 seconds?

Collins
New
Primary
Maths

Name _____ Date _____

That's odd!

● **Recognise odd and even numbers to 100**

 **Instructions**

- ● Choose a coloured pencil each.
- ● One player is odd, one player is even.
- ● Take turns to roll the dice.
- ● Starting at 1, move your playing piece the correct number of spaces.
- ● If the even player lands on an even number, colour the square. If not, leave it blank.
- ● If the odd player lands on an odd number, colour the square. If not, leave it blank.
- ● Continue until the even player reaches 100 and the odd player reaches 9*
- ● The player with the most squares coloured is the winner.

You need:

- ● playing piece (per player)
- ● 1–6 dice
- ● coloured pencil (per player)

1	2	3	4	5	6	7	8	9	10
11	12	13	14	15	16	17	18	19	20
21	22	23	24	25	26	27	28	29	30
31	32	33	34	35	36	37	38	39	40
41	42	43	44	45	46	47	48	49	50
51	52	53	54	55	56	57	58	59	60
61	62	63	64	65	66	67	68	69	70
71	72	73	74	75	76	77	78	79	80
81	82	83	84	85	86	87	88	89	90
91	92	93	94	95	96	97	98	99	100

 Play the game as described in the  section but start at 100.
Continue until the even player reaches 2 and the odd player reaches 1.

Collins
New
Primary
Maths

Name _____ Date _____

Revising × 2, × 5, × 10

- **Know by heart multiplication facts for the 2, 5 and 10 times tables**

Multiply the numbers in the first column by the number at the top.
Write the answer in the second column.

a × 5

7	35
3	
2	
8	
1	
6	
5	
9	
4	
10	

b × 2

4	
1	
7	
5	
9	
10	
2	
6	
8	
3	

c × 10

6	
2	
3	
7	
10	
8	
5	
1	
9	
4	

Write the missing numbers in each of these grids.

×	2	5	10
3			
4			
6			
7			
8			
9			

×					
2	4		6		
5		25			50
10				60	80

Collins New Primary Maths

Name _____ · Date _____

Multiples of 2, 5 and 10

- ● **Recognise two-digit and three-digit multiples of 2, 5 or 10**

a Colour all the numbers that are multiples of 5.

72	237	450	15
310	85	46	125
225	141	20	38

b Colour all the numbers that are multiples of 2.

216	80	101
25	22	69
138	16	207
164	33	448

c Colour all the numbers that are multiples of 10.

20	80	93	327
95	52	50	460
100	11	130	270

Find your way to the secret cave by writing the correct sequence by the footprints. Write the final number on the diamond.

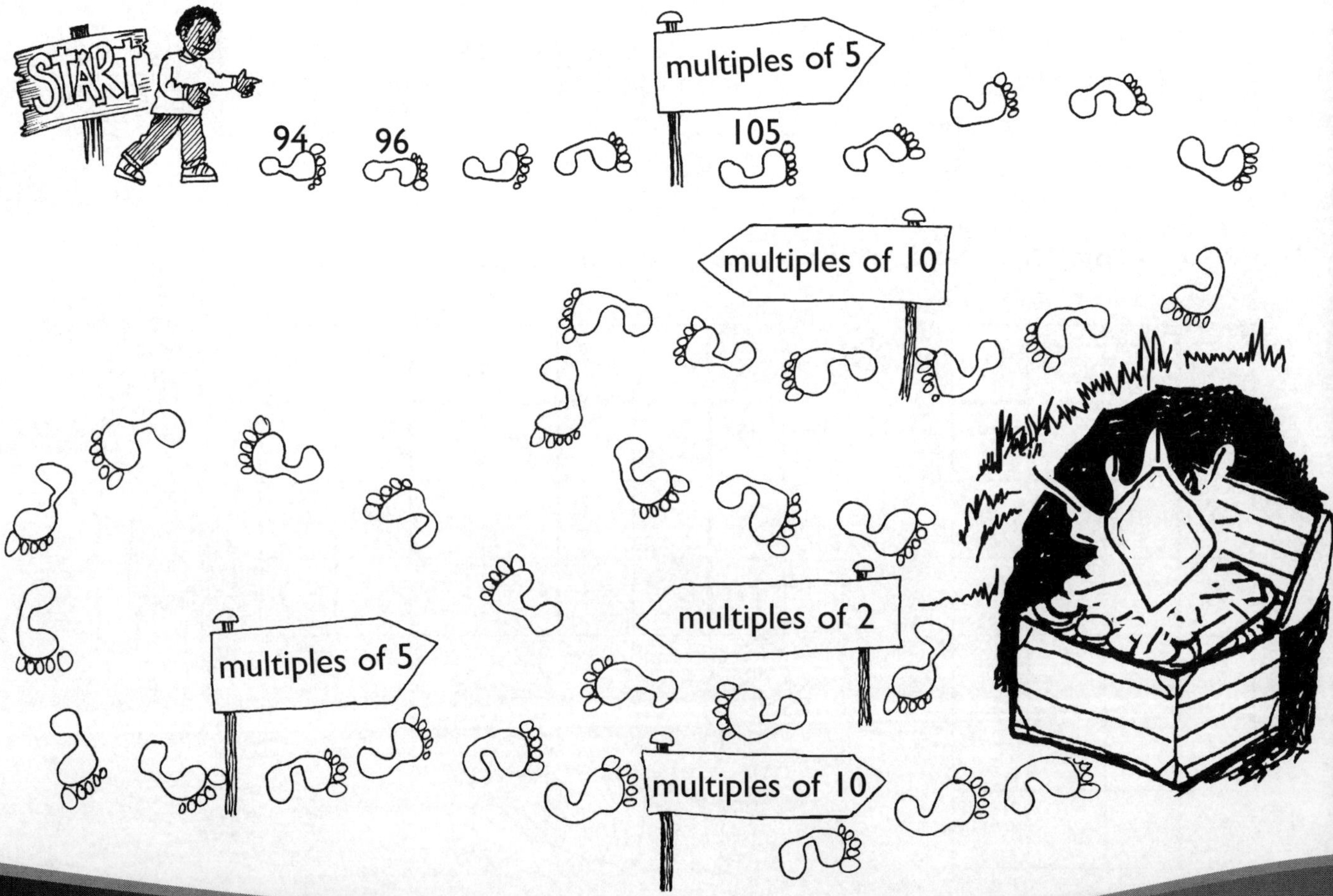

START

94   96

multiples of 5

105

multiples of 10

multiples of 5

multiples of 2

multiples of 10

Name _____ Date _____

Household shapes

• **Name and describe 3-D shapes**

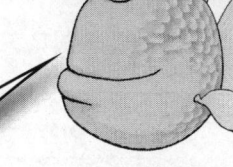

Find some containers in your kitchen which have these bases:

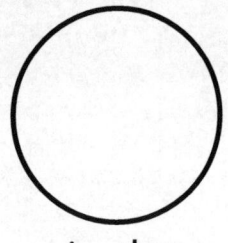  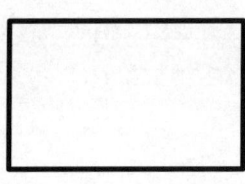 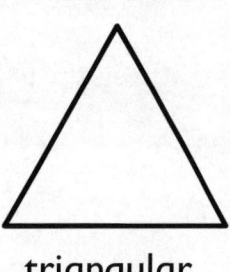

circular   square   rectangular   triangular

You need:
● household containers

Take each container and arrange them into 4 sets according to their base shape. Ask someone at home to check.

Tick the columns which describe the container.

Object	Base ⬭	Base ◻	Base ▭	Base △	is a prism
1 carton of juice			✔		✔
2 bottle of sauce	✔				✗
3					
4					
5					
6					
7					

Which type of base shape do most objects have? Why do you think this is? Write your explanation on the back of this sheet.

© Collins
New
Primary
Maths

Name _____ Date _____

Cutting corners (1)

● **Solve a puzzle about shapes**

'By joining the two pieces, edge to edge, you can make at least 6 different shapes.' Investigate.

You need:
● scissors
● ruler

Carefully cut out the square at the bottom of the sheet. Now cut along the dotted line so that you have two shapes. Join the shapes, edge to edge, to make new shapes. Ask someone at home to check.

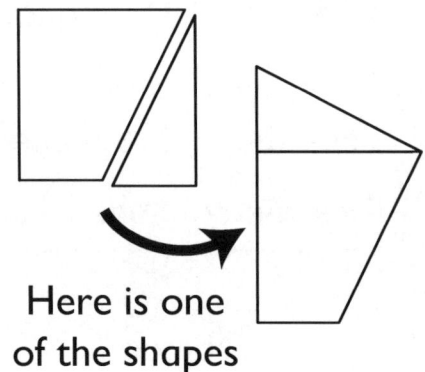

Here is one of the shapes

Draw the different shapes that you make.

Can you find more than six? Use the back of the sheet if necessary.

I made these shapes.

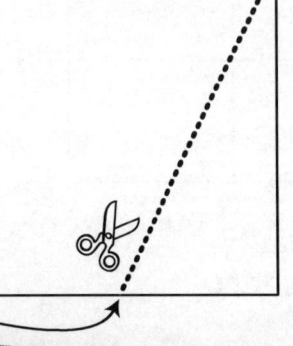

Halfway along side

An extra square if you need it

Collins
New
Primary
Maths

Name _____ Date _____

Candle lengths

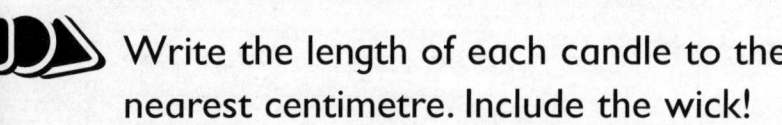

- **Read scales to the nearest division**

 Write the length of each candle to the nearest centimetre. Include the wick!

 Complete these sentences.

a Candle F is about [ ] cm longer than candle A.

b Candle E is about [ ] cm longer than candle C.

c Candle B is about [ ] cm shorter than candle D.

d Candle A is about [ ] cm shorter than candle E.

A is about [ ] cm long

B is about [ ] cm long

C is about [ ] cm long

D is about [ ] cm long

E is about [ ] cm long

F is about [ ] cm long

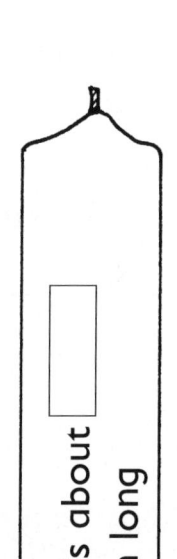
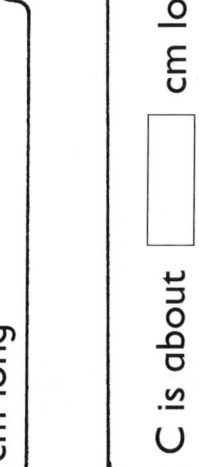
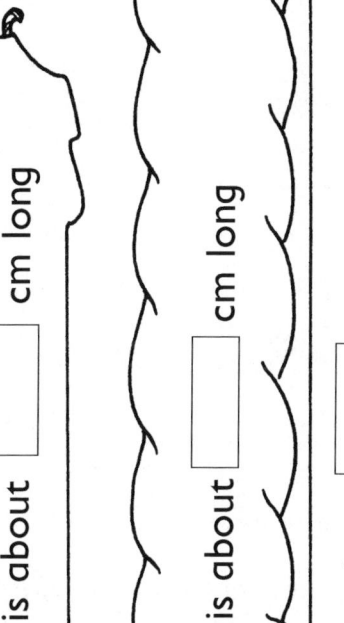
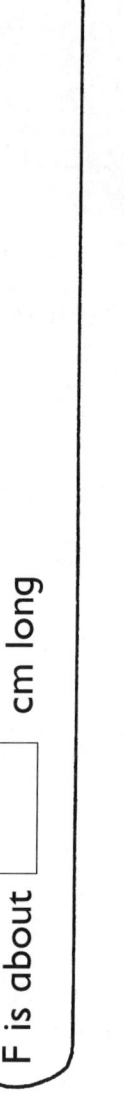

19
18
17
16
15
14
13
12
11
10
9
8
7
6
5
4
3
2
1
cm

When lit, Candle E will burn for 4 hours.

Write the length of the candle, to the nearest centimetre, after it has burned for I hour.

Collins
New
Primary
Maths

Name _____ Date _____

Tableware

- **Show what was found out using tables and diagrams**

Count the cups, mugs, dinner plates and drinking glasses that your family uses regularly. Write the totals in the table.

Tableware	Number
Cup	
Mug	
Dinner plate	
Drinking glass	

1 Complete the bar chart to show the tableware your family regularly uses.

2 Which are there more of: dinner plates or mugs?

How many more?

3 Write a sentence about the information displayed in your bar chart.

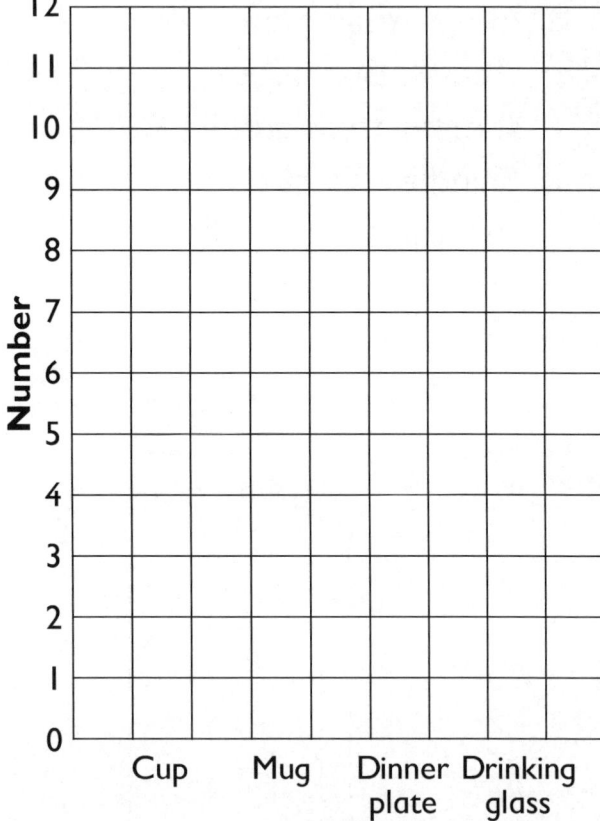

Tableware we use regularly

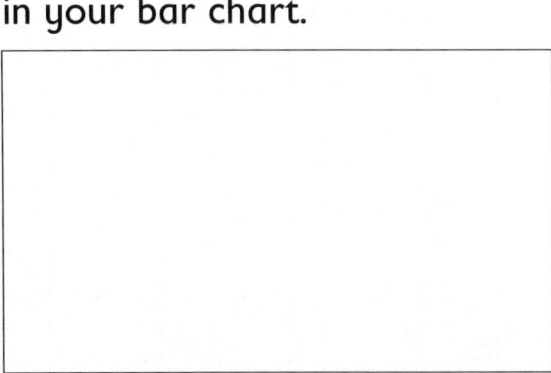

1 Count the knives, forks, dessert spoons and teaspoons your family uses regularly. Write the totals in a table.

2 Draw a bar chart to show the information.

3 Write a sentence about the information displayed in your bar chart.

You need:

- squared paper
- ruler

Collins
New
Primary
Maths

Name _____Date _____

Car boot sale

- **Show information using tables, pictograms and bar charts**

 Count the books, T-shirts and dolls. Complete the table.

You need:
- ruler

	Number
Books	
T-shirts	
Dolls	

 1 Draw a pictogram to show the things for sale.
Think of a simple picture to stand for the dolls, books and T-shirts.
Draw a picture for every two things for sale.
Write a key for your pictogram.

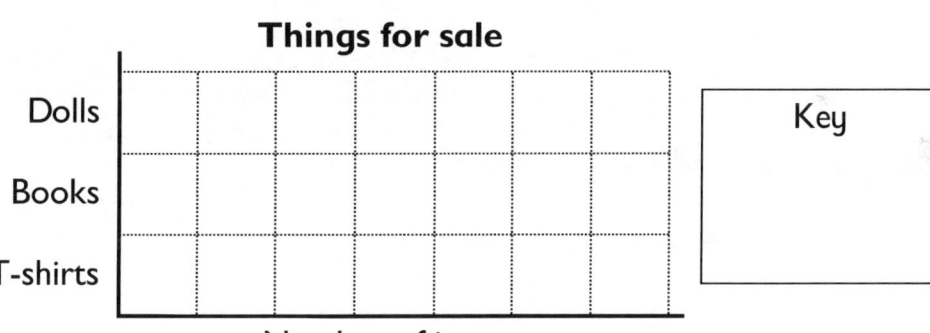

Things for sale

Dolls

Books

T-shirts

Number of items

Key

2 Use the information in your pictogram to answer these questions.

a How many dolls are for sale?

b How many T-shirts are for sale?

c Which is the most common thing for sale?

d How many more books than dolls are there?

e How many things for sale are not dolls?

f How many things are for sale altogether?

On the back of this sheet, draw a bar chart for the data.

Collins
New
Primary
Maths

Name _____ Date _____

Fresh food

- Use Venn diagrams to sort data and objects using one criterion

Food	Tick
Fruit	
Vegetable	
Dairy product	
Meat	
Other	

■ Make a tick for each item of fresh food in your house.

● 1 Using the table above, make a tick in the Venn diagram for each food item.

2 How many pieces of fruit are there? ▢

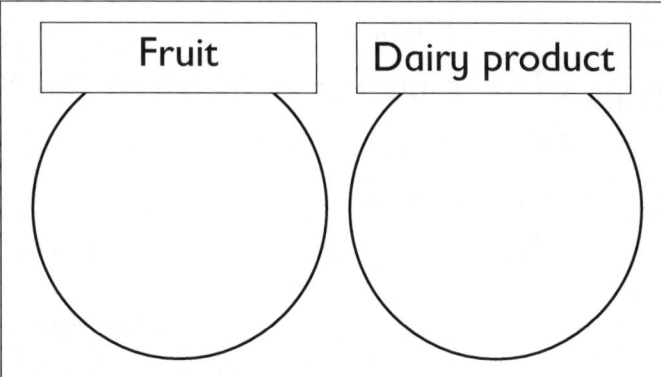

Fruit   Dairy product

3 How many dairy products are there? ▢

4 How many other items of fresh food are there? ▢

5 Write two sentences about the information in your diagram.

▲ 1 On the back of this sheet, make your own Venn diagram for the table of data.

2 Write two sentences about the information in your diagram.

Collins
New
Primary
Maths

Name _____ Date _____

Problems at home

- **Solve one-step and two-step problems involving numbers**

Work out these word problems. Show all your working.

a I have 3 dogs. Each dog eats 4 tins of food a week. How many tins do I buy each week?

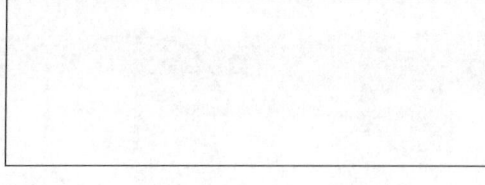

b Each twin received 18 birthday cards. How many did they receive altogether?

c I have grown 3 flowers. Each flower has 7 petals. How many petals are there altogether?

a Dad cooked 24 cakes. His 3 children ate 5 cakes each. How many cakes were left?

b I invited 16 friends to my party. Half of them couldn't come. Mum made 4 sandwiches for each friend at the party. How many sandwiches did she make?

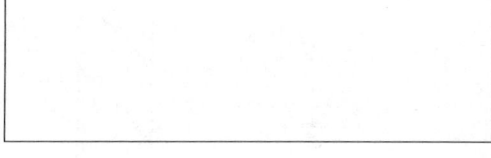

c Every week we eat 4 packets of crisps each. Mum buys 24 packets of crisps a week. How many people are in our family?

If I buy a bag of 50 sweets and I eat 3 a week, for how many weeks will I have 3 sweets?

How many more will I need for one more week?

Collins
New
Primary
Maths

Name _____ Date _____

Fraction tiles

- **Find unit fractions**

☐ Write the fraction shaded, in words and numbers.

a 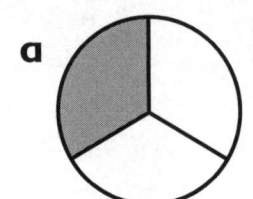 **b** 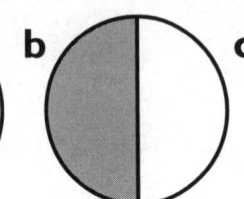 **c** 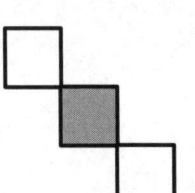 **d e**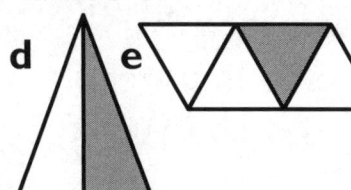

You need:
- colouring materials

| one third | $\frac{1}{3}$ | | | | | | | |

⬤ **I** Colour the fraction shown.

a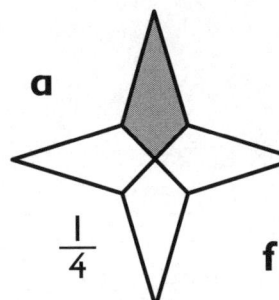
$\frac{1}{4}$

b
$\frac{1}{3}$

c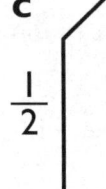
$\frac{1}{2}$

d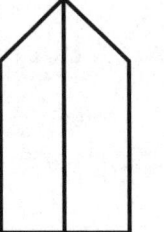
$\frac{1}{3}$

e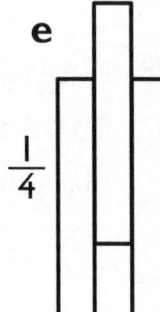
$\frac{1}{4}$

f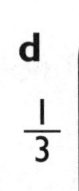
$\frac{1}{2}$

g
$\frac{1}{4}$

h
$\frac{1}{3}$

2 Circle the fraction of tiles shown and then fill in the box.

a

b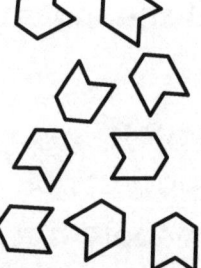

c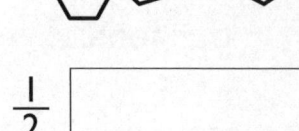

$\frac{1}{4}$ | $\frac{1}{4}$ of 8 is 2

$\frac{1}{3}$ |

$\frac{1}{2}$ |

△ On the back of this sheet, draw a shape and colour $\frac{1}{2}$.
Repeat for these fractions: $\frac{1}{3}$, $\frac{1}{4}$, $\frac{2}{3}$, $\frac{3}{4}$.

Collins
New
Primary
Maths

Name _____ Date _____

Which standard unit?

- **Choose suitable units to estimate or measure length**

Circle the standard unit you are most likely to measure:

a the length of your bed   cm   m   km

b the height of your house   cm   m   km

c the width of your front door   cm   m   km

d the thickness of a sandwich   cm   m   km

e the depth of a drawer   cm   m   km

f the distance to Big Ben   cm   m   km

I   Write two more things you would measure using kilometres.

a the distance from London to New York.

b the distance between [_____]

c [_____]

2   Write two more things that could be measured using metres.

a the depth of water in a swimming pool

b the height of [_____]

c the length of [_____]

3   Write two more things you would measure using centimetres.

a the length of your shoe

b the width of a [_____]

c the width of a [_____]

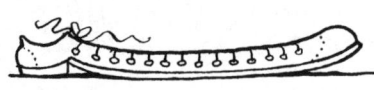

Write the best estimate from the box for:

a the length of a passenger train [_____]

b the height of a railway tunnel [_____]

c the distance between 2 railway stations [_____]

d the length of a passenger's train ticket [_____]

10 km
10 m
100 m
10 cm
I m

Collins
New
Primary
Maths

Name _____ Date _____

Money boxes

- Describe the position of a square on a grid

 **Instructions**

Place the coins on the grid so that:

- there is a coin in each row and column
- no two coins of the same value are next to each other either horizontally (⇔) or vertically (⇕).

You need:
- 4 × 1p coins
- 4 × 2p coins
- 4 × 5p coins
- 4 × 10p coins

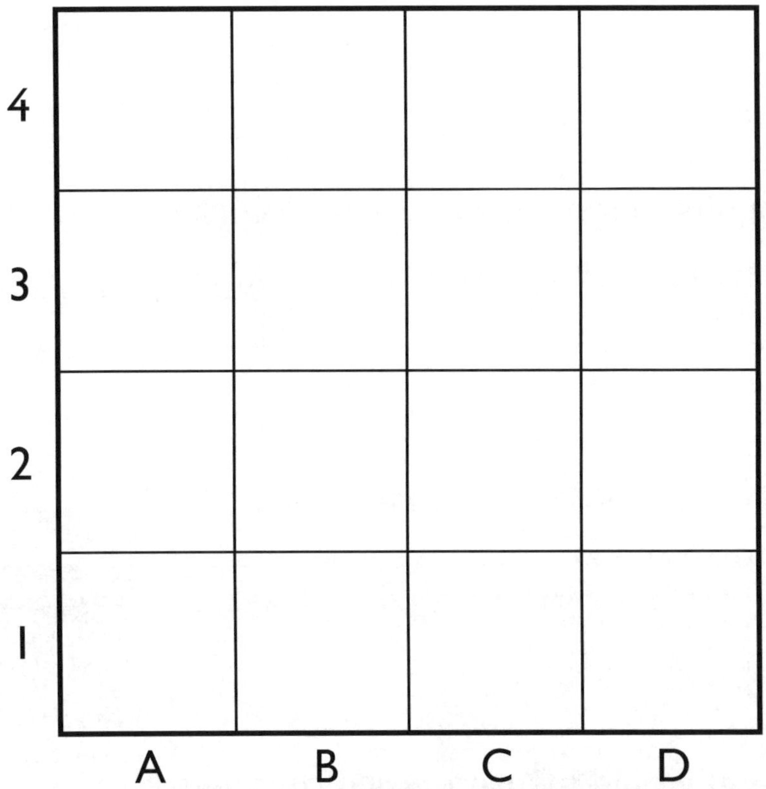

Remember

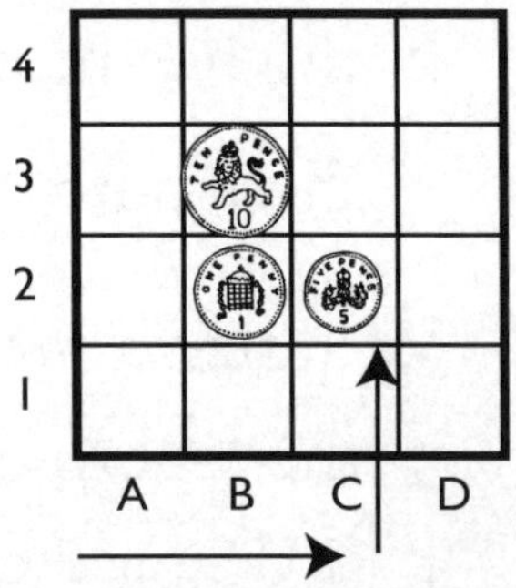

Across first, then up.
5p is in square C2

 Now complete these sentences for your grid.

a The 1p coins are in squares ☐ , ☐ , ☐ and ☐ .

b The 2p coins are in squares ☐ , ☐ , ☐ and ☐ .

c The 5p coins are in squares ☐ , ☐ , ☐ and ☐ .

d The 10p coins are in squares ☐ , ☐ , ☐ and ☐ .

Collins
New
Primary
Maths

Name _____ Date _____

Number pairs

Find the pairs of numbers that total 10. Circle them and then work out the answer to the whole sum.

a ⑥ + 11 + ④ = $\boxed{21}$
     10

b 5 + 2 + 5 = ☐

c 7 + 3 + 8 = ☐

d 5 + 2 + 8 = ☐

e 7 + 9 + 1 = ☐

f 5 + 5 + 6 = ☐

a 9 + 7 + 2 + 1 = ☐

b 5 + 1 + 9 + 5 = ☐

c 1 + 3 + 7 + 8 = ☐

d 5 + 7 + 5 + 3 = ☐

e 1 + 8 + 7 + 2 = ☐

f 4 + 0 + 6 + 10 = ☐

Can we use this strategy to make subtraction calculations easier? Explain your answer.

☐

Collins
New
Primary
Maths

Name _____ Date _____

Cloud subtraction

● **Know subtraction facts for each number to 20**

■ Write the answers to these subtraction calculations as quickly as you can.

a 8 – 3 = ☐

b 7 – 4 = ☐

c 6 – 2 = ☐

d 9 – 3 = ☐

e 10 – 1 = ☐

f 15 – 5 = ☐

g 6 – 3 = ☐

h 9 – 4 = ☐

i 17 – 1 = ☐

j 20 – 2 = ☐

● Write the answers to these subtraction calculations as quickly as you can.

a 15 – 4 = ☐

b 18 – 5 = ☐

c 20 – 6 = ☐

d 19 – 8 = ☐

e 13 – 5 = ☐

f 12 – 7 = ☐

g 15 – 8 = ☐

h 11 – 9 = ☐

i 17 – 9 = ☐

j 14 – 6 = ☐

▲ On the back of this sheet, write out the multiple of ten calculations that go with each question in the ● section.

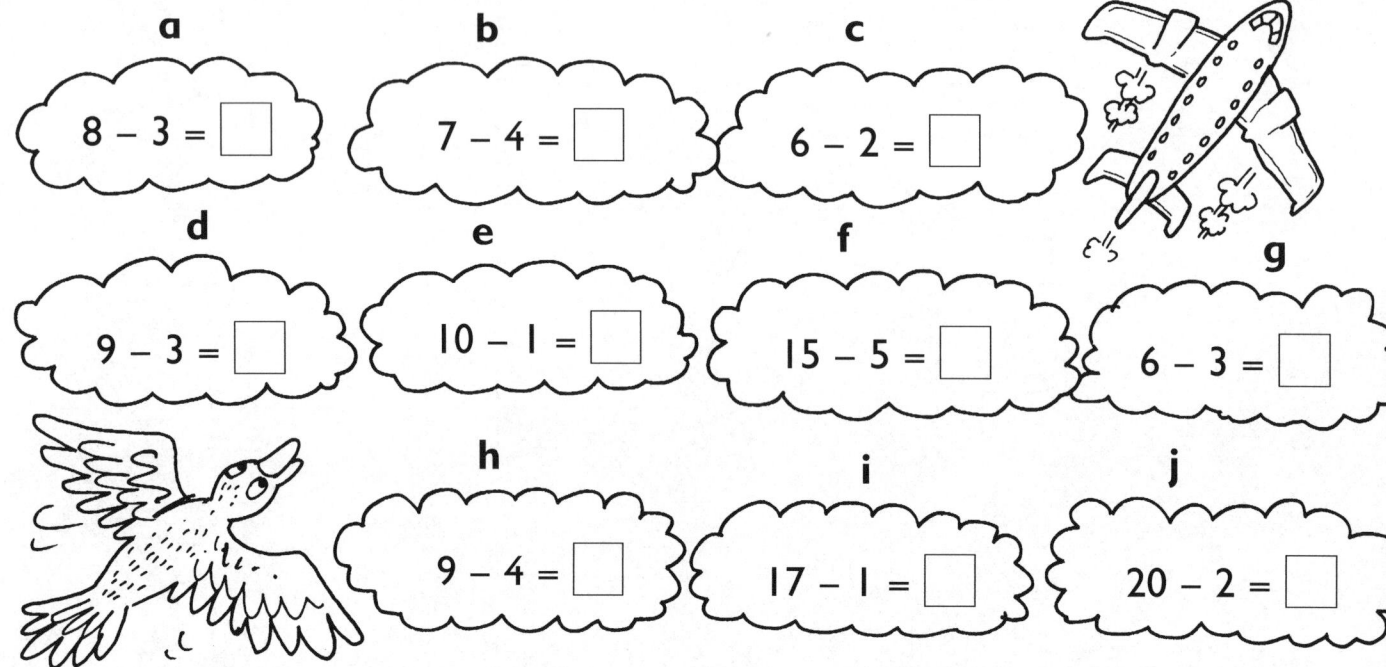

C. Collins
New
Primary
Maths

Name _____ Date _____

Multiple choices

- **Describe the pattern when counting in 2s, 3s, 4s or 5s**

 Find the missing numbers and complete each sequence.

a			6	8		12	14		
b		6		12	15				30
c	4					24		32	
d			15			30		45	
e		20					70	90	

 1 Look at the table above. List the numbers that are:

   a multiples of 2 and 3

   b multiples of 4 and 5

   c multiples of 4 and 10

2 Write **true**, **false** or **sometimes true** for these sentences.

   a Multiples of 10 are multiples of 5.

   b Multiples of 5 are multiples of 10.

   c Multiples of 3 are even numbers.

   d Multiples of 4 are never odd.

   e Multiples of 10 are multiples of 2 and of 5.

Collins New Primary Maths

Name _____ Date _____

Multiplication machines

● **Know the 2, 3, 5 and 10 times tables**

■ Follow the instructions on each machine. Fill in the missing numbers.

a

In	Out
5	
7	
10	
9	
4	

× 2

b

In	Out
8	
3	
6	
7	
9	

× 5

● **a**

In	Out
5	
7	
10	
9	
4	

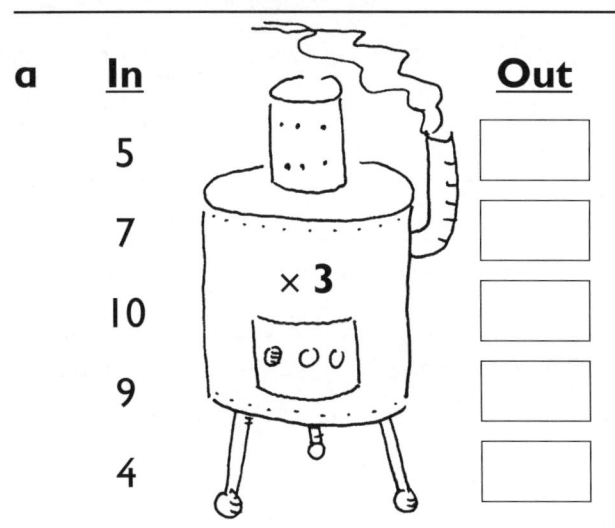
× 3

b

In	Out
3	
6	
1	
8	
0	

× 10

---

 a

In	Out
7	
4	
2	
	25
	15

× 5

b

In	Out
	15
8	
	27
	18
	21

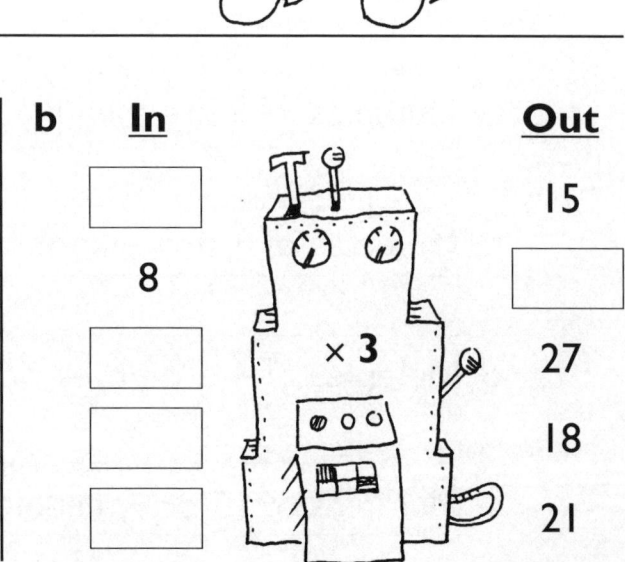
× 3

Collins
New
Primary
Maths

Name _____ Date _____

Know your 4 times table

- **Know the 4 times table**

Quickly do these calculations in your head. Write the answers.

a $1 \times 4 =$ ⬚ **b** $6 \times 4 =$ ⬚ **c** ⬚ $\times 4 = 20$

d $2 \times 4 =$ ⬚ **e** $9 \times 4 =$ ⬚ **f** ⬚ $\times 4 = 16$

g $5 \times 4 =$ ⬚ **h** $3 \times 4 =$ ⬚ **i** $7 \times$ ⬚ $= 28$

j $10 \times 4 =$ ⬚ **k** $8 \times 4 =$ ⬚ **l** $6 \times$ ⬚ $= 24$

Cut out the star along the dotted lines.

Jumble up the pieces.

Work out the answers to the 4 times table to put the puzzle back together.

You need:
- scissors

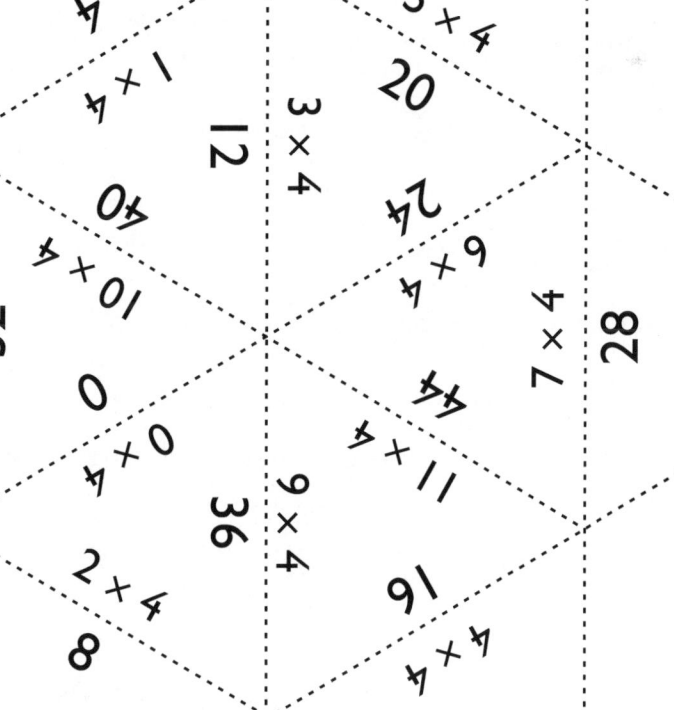

Collins New Primary Maths

Name _____ Date _____

Multiplying two-digit numbers

- **Multiply a two-digit number by a one-digit number**

Example
$17 \times 6 = (10 \times 6) + (7 \times 6)$
$= 60 + 42$
$= 102$

Complete each of these calculations.

a $13 \times 8 = (10 \times 8) + (3 \times 8)$
$= \boxed{} + \boxed{}$
$= \boxed{}$

b $15 \times 6 = (10 \times 6) + (5 \times 6)$
$= \boxed{} + \boxed{}$
$= \boxed{}$

c $19 \times 3 = (10 \times 3) + (9 \times 3)$
$= \boxed{} + \boxed{}$
$= \boxed{}$

d $16 \times 4 = (10 \times 4) + (6 \times 4)$
$= \boxed{} + \boxed{}$
$= \boxed{}$

Work out the answer to each of these calculations. Show all your working.

a $14 \times 8 =$

b $18 \times 5 =$

c $17 \times 7 =$

d $18 \times 4 =$

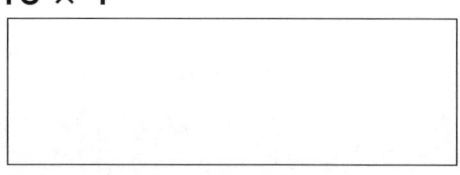

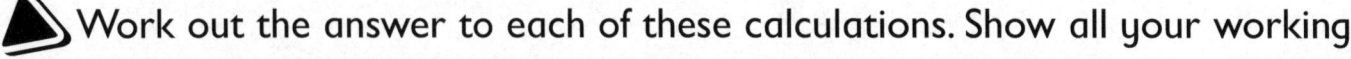

Work out the answer to each of these calculations. Show all your working.

a $25 \times 7 =$

b $24 \times 8 =$

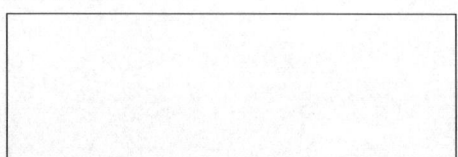

c $23 \times 6 =$

d $22 \times 9 =$

Collins New Primary Maths

Name _____ Date _____

Using 10 and 100

- **Explain how the digits in a number change when counting in 10s or 100s**

Do these quickly in your head. Write the answer.

a 127 − 100 = ☐ **b** 371 − 100 = ☐ **c** 371 − 10 = ☐

d 235 + 100 = ☐ **e** 12 + 10 = ☐ **f** 455 − 10 = ☐

g 360 − 100 = ☐ **h** 45 + 10 = ☐ **i** 67 − 10 = ☐

j 452 + 100 = ☐ **k** 260 − 10 = ☐ **l** 670 − 100 = ☐

Find your way to the end of the maze by adding or subtracting 10 or 100 as shown. Write the new number in the circle.

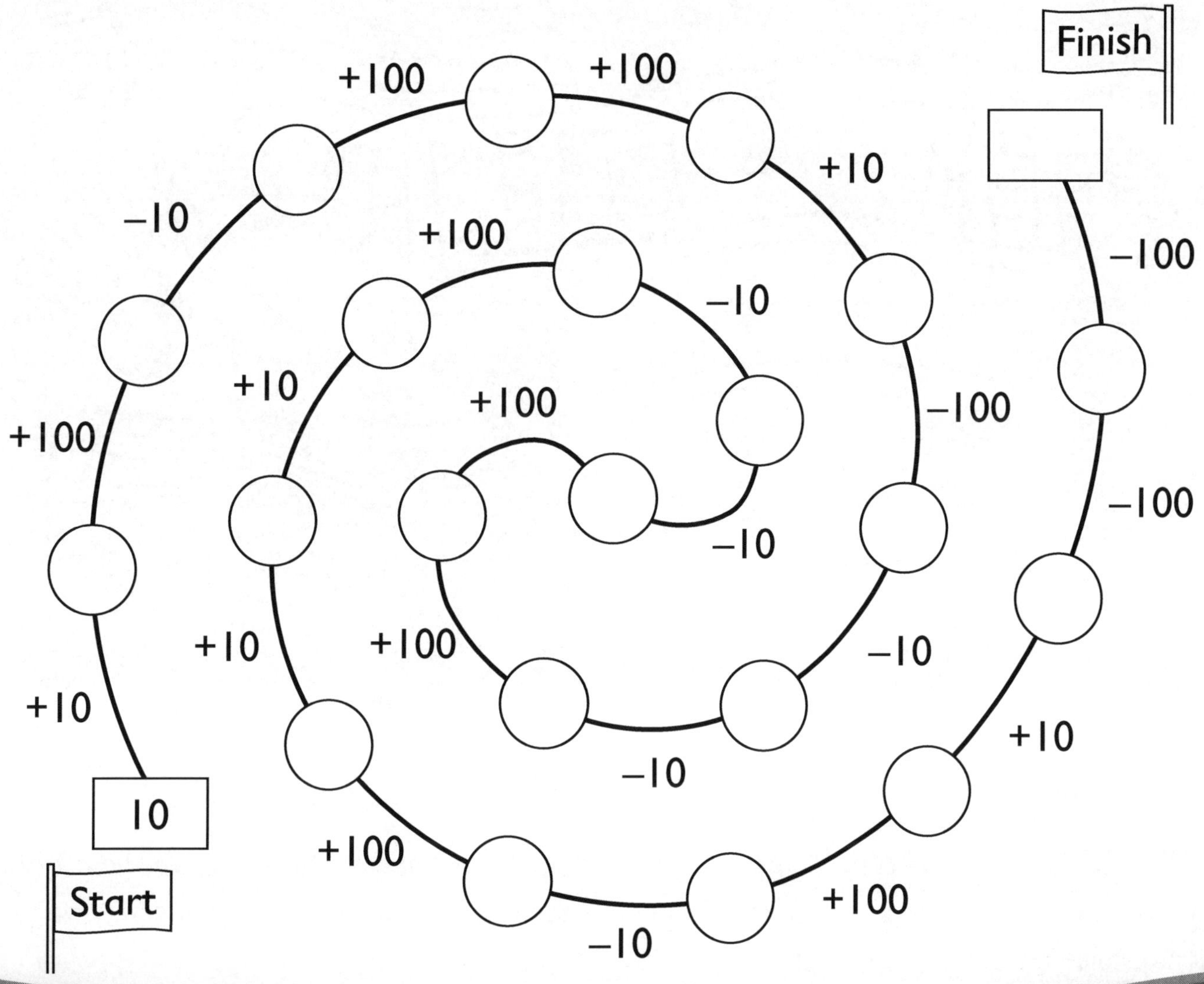

Finish

+100   +100   +10   −100

−10   +100   −10   −100

+100   +10   +100   −10   −100

+10   +10   +100   −10

+10   −10   +10

10

Start   +100   −10   +100

Name _____ Date _____

Scarf addition

● Add or subtract mentally two-digit numbers

■ Complete these calculations.

a $38 - 13 = \square$

b $46 + 12 = \square$

c $56 + 13 = \square$

◖◣

a $63 - 24 = \square$

b $67 + 25 = \square$

c $55 - 18 = \square$

d $85 + 56 = \square$

e $78 - 29 = \square$

f $92 + 37 = \square$

▲ Choose 2 addition and 2 subtraction calculations from the **◖◣** section and, on the back of this sheet, explain your method for adding and subtracting mentally two-digit numbers.

Collins
New
Primary
Maths

Name _____ Date _____

Revising the 2, 3, 4, 5, 6 and 10 times tables

- **Know the 2, 3, 4, 5, 6 and 10 times tables**

Complete the flowers by filling in the missing factor or product.

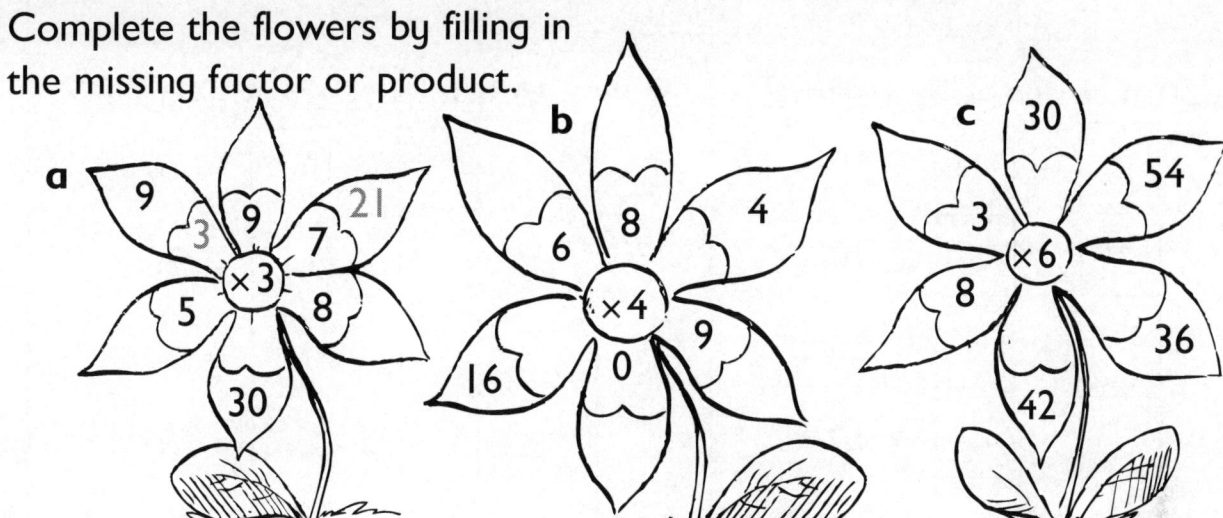

Colour the flower petals which are multiples of 3 red.
Colour the flower centres which are multiples of 4 yellow.

1 Write the numbers that are multiples of both 3 and 4.

2 Write the numbers that are multiples of both 3 and 6.

3 Write the numbers that are multiples of both 2 and 3.

4 Write the numbers that are multiples of both 4 and 6.

5 Write the numbers that are multiples of both 2 and 4.

6 Write the numbers that are multiples of both 2 and 6.

Name _____ Date _____

What was the question?

- **Solve mathematical puzzles**

1

The answer is

10

What was the question?

☐ + ☐ = 10

☐ + ☐ = 10

☐ + ☐ = 10

☐ − ☐ = 10

☐ − ☐ = 10

☐ × ☐ = 10

2

The answer is

20

What was the question?

☐ + ☐ = 20

☐ + ☐ = 20

☐ − ☐ = 20

☐ − ☐ = 20

☐ × ☐ = 20

☐ × ☐ = 20

1

The answer is

14

What was the question?

☐ + ☐ = 14

☐ + ☐ = 14

☐ + ☐ = 14

☐ − ☐ = 14

☐ − ☐ = 14

☐ × ☐ = 14

2

The answer is

15

What was the question?

☐ + ☐ = 15

☐ + ☐ = 15

☐ + ☐ = 15

☐ − ☐ = 15

☐ − ☐ = 15

☐ × ☐ = 15

On the back of this sheet, write down as many calculations as you can think of with an answer of 18. Use +, −, × and ÷. Can you use a combination of these operations?

Collins New Primary Maths

Name _____ Date _____

Cut out fractions

● **Identify fractions of shapes**

 Cut out the first four shapes. Fold them in half and then into quarters. Colour half red, a quarter blue and a quarter yellow.

 Label the fractions $\frac{1}{2}$, $\frac{1}{4}$, $\frac{1}{4}$.

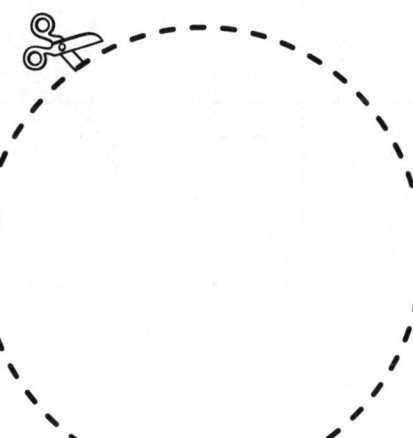

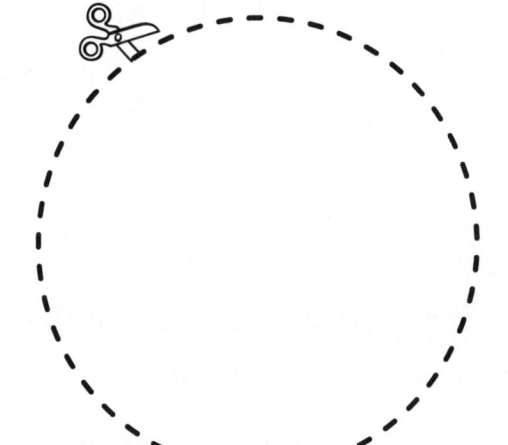

Cut out another circle.
Can you fold it into sixths?

Name _____ Date _____

Great grids

- Use multiples of 2, 3, 4, 5, 6 or 10 to solve a puzzle

■ Multiply the numbers in the first grid by 2.
Write the answers in the second grid.

1	9	3
7	4	6
5	8	2

×2 →

2		
	8	
		4

● Multiply the number in the first grid by 3, 4, 5 or 10 as shown.
Write the answers in the second grid.

a

2	9	4
7	5	10
8	3	6

×5 →

b

4	8	3
7	2	9
5	6	10

×10 →

c

9	2	6
8	3	7
5	4	10

×3 →

d

9	2	6
4	7	3
8	5	10

×4 →

▲ On the back of this sheet, draw two 3 × 3 grids like
those above. Write the nine numbers from 2 to 10 in
the first grid. Then multiply each of these numbers
by 6 and write the answers in the second grid.

© Collins
New
Primary
Maths

Name _____ Date _____

Odd ones out

- Recognise multiples of 2, 3, 4, 5 and 10 up to the tenth multiple

You need:
- colouring materials

Each bag has at least one ball that does not belong.

Colour all the multiples that do not belong in each bag.

a

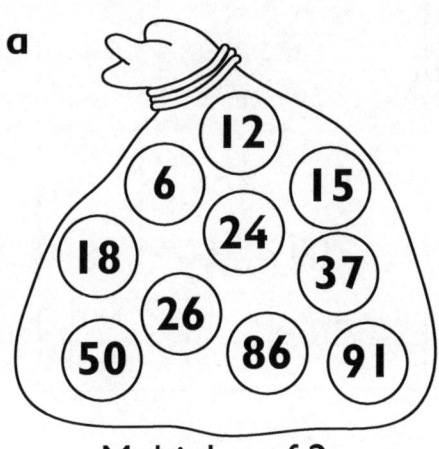

Multiples of 2

b

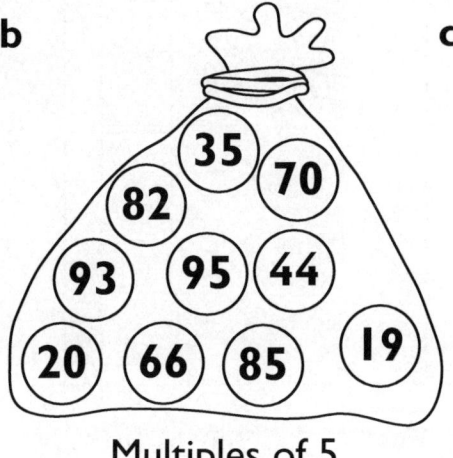

Multiples of 5

c

Multiples of 10

Each bag has at least one ball that does not belong.

Colour all the multiples that do not belong in each bag.

a

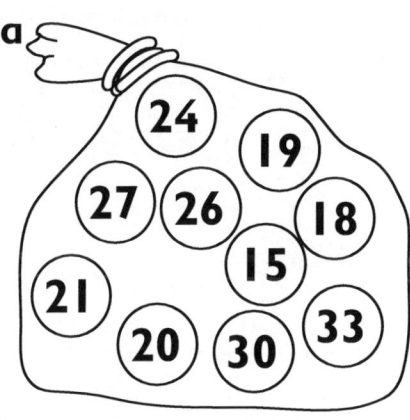

Multiples of 3

b

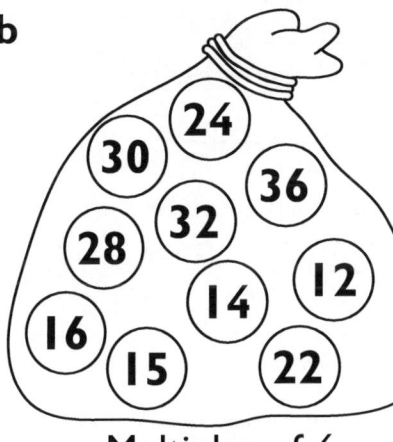

Multiples of 4

c

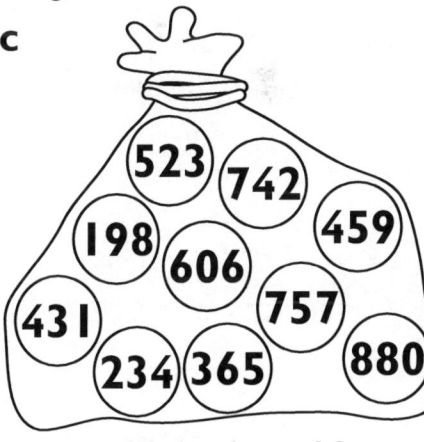

Multiples of 2

On the back of this sheet, draw a Venn diagram. Sort the numbers in **a** and **b** of the ● section above.

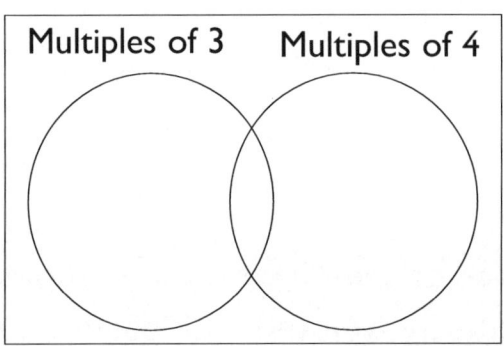

Multiples of 3   Multiples of 4

Name _____ Date _____

Knowing division facts

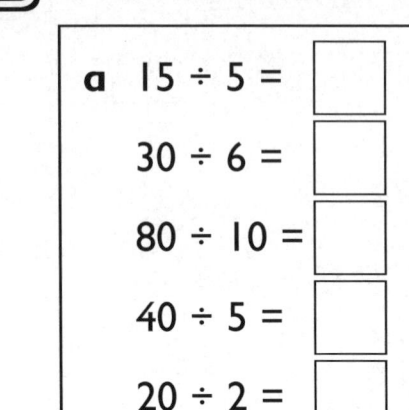

- Work out division facts corresponding to the 2, 3, 4, 5, 6 and 10 times tables

■ Write the answers to these division facts.

a	15 ÷ 5 = ☐	b	14 ÷ 2 = ☐	c	18 ÷ 6 = ☐
	30 ÷ 6 = ☐		36 ÷ 6 = ☐		9 ÷ 3 = ☐
	80 ÷ 10 = ☐		50 ÷ 5 = ☐		12 ÷ 4 = ☐
	40 ÷ 5 = ☐		16 ÷ 2 = ☐		40 ÷ 4 = ☐
	20 ÷ 2 = ☐		12 ÷ 3 = ☐		100 ÷ 10 = ☐
	60 ÷ 10 = ☐		24 ÷ 4 = ☐		30 ÷ 3 = ☐

● Read each word problem. Write a division number sentence for each problem and then write the answer.

a A square has 4 sides. The total length of the sides is 20 cm. What is the length of each side?

[_____]

b Fairground rides cost £10 for 5 rides. How much does it cost per ride?

[_____]

c Alex has made a pattern of 24 tiles. One tile in every 6 has a pattern. How many tiles have a pattern?

[_____]

d How many sweets are left over if 16 sweets are shared equally into 3 bags?

[_____]

e How many balls are left over if 33 balls are shared out equally between 5 teams?

[_____]

 Look at the division calculations in the ■ section. On the back of this sheet, write the related multiplication calculation for each division calculation.

Collins
New
Primary
Maths

Name _____   Date _____

Pinboard puzzles

- **Name and describe 2-D shapes**

You need:
- ruler
- set-square

1 Read the description above each pinboard. Draw the shape on the pinboard.

a 4 right angles and opposite sides equal

b A quadrilateral with one right angle

c 5 vertices, 2 of which are right angles

d A triangle with 2 equal sides but no right angle

d

2 Write a description for these shapes on the back of this sheet.

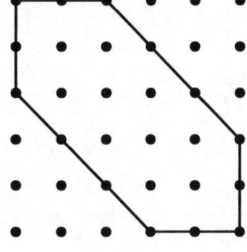

c

b

a

Collins New Primary Maths

Name _____ Date _____

Duvet patterns

- **Reflect a shape when the mirror line is along one edge**

 These duvet patterns are only half made. Finish the other half in the same pattern.

Place a mirror on this line to check your pattern.

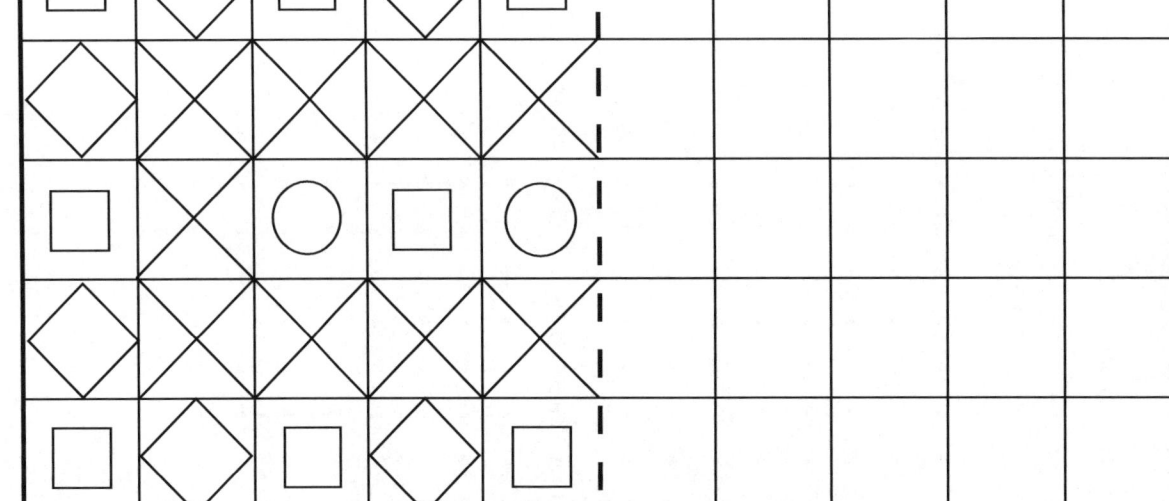

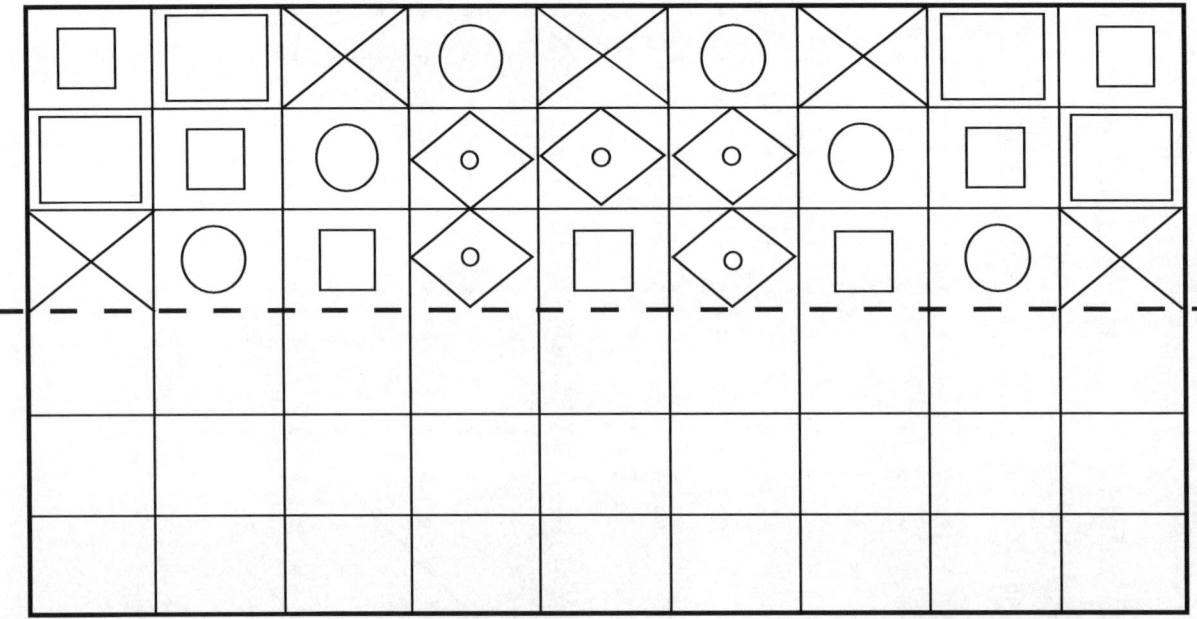

 Colour the top duvet pattern making sure that it is still symmetrical.

You need:

- coloured pencils

Collins New Primary Maths

Name _____ Date _____

Right on time

● **Tell the time to the nearest 5 minutes**

Write what time each clock face shows.

a

b

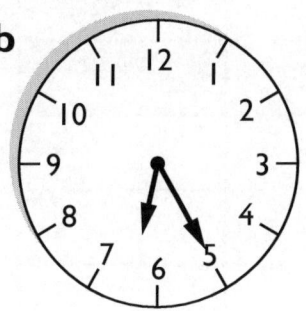

c

d

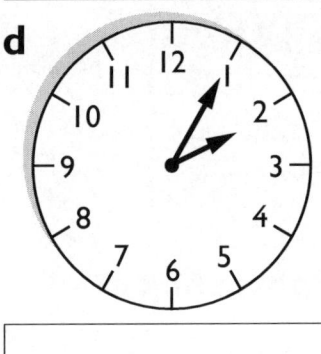

e

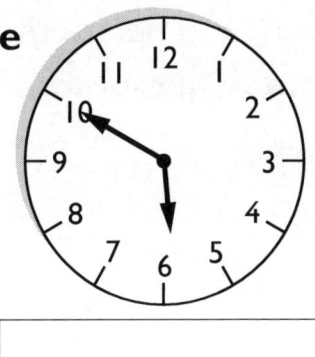

f

1   Show the time on both clocks.

| 10 past 4 | 25 to 9 | 20 past 3 | 10 to 11 |

a

b

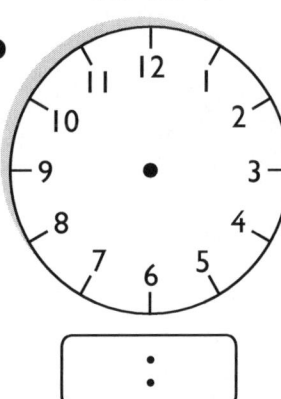

c

d

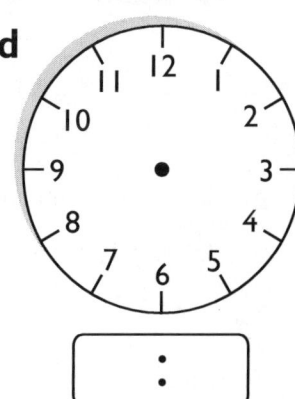

4 : 10   :   :   :

2   This is Abi's digital alarm clock.

  a Write the time it showed:

    10 minutes ago [:]   30 minutes ago. [:]

  b In 15 minutes time when the alarm bell rings it will be: [:]

Name _____ Date _____

Sport shop data

● Show information in tables, bar charts and pictograms

■ Count the things for sale in the sport shop. Write the numbers in the table.

Item	Number
footballs	
rackets	
bats	
goggles	

 **1** Using the information above, complete the bar chart. Now answer these questions.

a What is the most common item for sale?

b How many more footballs than bats are there?

c If the shop sells half the rackets, how many will it have left?

2 Write two sentences about the information presented in the bar chart.

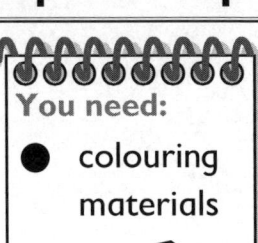

You need:
● colouring materials

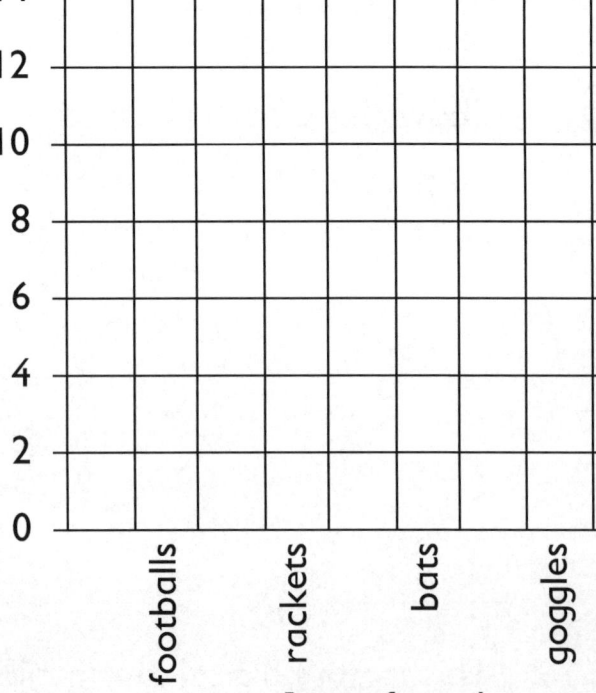

On the back of this sheet, draw a pictogram for the data.

You need:
● ruler

Collins New Primary Maths

Name _____ Date _____

Dinosaur pictograms

- **Show information in a pictogram where a picture represents 2 objects**

Count the dinosaurs and complete the table.

Dinosaur	Number
Brontosaurus	
Tyrannosaurus	
Stegosaurus	
Pterodactyl	

Pterodactyl

Stegosaurus

Brontosaurus

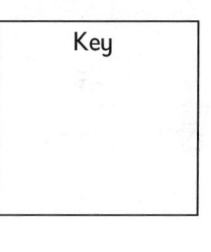

Tyrannosaurus

1 Complete the pictogram.
Draw a dinosaur egg $\bigcirc$ to stand for
2 dinosaurs.

Title: _____

Brontosaurus

Tyrannosaurus

Stegosaurus

Pterodactyl

Key

2 Use the information in your completed pictogram to answer these questions.

a How many Brontosaurus are there? ⬚

b How many Pterodactyls and Tyranosaurus are there? ⬚

c Which is the most common dinosaur? ⬚

d How many more Stegosaurus than Pterodactyls are there? ⬚

e How many dinosaurs are not Pterodactyls? ⬚

f How many dinosaurs are there altogether? ⬚

You need:
- colouring materials
- ruler

On the back of this sheet, draw a bar chart for the data.

Collins
New
Primary
Maths

Name _____ Date _____

Cutting corners (2)

- **Sort objects using Carroll diagrams**

 **1** Cut off the bottom left corner of your A4 sheet of paper.

2 Use a red pen to write a different name on each side.

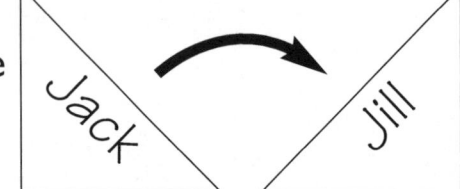

3 Copy the Carroll diagram.

4 Drop the corner of paper 20 times. Each time, make a tick in the Carroll diagram.

5 Write the totals in the Carroll diagram.

You need:
- scissors
- red and blue colouring materials
- ruler
- A4 paper

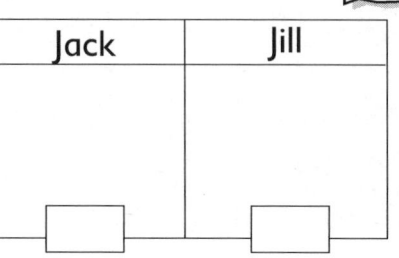

 **1** Cut off the bottom right corner of this sheet.

2 Use a blue pen to write the above names on each side.

3 Copy the Carroll diagram.

4 Drop both corners of paper 20 times. Each time, record the results using ticks in the Carroll diagram.

5 Write the totals in the Carroll diagram.

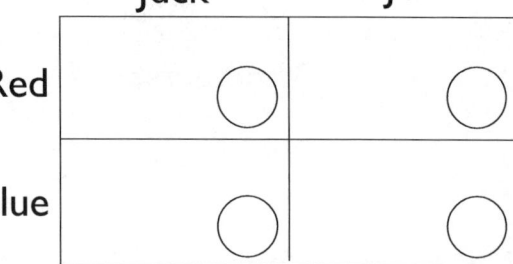

 1 Cut off the top two corners of this sheet.

2 Write a different name on each side of the left corner.

3 Write a different number on each side of the right corner.

4 Copy the Carroll diagram. Label the Carroll diagram with your names and numbers.

5 Drop both corners of paper 20 times. Record the results using ticks. Then write in the totals.

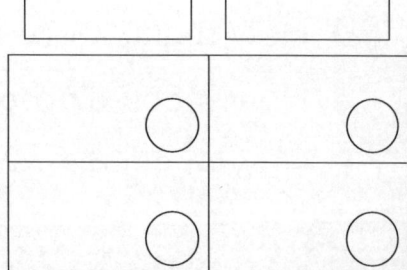

Name _____   Date _____

Plant subtraction

- **Use written methods to explain subtraction**

Find the difference by counting on to work out the calculations.

93 94 95 96 97 98 99 100 101 102 103 104 105 106 107

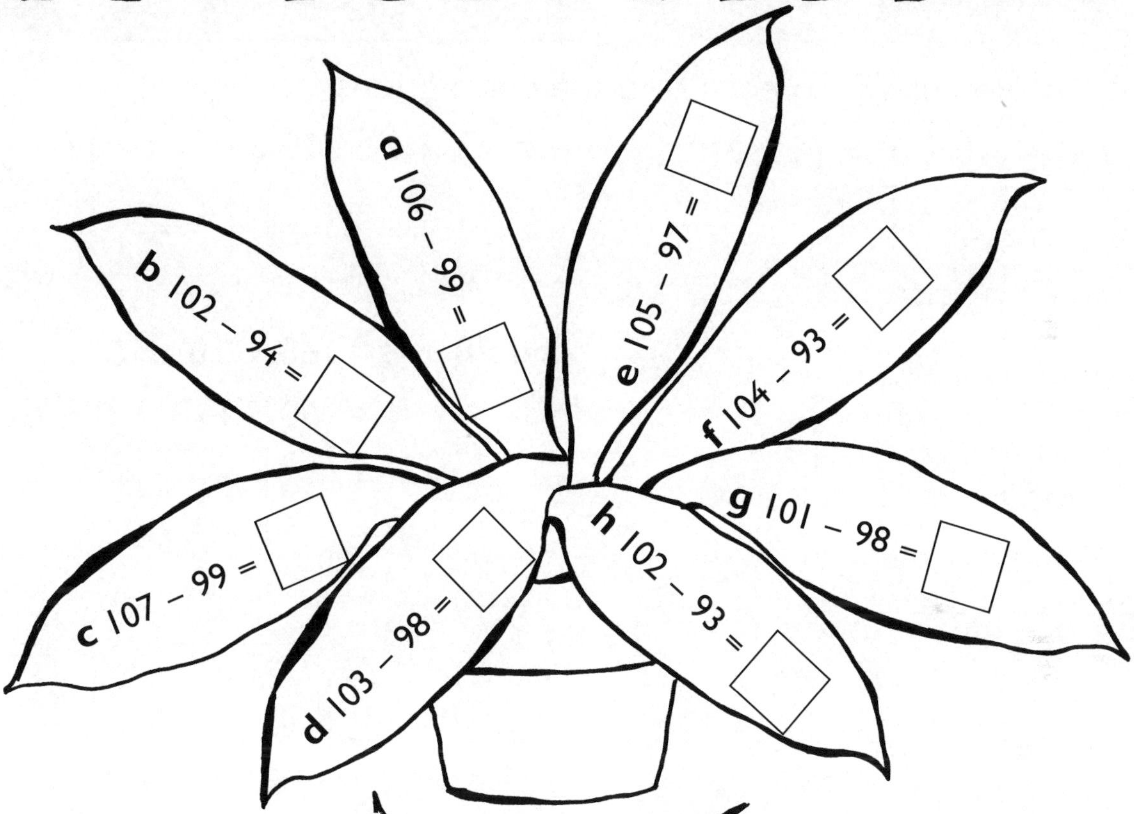

a 106 – 99 = ☐

b 102 – 94 = ☐

c 107 – 99 = ☐

d 103 – 98 = ☐

e 105 – 97 = ☐

f 104 – 93 = ☐

g 101 – 98 = ☐

h 102 – 93 = ☐

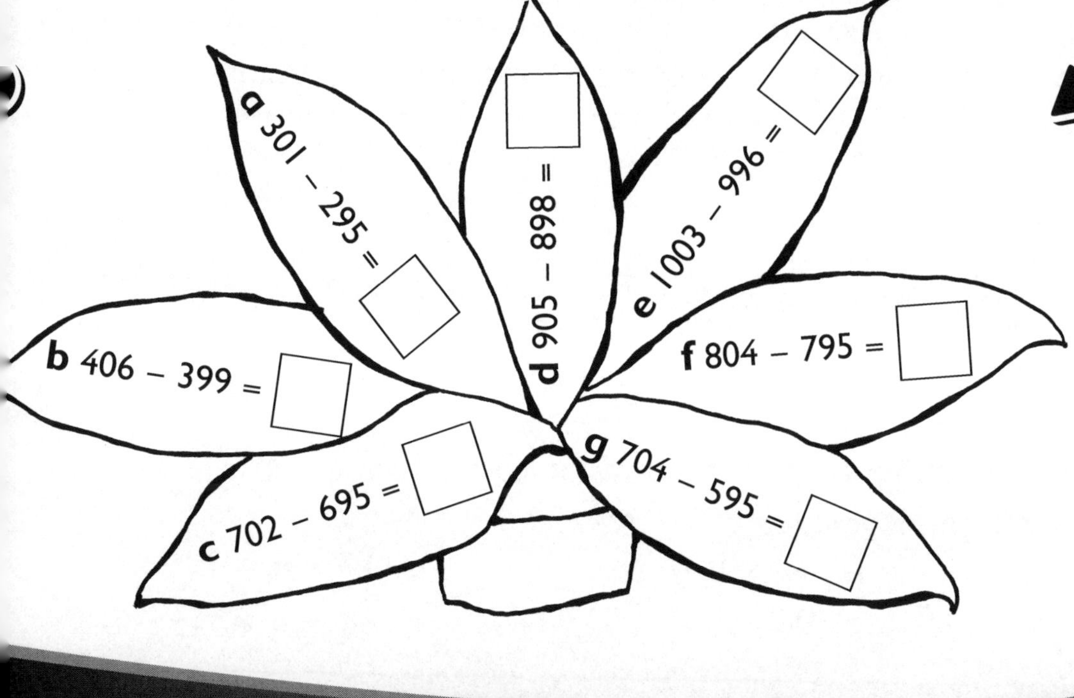

a 301 – 295 = ☐

b 406 – 399 = ☐

c 702 – 695 = ☐

d 905 – 898 = ☐

e 1003 – 996 = ☐

f 804 – 795 = ☐

g 704 – 595 = ☐

On the back of this sheet, make up 10 subtraction calculations for yourself.

Collins
New
Primary
Maths

Name _____ Date _____

Multiplying and dividing two-digit numbers

- Multiply and divide a two-digit number by a one-digit number

Example

$17 \times 3 = (10 \times 3) + (7 \times 3)$	$90 \div 5 = (50 + 40) \div 5$
$\quad = 30 + 21$	$\quad = (50 \div 5) + (40 \div 5)$
$\quad = 51$	$\quad = 18$

■ Work out the answer to each of these calculations.

a $14 \times 8 = (10 \times 8) + (4 \times 8)$

$= \boxed{} + \boxed{}$

$= \boxed{}$

b $17 \times 6 = (10 \times \boxed{}) + (7 \times \boxed{})$

$= \boxed{} + \boxed{}$

$= \boxed{}$

c $19 \times 4 = (\boxed{} \times \boxed{}) + (\boxed{} \times \boxed{})$

$= \boxed{} + \boxed{}$

$= \boxed{}$

d $78 \div 6 = (60 + 18) \div 6$

$= (60 \div 6) + (18 \div 6)$

$= \boxed{} + \boxed{}$

$= \boxed{}$

e $92 \div 4 = (80 + 12) \div 4$

$= (\boxed{} \div \boxed{}) + (\boxed{} \div \boxed{})$

$= \boxed{} + \boxed{}$

$= \boxed{}$

f $72 \div 3 = (\boxed{} + \boxed{}) \div \boxed{}$

$= (\boxed{} \div \boxed{}) + (\boxed{} \div \boxed{})$

$= \boxed{} + \boxed{}$

$= \boxed{}$

● Work out the answer to each of these calculations. Show all your working.

a $18 \times 4 =$	**b** $15 \times 6 =$	**c** $13 \times 7 =$
d $54 \div 3 =$	**e** $64 \div 4 =$	**f** $95 \div 5 =$

▲ On the back of this sheet, work out the answer to each of these calculations. Show all your working.

a $18 \times 9 =$ **b** $16 \times 8 =$ **c** $17 \times 4 =$

d $98 \div 7 =$ **e** $96 \div 6 =$ **f** $84 \div 4 =$

Collins
New
Primary
Maths

Name _____ Date _____

Grocery grams

- **Know how many grams make 1 kg**

Look for the weight label on packets, tins and jars.
Find three items for each set.
Write the name and weight in grams of each item in the appropriate column.

grocery item	Less than $\frac{1}{2}$ kg	weight in grams
e.g. jar marmalade		454 g
1		
2		
3		

grocery item	$\frac{1}{2}$ kg	weight in grams
e.g. low fat spread		500 g
1		
2		
3		

grocery item	more than $\frac{1}{2}$ kg	weight in grams
e.g. cereal		750 g
1		
2		
3		

 Find a set of items from the ▶ section which together will weigh
about $1\frac{1}{2}$ kg Draw each item and write its weight in the box.

☐ + ☐ + ☐ = about $1\frac{1}{2}$ kg

Can you find other combinations of groceries that weigh about $1\frac{1}{2}$ kg?
Write any combinations on the back of this sheet.

Collins
New
Primary
Maths

Name _____ Date _____

Helicopter directions

- Use the four compass directions, N, S, E, W, to describe a direction

■ You are in a helicopter hovering over Alpha rig. Look at the map then complete these sentences.

1 I can see [ ] rig to the south.

2 I can see [ ] rig to the east.

3 The supply ship is to the [ ].

4 If I want to fly to Aberton Port, I will have to face [ ].

Map:
Gamma rig | Supply ship
Aberton Port
Alpha rig | Delta rig
Beta rig | Fishing boats

N
W—E
S

● Answer these questions.

1 I am hovering over an oil rig. I can see the supply ship in front of me. Behind me is Beta rig.

 a In which direction am I facing? [ ]

 b If I make a quarter turn to the right, which oil rig will I see? [ ]

2 I am flying over the fishing boats. Behind me is Beta rig.

 a In which direction am I flying? [ ]

 b I want to land on Delta rig. Write down the directions. [ ]

3 I am hovering over an oil rig. I can see Aberton Port in front of me. Behind me is Delta rig.

 a In which direction am I facing? [ ]

 b If I make a quarter turn to the left, which rig will I see? [ ]

▲ On the back of this sheet, write a description of how to get from one rig to another. Include directions and turns in your description.

Collins New Primary Maths

Name _____	Date _____

Cut out fractions

- **Use diagrams to compare fractions and establish equivalents**

Cut out the circles and then cut them into their fraction pieces. How many new circles can you make?

On a piece of paper, draw each of your circles and label the fractions you have used.

You need:
- scissors
- sheet of paper

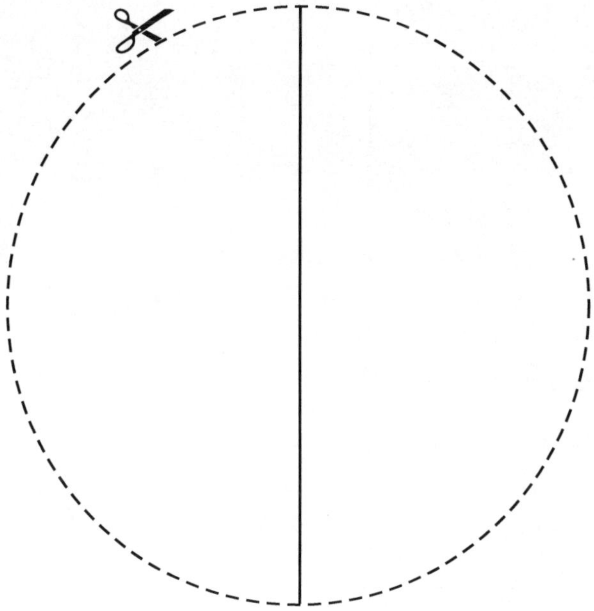

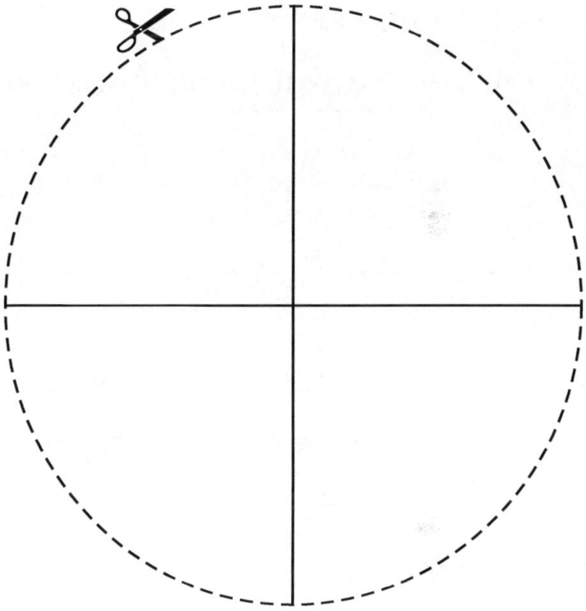

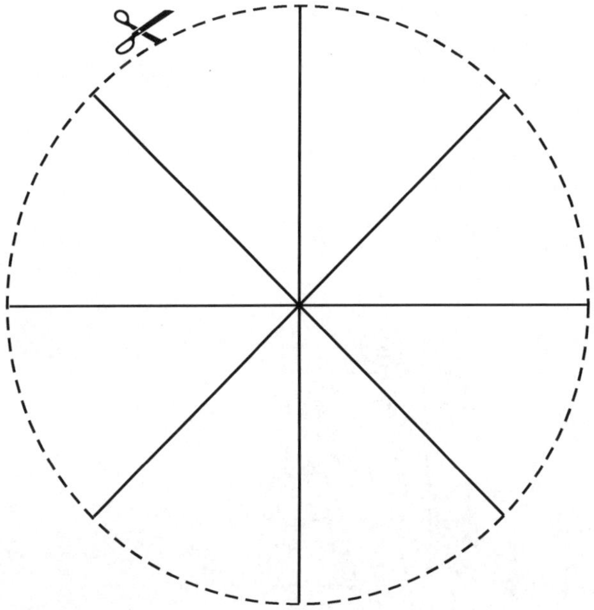

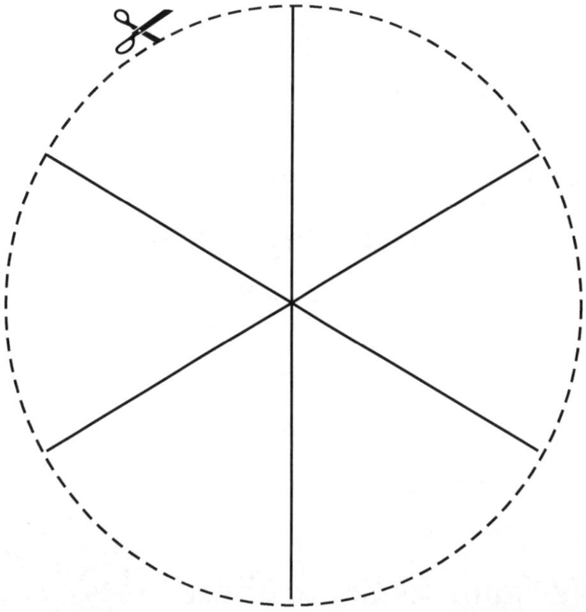

Collins
New
Primary
Maths

Name _____ Date _____

Problems with the Williams family

● Solve one-step and two-step word problems

■ 1 Mrs Williams dug up 27 potatoes and 17 carrots. How many vegetables does she have altogther? ☐

2 Sarah is watching TV. The first programme lasted for 15 minutes and the second programme for 20 minutes. How long did Sarah watch TV for?
☐

3 Mr William baked 15 jam tarts. He ate 7 of them. How many were left? ☐

● 1 Simon has collected 63 stickers. He has 18 in a box and the rest in an album. How many are in the album? ☐

2 Mrs Williams has 4 pots and she has planted 13 bulbs in each. She wants to plant 75 bulbs altogether. How many more bulbs does she need to buy? ☐

3 Mr Williams bought 56 biscuits to last the family for a week. How many can each member of the family eat a day? ☐

Working out

▲ On the back of this sheet, write a word problem about the Williams family to share with your class.

Collins New Primary Maths

Name _____ Date _____

Division deckchairs

> ● Know by heart the multiplication facts for the 2, 3, 4,
> 5, 6 and 10 times tables and the related division facts

Write the answers for these divison facts.

$20 \div 2 = \boxed{}$

$16 \div 4 = \boxed{}$

$40 \div 5 = \boxed{}$

$40 \div 10 = \boxed{}$

$30 \div 6 = \boxed{}$

$30 \div 3 = \boxed{}$

$18 \div 2 = \boxed{}$

$50 \div 10 = \boxed{}$

$15 \div 3 = \boxed{}$

$32 \div 4 = \boxed{}$

$50 \div 5 = \boxed{}$

$12 \div 6 = \boxed{}$

$14 \div \boxed{} = 7$

$50 \div \boxed{} = 10$

$20 \div \boxed{} = 5$

$35 \div \boxed{} = 5$

$\boxed{} \div 3 = 6$

$\boxed{} \div 4 = 2$

Here are some multiplication and division number families.
Write the multiplication and division facts for each.

Example

60	$6 \times 10 = 60$
10	$10 \times 6 = 60$
60	$60 \div 10 = 6$
	$60 \div 6 = 10$

a
| 5 |
| 8 |
| 40 |

b
| 3 |
| 8 |
| 24 |

c
| 4 |
| 7 |
| 28 |

One number in the family has gone missing. Find the
missing number then write the multiplication and
division facts for each family.

a
| |
| 2 |
| 14 |

b
| 9 |
| 10 |
| |

c
| |
| 5 |
| 30 |

d
| 3 |
| |
| 21 |

Collins
New
Primary
Maths

Name _____ Date _____

Webs of doubles and halves

- **Double whole numbers, multiples of 5 and multiples of 10 and the related halves**

■ Double each number on the spider's web.

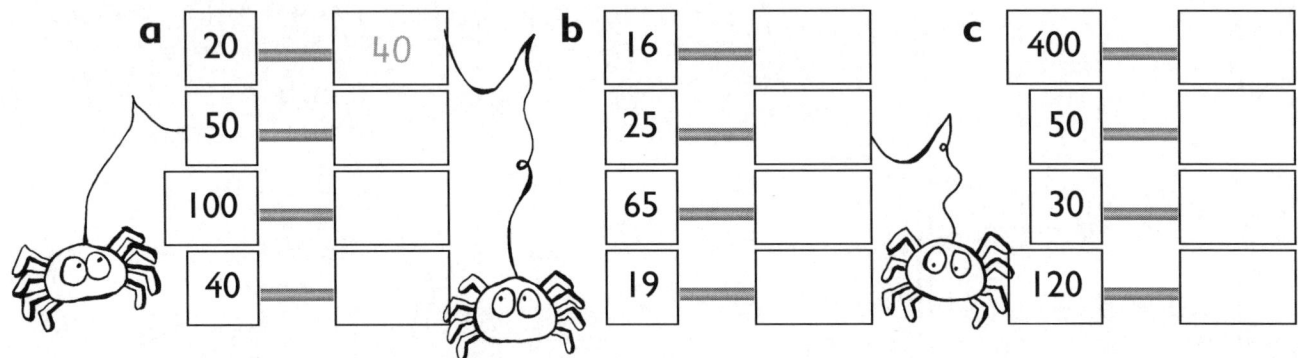

a
20	40
50	
100	
40	

b
16	
25	
65	
19	

c
400	
50	
30	
120	

● Complete each number web by following the instruction in the centre.

a
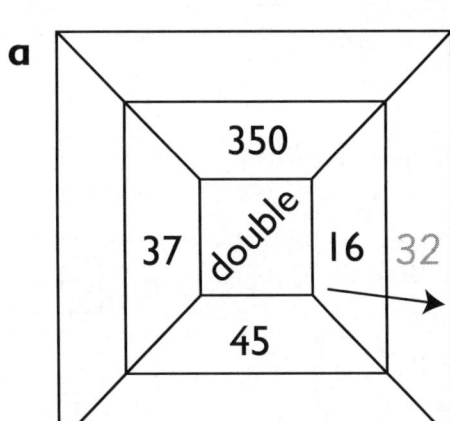

350

37 double 16 → 32

45

b

900

500 halve 170

38

19 ↓

▲ **a**
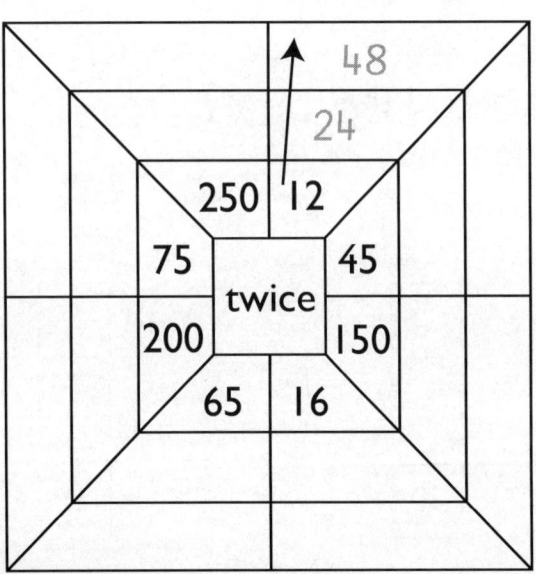

48
24

250 12
75 twice 45
200 150
65 16

b

6
12

500 24
48 $\frac{1}{2}$ 180
140 600
32 1000

C. Collins New Primary Maths

Name _____ Date _____

Multiplying multiples of 10 and 100

- Know by heart the multiplication facts for the 2, 3, 4, 5, 6 and 10 times tables and the related division facts
- Multiply one-digit numbers by multiples of 10 and 100

a $7 \times 5 =$ ☐   b $6 \times 2 =$ ☐   c $8 \times 10 =$ ☐

d $3 \times 10 =$ ☐   e $7 \times 3 =$ ☐   f $8 \times 4 =$ ☐

g $6 \times 4 =$ ☐   h $4 \times 5 =$ ☐   i $3 \times 6 =$ ☐

j $8 \times 6 =$ ☐   k $7 \times 6 =$ ☐   l $9 \times 3 =$ ☐

Use your knowledge of the times tables facts to help you work out the answers to these calculations.

1 a
$8 \times 3 =$
$80 \times 3 =$
$8 \times 300 =$

b
$9 \times 5 =$
$90 \times 5 =$
$9 \times 50 =$

c
$2 \times 7 =$
$2 \times 700 =$
$20 \times 7 =$

d
$4 \times 4 =$
$40 \times 4 =$
$4 \times 400 =$

e
$9 \times 6 =$
$900 \times 6 =$
$9 \times 60 =$

f
$10 \times 8 =$
$8 \times 100 =$
$80 \times 10 =$

2 a $70 \times 3 =$ ☐   **b** $7 \times 400 =$ ☐   **c** $4 \times 600 =$ ☐

d $2 \times 400 =$ ☐   **e** $6 \times 90 =$ ☐   **f** $8 \times 30 =$ ☐

g $800 \times 2 =$ ☐   **h** $30 \times 9 =$ ☐   **i** $80 \times 4 =$ ☐

Use your knowledge of the times tables facts to help you work out the answers to these calculations.

a $60 \times$ ☐ $= 420$ b $4 \times$ ☐ $= 280$ c ☐ $\times 3 = 270$

d ☐ $\times 8 = 320$ e $20 \times$ ☐ $= 180$ f ☐ $\times 900 = 3600$

g $8 \times$ ☐ $= 1600$ h $400 \times$ ☐ $= 2000$ i ☐ $\times 6 = 3600$

© Collins
New
Primary
Maths

Name _____ Date _____

Finding remainders

● **Divide a two-digit number by a one-digit number**

■ Group each set of objects. Write how many groups there are.
Write how many are left over.

a 13 ÷ 3 = ☐ R ☐

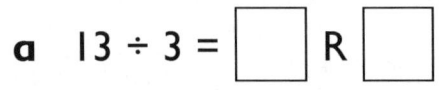

b 22 ÷ 10 = ☐ R ☐

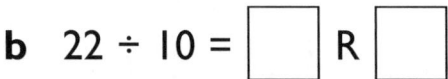

c 17 ÷ 5 = ☐ R ☐

d 14 ÷ 4 = ☐ R ☐

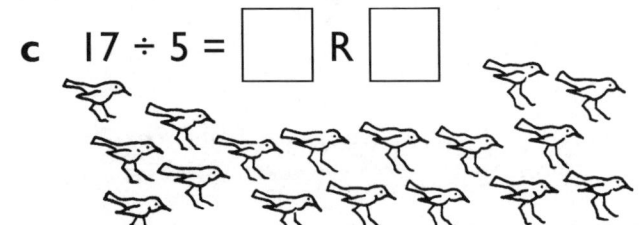

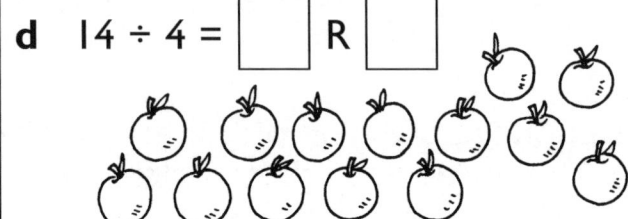

e 11 ÷ 2 = ☐ R ☐

f 23 ÷ 5 = ☐ R ☐

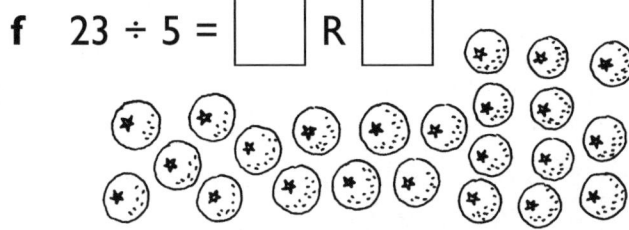

◆ Look at each division calculation. Write what multiplication fact you think
of to answer the question. Write the answer and any remainders.

a ☐ 16 ÷ 5 ☐
Think

3 × 5 = 15
So 16 ÷ 5 = 3 R 1

b ☐ 23 ÷ 10 ☐
Think

_____
So _____

c ☐ 32 ÷ 3 ☐
Think

_____
So _____

d ☐ 26 ÷ 4 ☐
Think

_____
So _____

e ☐ 38 ÷ 5 ☐
Think

_____
So _____

f ☐ 29 ÷ 3 ☐
Think

_____
So _____

Name _____ Date _____

Rounding weights

● Round any three-digit number to the nearest 10 or 100

Round the weights to the nearest 100 g.

a	b	c	d	e
		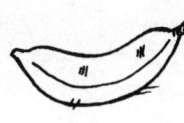		
760 g	315 g	123 g	650 g	93 g

1 Round each weight to the
nearest 100 kg. Write your
answer in the box.

2 Round each weight to the
nearest 10 kg. Write your
answer in the oval.

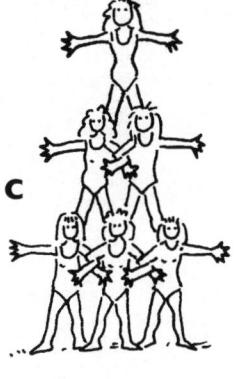

a	b	c	d	e
			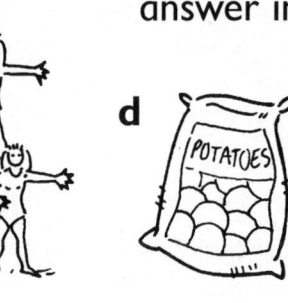	
550 kg	223 kg	385 kg	32 kg	158 kg

These weights have been rounded to the nearest 100 kg.

Write down two possible weights.

a	b	c	d	e

400 kg	200 kg	100 kg	800 kg	0 kg

Collins
New
Primary
Maths

Name _____ Date _____

Thoughtful numbers

- **Develop and use written methods**

First work out each calculation in your head.
Then write down how you did it.

a 16 + 21 = 37

10 + 20 + 6 + 1

b 36 + 22 =

c 45 + 31 =

d 64 + 35 =

e 23 + 54 =

f 72 + 26 =

a 39 + 43 =

b 68 + 25 =

c 76 + 24 =

d 53 + 64 =

e 87 + 34 =

f 95 + 56 =

a 58 + 27 =

b 84 + 77 =

Name _____ Date _____

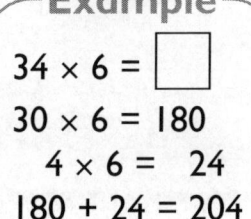

Multiplying larger numbers

● **Multiply a two-digit number by a one-digit number**

Example

34 × 6 = ☐
30 × 6 = 180
  4 × 6 =   24
180 + 24 = 204

Work out the answers to the calculations.
Show all your working.

a 23 × 2 = ☐

b 2 × 24 = ☐

c 3 × 32 = ☐

d 3 × 13 = ☐

e 4 × 12 = ☐

f 4 × 42 = ☐

a 6 × 23 = ☐

b 33 × 9 = ☐

c 87 × 4 = ☐

d 43 × 5 = ☐

e 58 × 4 = ☐

f 64 × 8 = ☐

Write the answers.

a Twice 24 ☐

b The product of 23 and 2 ☐

c Multiply 4 by 22 ☐

d 15 lots of 2 ☐

e 4 times 11 ☐

f Twice 43 ☐

g 33 multiplied by 3 ☐

h Double 44 ☐

i Double 34 ☐

j Multiply 33 by 2 ☐

k What is the product of 2 and 25? ☐

l 3 times 12 ☐

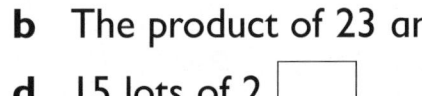

Collins
New
Primary
Maths

Name _____ Date _____

Dividing larger numbers

- **Divide a two-digit number by a one-digit number**

Example
$87 \div 4 = (80 + 7) \div 4$
$= (80 \div 4) + (7 \div 4)$
$= 20 + 1 \text{ R3}$
$= 21 \text{ R3}$

■ Work out the answer to each of these calculations.

a $98 \div 3 = (90 + 8) \div 3$
$= (90 \div 3) + (8 \div 3)$
$= \boxed{} + \boxed{} \text{ R} \boxed{}$
$= \boxed{} \text{ R} \boxed{}$

b $72 \div 5 = (50 + 22) \div 5$
$= (50 \div 5) + (22 \div 5)$
$= \boxed{} + \boxed{} \text{ R} \boxed{}$
$= \boxed{}$

c $81 \div 6 = (\boxed{} + \boxed{}) \div \boxed{}$
$= (\boxed{} \div \boxed{}) + (\boxed{} \div \boxed{})$
$= \boxed{} + \boxed{}$
$= \boxed{} \text{ R} \boxed{}$

d $93 \div 4 = (\boxed{} + \boxed{}) \div \boxed{}$
$= (\boxed{} \div \boxed{}) + (\boxed{} \div \boxed{})$
$= \boxed{} + \boxed{}$
$= \boxed{} \text{ R} \boxed{}$

● Work out the answer to each of these calculations. Show all your working

a $95 \div 6 =$	**b** $70 \div 4 =$	**c** $68 \div 3 =$
d $87 \div 5 =$	**e** $74 \div 3 =$	**f** $89 \div 6 =$

 Divide 98 by 7, 8 and 9.

98

7	8	9

Name _____ Date _____

Similar calculations

- **Identify patterns of numbers**

 Choose six calculations that you know, then write other calculations they can help you to work out.

a +

I know
7 + 4 = 11

so
I can
work out

17 + 4 = 21
27 + 4 = 31
37 + 4 = 41
47 + 4 = 51
57 + 4 = 61
87 + 4 = 91

b +

I know

so
I can
work out

_____
_____
_____
_____
_____
_____

c +

I know

so
I can
work out

_____
_____
_____
_____
_____
_____

d +

I know

so
I can
work out

_____
_____
_____
_____
_____
_____

e –

I know
5 – 2 = 3

so
I can
work out

25 – 2 = 23
35 – 2 = 33
45 – 2 = 43
55 – 2 = 53
85 – 2 = 83
95 – 2 = 93

f –

I know

so
I can
work out

_____
_____
_____
_____
_____
_____

g –

I know

so
I can
work out

_____
_____
_____
_____
_____
_____

h –

I know

so
I can
work out

_____
_____
_____
_____
_____
_____

On the back of this sheet, explain the patterns in the calculations.
What is the same about them?

€ Collins
New
Primary
Maths

Name _____ Date _____

Magic squares

● **In a puzzle find numbers that match a property**

■ Find the total of each of these rows, columns and diagonals.

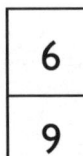
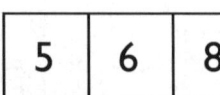
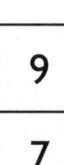
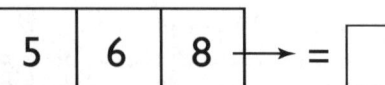
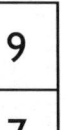

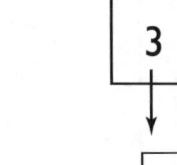

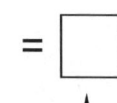

a
| 6 |
| 9 |
| 1 |
= ☐

b
| 5 | 6 | 8 | → = ☐

e
| 9 |
| 7 |
| 6 |
= ☐

f
| 20 |
| 30 |
| 10 |
= ☐

c
| 10 |
| 7 |
| 3 |
= ☐

| 5 | = ☐
| 13 |
d
| 12 |

g
☐ = ← | 11 | 21 | 31 |

● Fill in the missing numbers to make these magic squares.

a Magic number = ☐

	2	
	4	
	6	1

b Magic number = ☐

3	8	7
	6	

c Magic number = ☐

		1
2	7	6

d Magic number = 30

13	6	
	14	

e Magic number = 27

8		12
		10

f Magic number = ☐

26	21	
	25	
		24

▲ On the back of this sheet, make a magic square of your own.
What is the magic number?

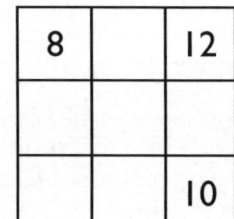

Name _____ Date _____

Know your division facts

- **Know by heart the division facts related to the 2, 3, 4, 5, 6 and 10 times tables**

- Take turns to spin the spinner.

- If the number spun shows the answer to a division calculation on the game board, then cover it with one of your counters. If not, miss a turn.

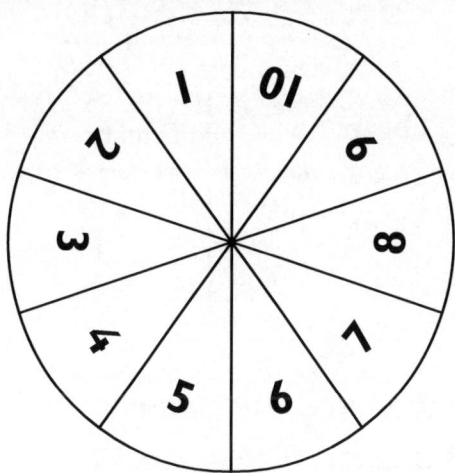

You need:

- paper clip
- pencil
- 40 counters: 20 in one colour, 20 in another

- The winner is the first player to place 5 of their counters in a column, row or diagonal.

	32 ÷ 4	20 ÷ 10	10 ÷ 5	20 ÷ 4	18 ÷ 6	30 ÷ 10	
16 ÷ 4	5 ÷ 5	2 ÷ 2	21 ÷ 3	6 ÷ 3	14 ÷ 2	4 ÷ 4	24 ÷ 3
70 ÷ 10	27 ÷ 3	36 ÷ 4	40 ÷ 5	60 ÷ 10	28 ÷ 4	12 ÷ 2	18 ÷ 2
8 ÷ 2	24 ÷ 6	100 ÷ 10	12 ÷ 3	18 ÷ 3	15 ÷ 5	6 ÷ 2	60 ÷ 6
42 ÷ 6	15 ÷ 3	4 ÷ 2	16 ÷ 2	12 ÷ 4	54 ÷ 6	90 ÷ 10	8 ÷ 4
20 ÷ 5	24 ÷ 4	50 ÷ 5	10 ÷ 2	6 ÷ 6	3 ÷ 3	30 ÷ 5	40 ÷ 10
50 ÷ 10	25 ÷ 5	30 ÷ 6	48 ÷ 6	30 ÷ 3	12 ÷ 6	80 ÷ 10	35 ÷ 5
	40 ÷ 4	20 ÷ 2	45 ÷ 5	9 ÷ 3	36 ÷ 6	10 ÷ 10	

Collins New Primary Maths

Name _____ Date _____

Estimating and checking

- **Estimate and check calculations**

Examples

Example 1

27 × 4 =

Estimate	Calculate	Check
30 × 4 = 120	20 × 4 = 80	27 × 2 = 54
	7 × 4 = 28	54 × 2 = 108
	80 + 28 = 108	

Example 2

73 ÷ 3 =

Estimate	Calculate	Check
75 ÷ 3 = 25	(60 + 13) ÷ 3	24 × 3
	= (60 ÷ 3) + (13 ÷ 3)	20 × 3 = 60
	= 20 + 4 R1	4 × 3 = 12
	= 24 R1	60 + 12 + 1 = 73

Estimate, calculate and check the answers to each of these calculations. Show all your working.

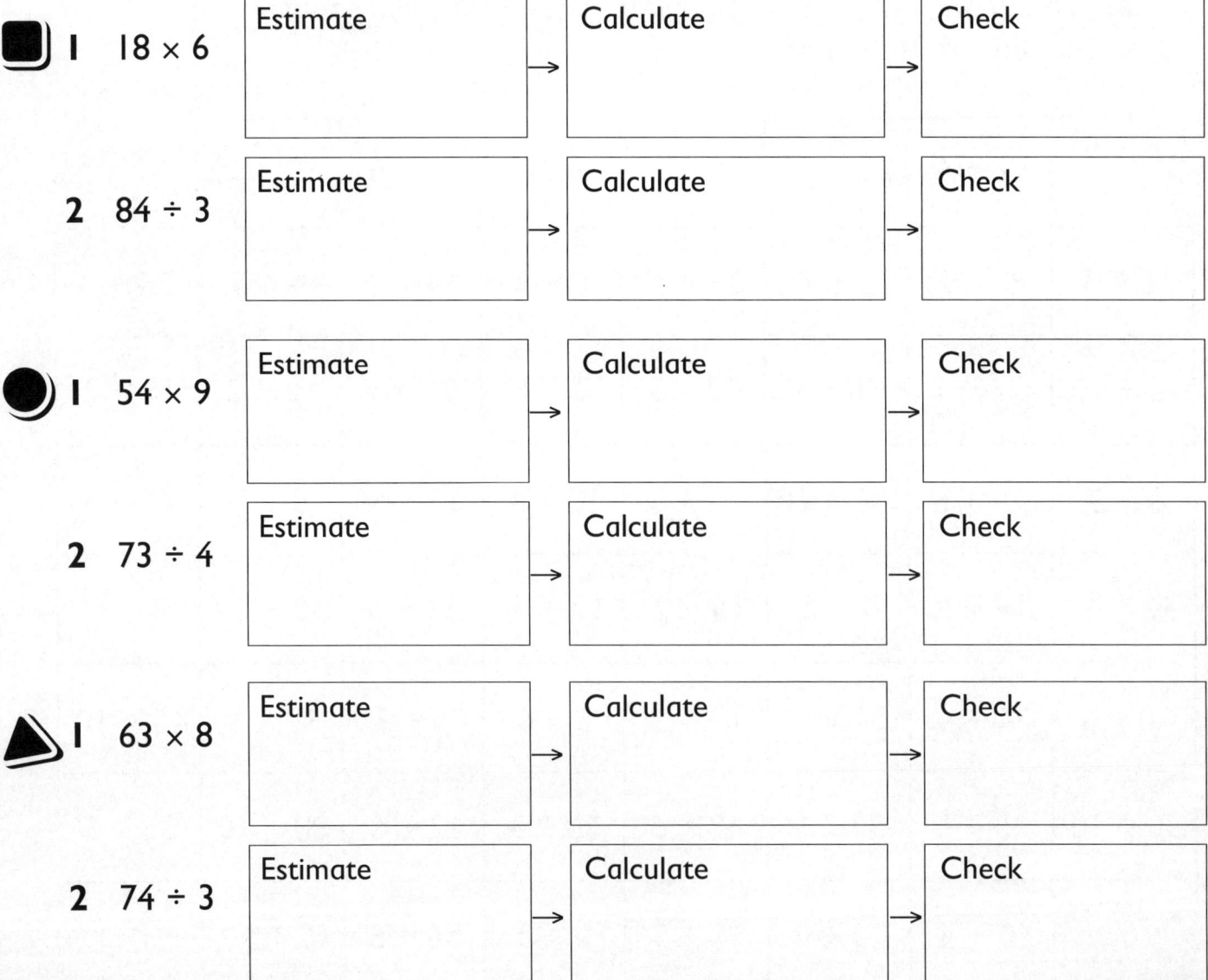

■ 1   18 × 6   Estimate → Calculate → Check

2   84 ÷ 3   Estimate → Calculate → Check

● 1   54 × 9   Estimate → Calculate → Check

2   73 ÷ 4   Estimate → Calculate → Check

▲ 1   63 × 8   Estimate → Calculate → Check

2   74 ÷ 3   Estimate → Calculate → Check

Name _____ Date _____

Four way fit

1 Cut out the eight shapes at the foot of the page.

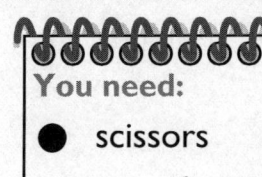

You need:
● scissors

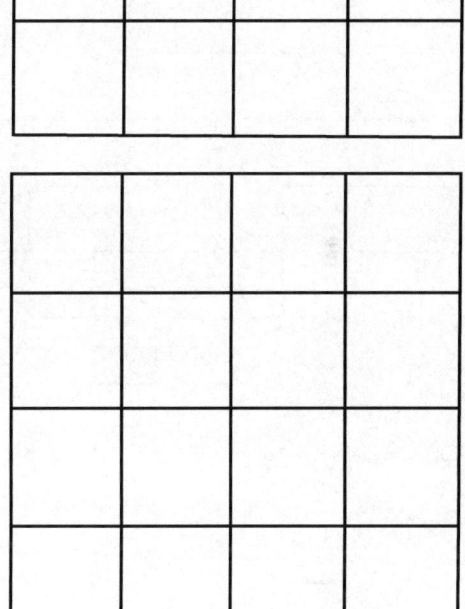

2 Use four 'T-shapes'.
Fit them on this grid.

Now use colour to show how the shapes fitted on the grid.

3 Use four 'L-shapes'.
Fit them on this grid.

Colour the grid to show how the shapes covered the grid.

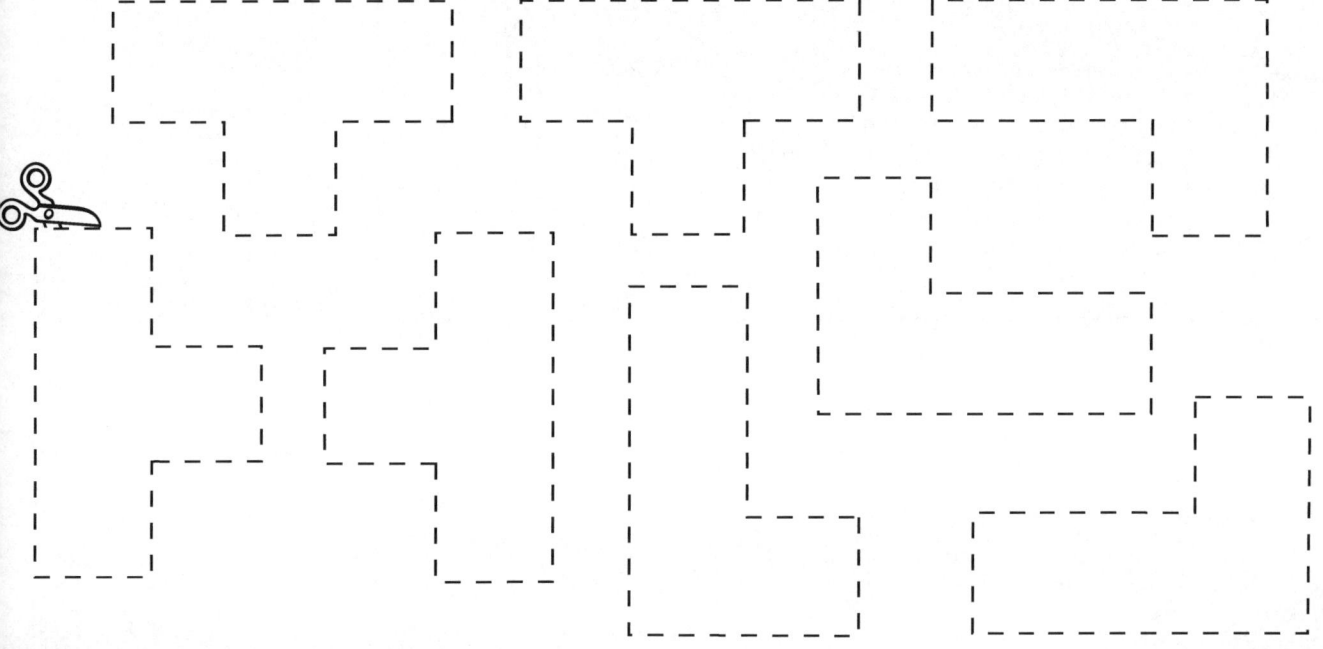

Collins
New
Primary
Maths

Name _____ Date _____

Rectangular patterns

● **Describe shapes and patterns**

Continue these patterns as far as you can go.

Use two colours for each pattern.

You need:
● colouring materials

 Pattern 1   Pattern 2

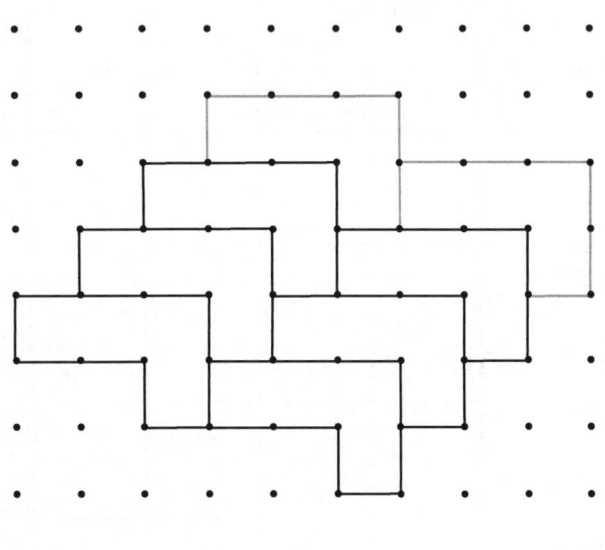

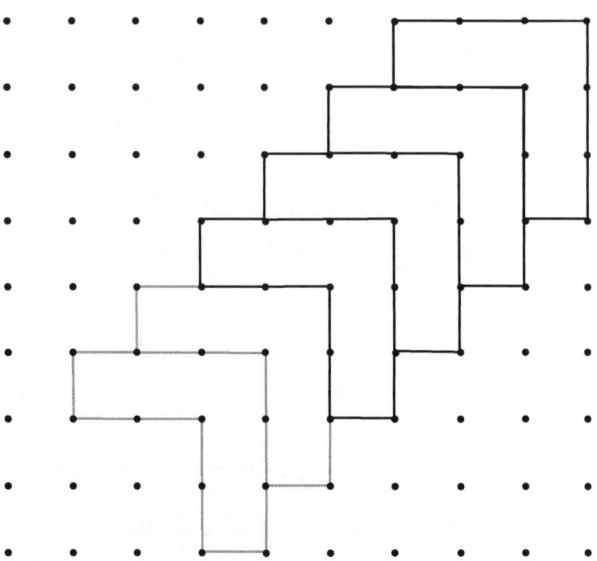

■ Pattern 1   Pattern 2

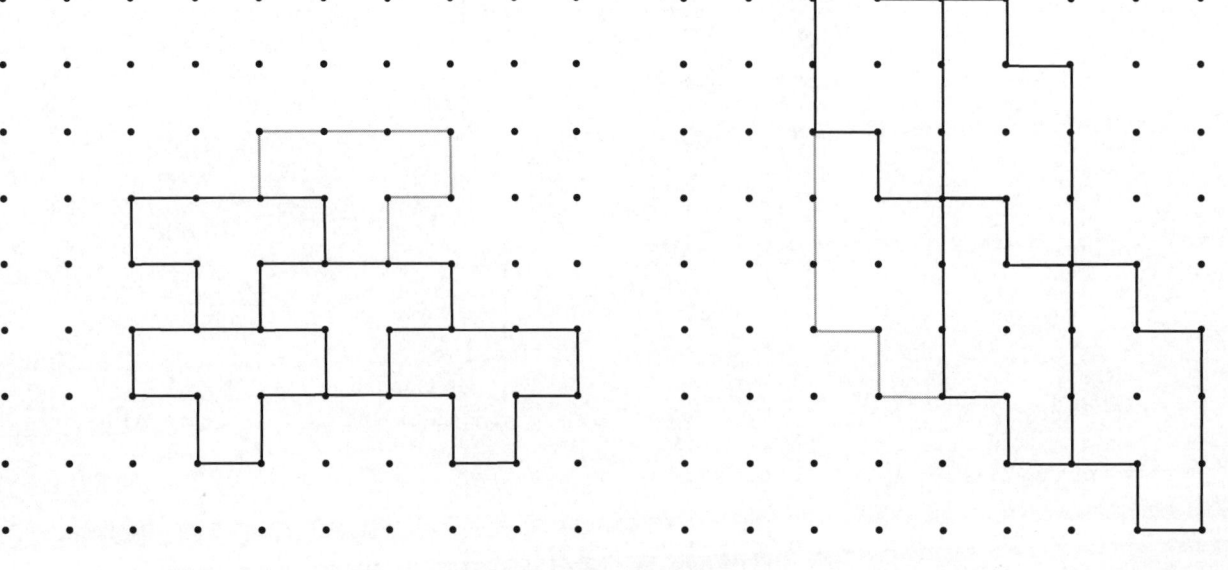

Name _____ Date _____

Kitchen capacities

● **Know how many millilitres are the same as one litre**

 Find these containers in your kitchen.
Estimate how much each holds and complete the table.

Container	I estimate
Kettle	
Teapot	
Saucepan	
Teacup	
My favourite mug	

You need:
● variety of kitchen containers

Catherine uses these containers in her kitchen.

800 ml $1\frac{1}{2}$ l   200 ml   300 ml

1 Fill the kettle.
A full kettle holds [ ] litres or [ ] millilitres.

2 Fill the teapot from the kettle.
The teapot holds [ ] ml.
There are [ ] ml left in the kettle.

3 Pour out a cup of tea.
The cup holds [ ] ml.
There are [ ] ml left in the teapot.

4 The teapot will fill [ ] cups.

5 Catherine has made a pot of tea.
How many mugs can she fill? [ ]
How much tea is left in the teapot? [ ]

 On the back of this sheet, write three statements comparing the capacities of the five containers in the section.

Collins
New
Primary
Maths

Name _____ Date _____

Skittles

● **Show information in a tally chart or bar chart**

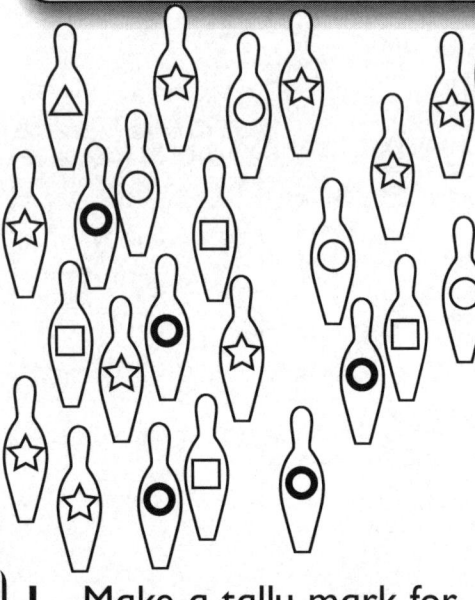

Skittle shape	Tally	Frequency
□		
△		
○		
☆		
◎		

■ **1** Make a tally mark for each skittle. Remember to group the tally marks in fives. Write down the frequencies.

2 Which skittle shape has the highest frequency? ☐

3 How many skittles are there altogether? ☐

4 Write your answer to question 3 using tally marks grouped in fives.

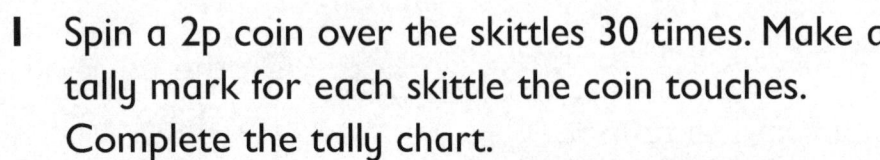

● Copy the empty tally chart from the ■ activity.

1 Spin a 2p coin over the skittles 30 times. Make a tally mark for each skittle the coin touches. Complete the tally chart.

2 Write two sentences about the information displayed in your table.

▲ Draw a bar chart for the tally chart in the ● section.

You need:
● 2p coin

You need:
● squared paper
● ruler
● colouring materials

Collins
New
Primary
Maths

Name _____ Date _____

Ladybird bar chart

- **Show information using tally charts, bar charts and pictograms**

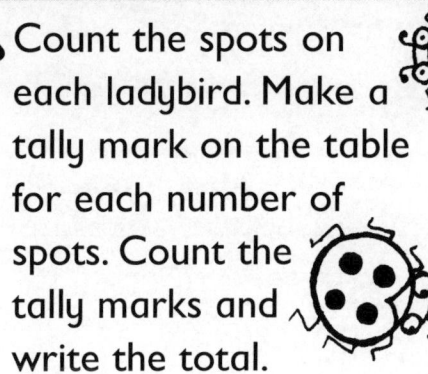

Count the spots on each ladybird. Make a tally mark on the table for each number of spots. Count the tally marks and write the total.

Spots	Tally	Total
2		
3		
4		
5		
6		

Spots on ladybirds

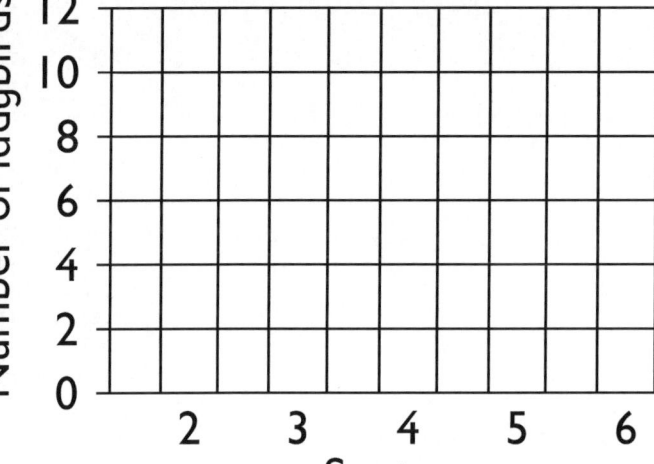

Number of ladybirds (vertical axis: 0, 2, 4, 6, 8, 10, 12)
Spots (horizontal axis: 2, 3, 4, 5, 6)

You need:
- colouring materials

1 Using the information above, complete the bar chart.

2 a What does the shortest bar tell you?

b Which are more common – 4 spots or 5 spots?

c How many ladybirds have more than 4 spots?

Draw a pictogram for the tally chart in the ● section.

You need:
- squared paper
- ruler
- colouring materials

Collins New Primary Maths

Name _____ Date _____

Carroll characters

- **Sort objects using Carroll diagrams**

■ These capital letters are drawn using straight lines and curved lines.

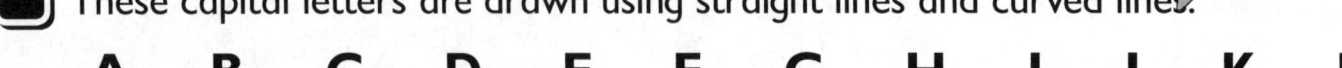

A B C D E F G H I J K L

Copy them into the correct part of the Carroll diagram.

Curved	Not curved

● 1 Sort the above capital letters using the Carroll diagram.
2 Write the totals in the circles.

	Curved	Not curved
Symmetry		
No symmetry		

3 How many letters have straight lines but no symmetry? ☐

▲ 1 Decide how to sort these symbols. On the back of this sheet, draw a Carroll diagram and sort the symbols.

! £ = % / & + (@ ✗ ?

2 Write two sentences about your diagram.

C. Collins
New
Primary
Maths

Name _____ Date _____

Partition and add

- **Develop and use written methods for addition**

Make up five addition calculations for yourself and work them out using the written partitioning method. Use a combination of 2-digit and 3-digit numbers.

Example	1
37 + 56 = 93 30 + 7 50 + 6 ———— 80 + 13	
2	**3**
4	**5**

Explain to someone at home how this method works and ask them if they think it is a good method. Write down what they say.

Name _____ Date _____

Which operation?

- Solve word problems in 'real life' and money, using
  one or more steps

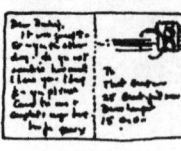

| 22p | 13p | 2p | £10 |
| stamps | postcards | envelopes | phonecards |

 1 Write in the circle the sign for the operation you will use.

2 Write the calculation necessary to answer the question.

3 Write the answer to the problem.

a John bought 4 stamps. ⊗
How much did he spend?

Calculation: [＿＿＿＿＿]

Answer: [＿＿]

b Mr Ali bought 35 phonecards. ◯
How much did he spend?

Calculation: [＿＿＿＿＿]

Answer: [＿＿]

c Sylvia has 90p to spend. ◯
How many envelopes can she
buy?

Calculation: [＿＿＿＿＿]

Answer: [＿＿]

d The postman has delivered a box ◯
of envelopes. There are 450 inside.
How much is the whole box worth?

Calculation: [＿＿＿＿＿]

Answer: [＿＿]

e Sebastian has saved £450. How ◯
many phonecards can he buy?

Calculation: [＿＿＿＿＿]

Answer: [＿＿]

f Seven people buy 5 phonecards ◯
each. How many phonecards are sold?

Calculation: [＿＿＿＿＿]

Answer: [＿＿]

g Susan bought 4 rows of stamps. ◯
There were 12 stamps in each
row. How many did she buy?

Calculation: [＿＿＿＿＿]

Answer: [＿＿]

h Carol bought 3 postcards, ◯
3 envelopes and 3 stamps.
How much did she spend?

Calculation: [＿＿＿＿＿]

Answer: [＿＿]

Collins
New
Primary
Maths

Name _____ Date _____

Measuring in millilitres

- **Read scales to the nearest division or half division**

 On Monday, Carlo the ice-cream maker carefully measured out these fruit juices. Write on the label how much juice there is in each container.

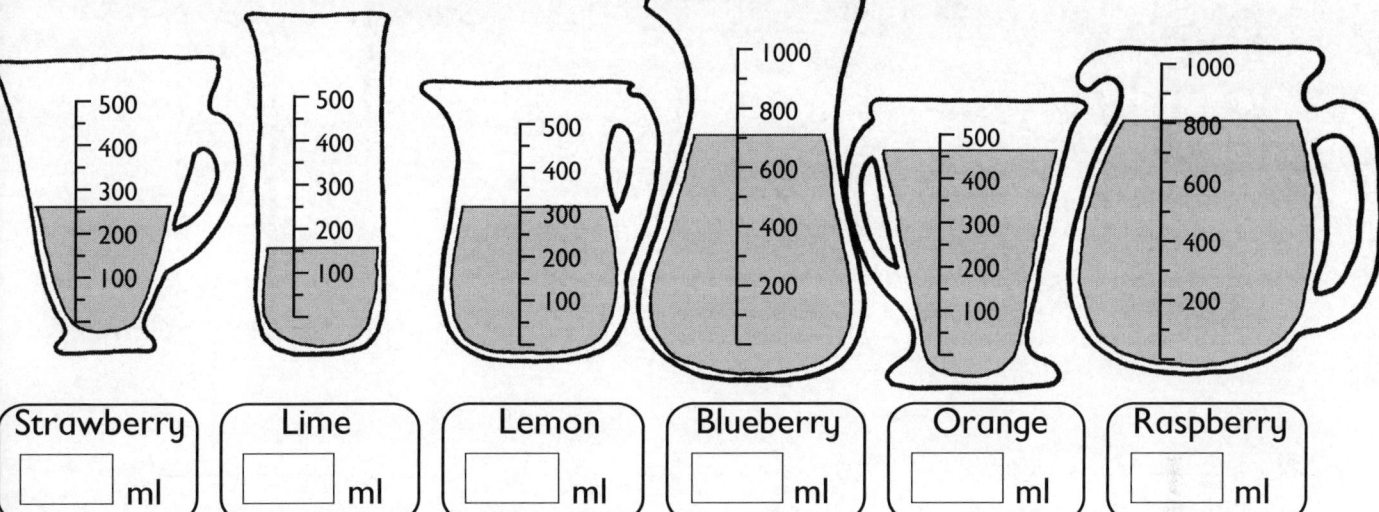

Strawberry	Lime	Lemon	Blueberry	Orange	Raspberry
⬚ ml	⬚ ml	⬚ ml	⬚ ml	⬚ ml	⬚ ml

The weather is very warm. Carlo has to make twice as much ice cream as on Monday. Fill each container with the correct amount of fruit juice. Write the flavour of the fruit juice underneath, and the amount of juice in the container. Remember to choose a suitable container for each amount.

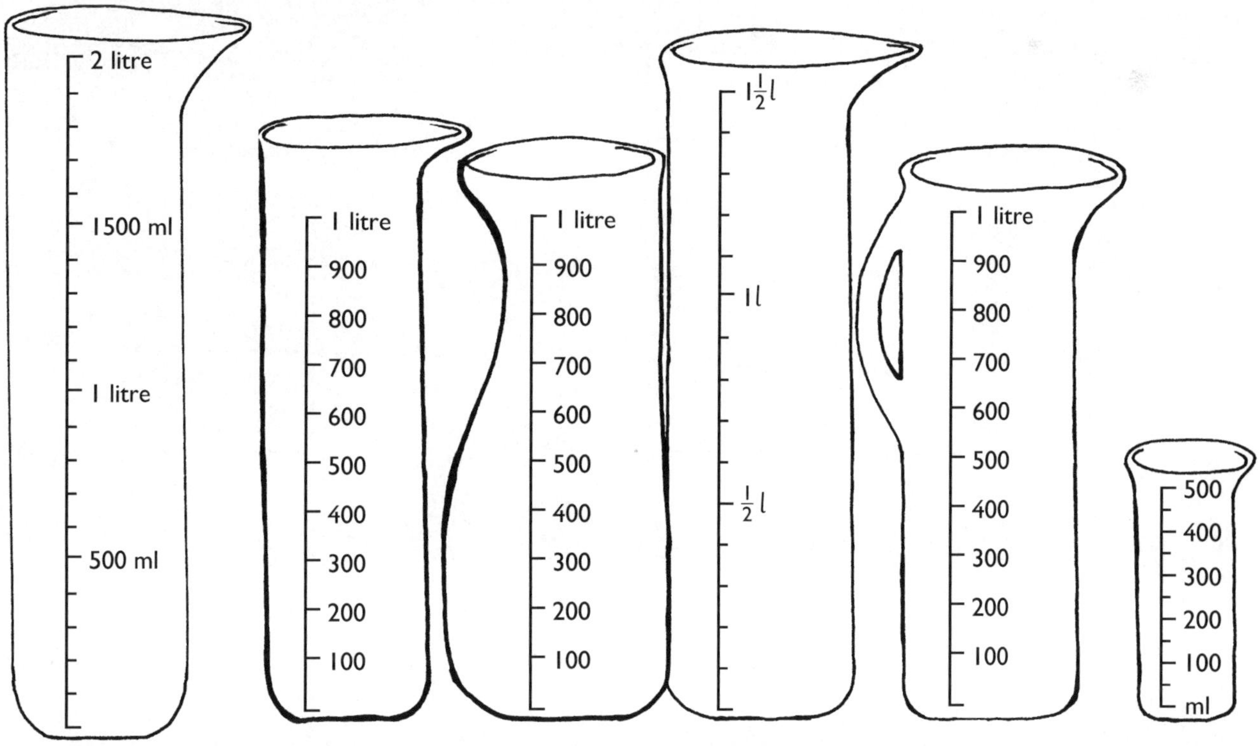

⬚ ml	⬚ ml	⬚ ml	⬚ ml	⬚ ml	⬚ ml

© HarperCollins*Publishers* Ltd 2008

Collins
New
Primary
Maths

Name _____ Date _____

Robot routes

- **Solve a puzzle involving right-angled turns**

You need:
- ruler

I can navigate 10 different routes from start to finish.

Here is one route.
Can you find the other 9?

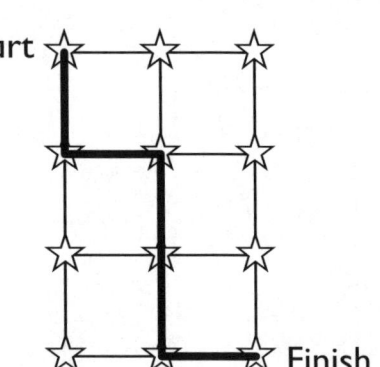

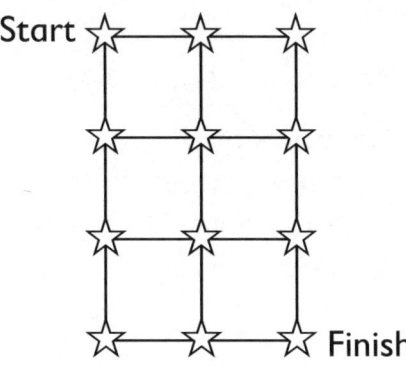

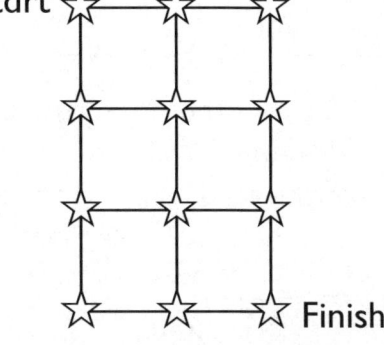

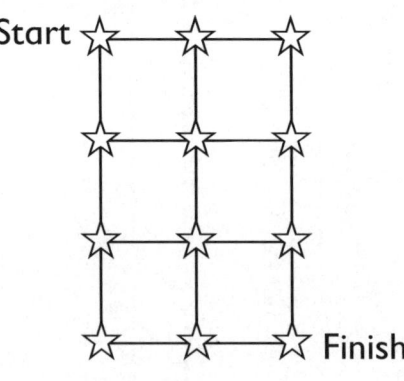

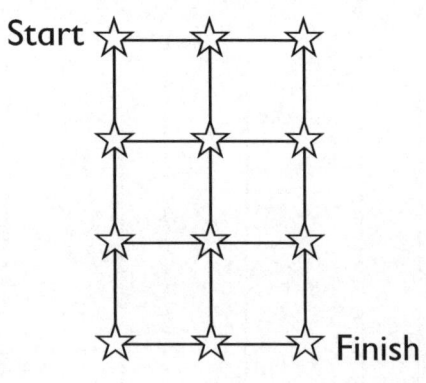

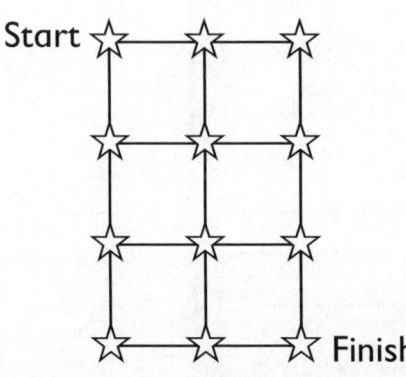

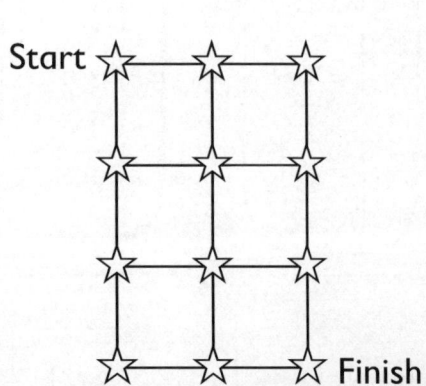

Collins
New
Primary
Maths

Name _____ Date _____

Coin change

• **Partition numbers in different ways**

Make up the amounts in each purse by choosing coins from each bag.

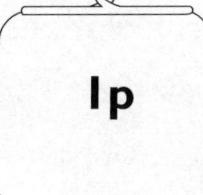

a 59p → ☐ p in 10p coins
→ ☐ p in 1p coins

b 83p → ☐ p in 10p coins
→ ☐ p in 1p coins

c 75p → ☐ p in 10p coins
→ ☐ p in 1p coins

d 96p → ☐ p in 10p coins
→ ☐ p in 1p coins

Make up the amounts in each purse by choosing coins from all 3 bags.

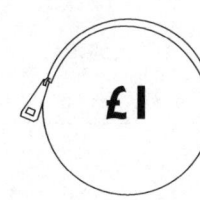

a

£5.25

b
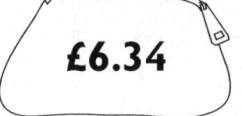
£6.34

c

£7.06

→ £ ☐ in £1 coins
→ ☐ p in 10p coins
→ ☐ p in 1p coins

→ £ ☐ in £1 coins
→ ☐ p in 10p coins
→ ☐ p in 1p coins

→ £ ☐ in £1 coins
→ ☐ p in 10p coins
→ ☐ p in 1p coins

Carrie, Kerry and Kiri paid £3.50 for their ticket to the cinema. Each paid with a different number of £1, 10p and 1p coins. Which coins might each girl have used?

Carrie
→ £ ☐ in £1 coins
→ ☐ p in 10p coins
→ ☐ p in 1p coins

Kerry
→ £ ☐ in £1 coins
→ ☐ p in 10p coins
→ ☐ p in 1p coins

Kiri
→ £ ☐ in £1 coins
→ ☐ p in 10p coins
→ ☐ p in 1p coins

© Collins
New
Primary
Maths

Clever calculations

● **Develop and use written methods for addition**

Name _____ Date _____

Write out the calculations and work out the answers.

 a 31 + 25

	3	1		
	2	5	+	
tens	5	0		
units		6		
answer	5	6		

b 42 + 34
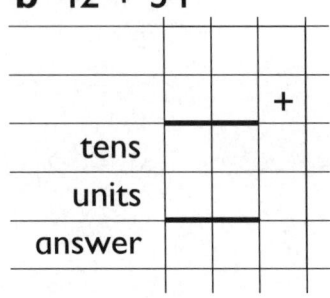

c 62 + 27
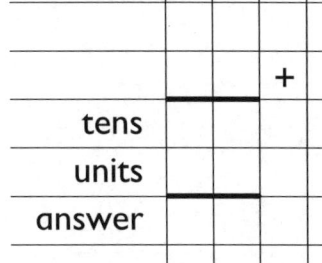

d 13 + 26
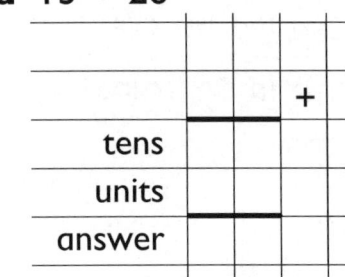

e 52 + 17
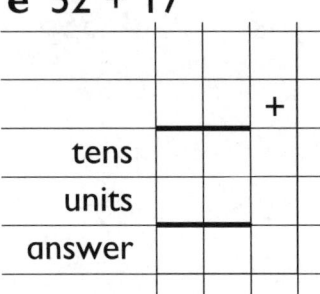

f 43 + 36
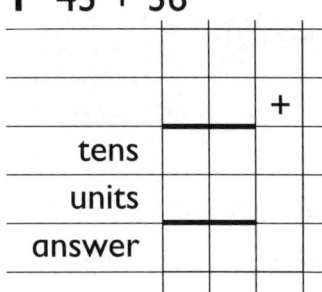

 **a** 137 + 42

	1	3	7		
		4	2	+	
hundreds	1	0	0		
tens		7	0		
units			9		
answer	1	7	9		

b 153 + 25
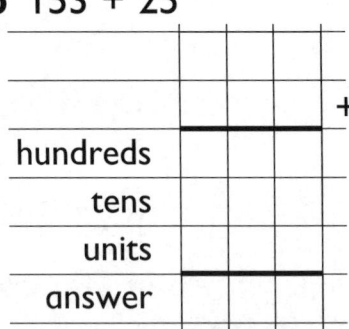

c 146 + 33
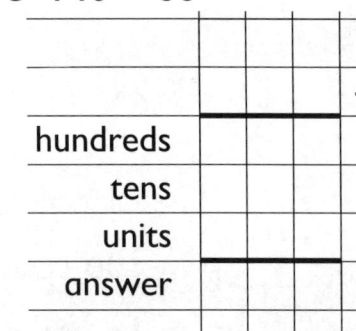

d 139 + 46
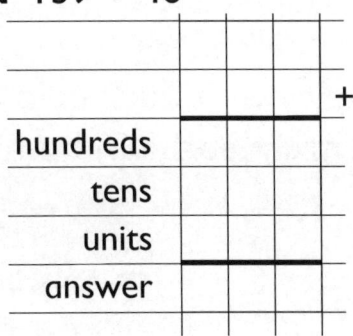

e 162 + 29
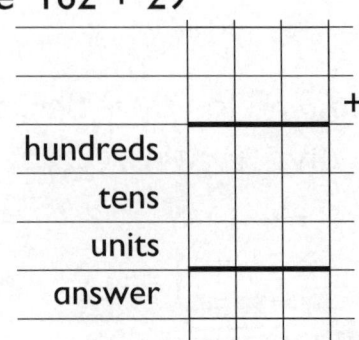

f 155 + 38
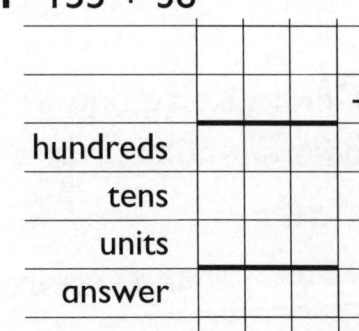

 On the back of this sheet, make up five HTU + HTU calculations for yourself.

Name _____ Date _____

Pie fractions

- **Use diagrams to compare fractions**

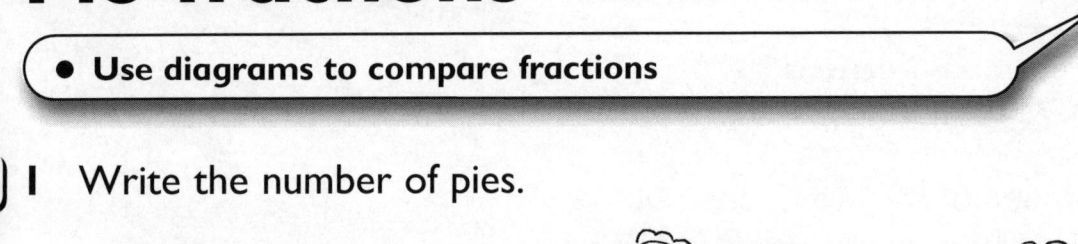

1 Write the number of pies.

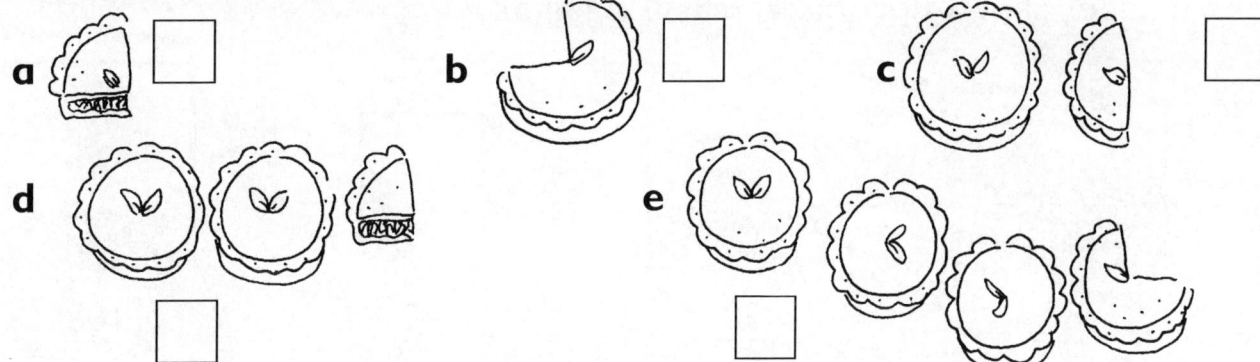

a ☐   b ☐   c ☐

d ☐   e ☐

2 Fill in the missing fractions.

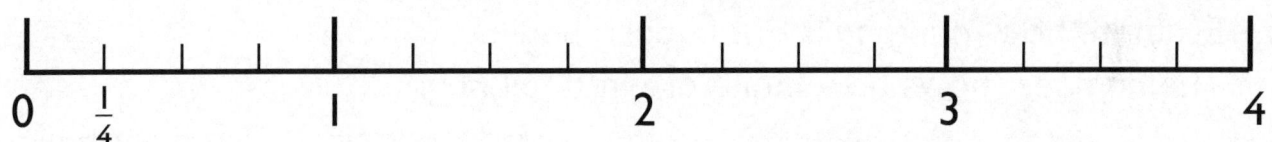

0    $\frac{1}{4}$ 1   2   3   4

1 Complete the number line in the ■ section and use it to help you answer these questions. Write the larger fraction.

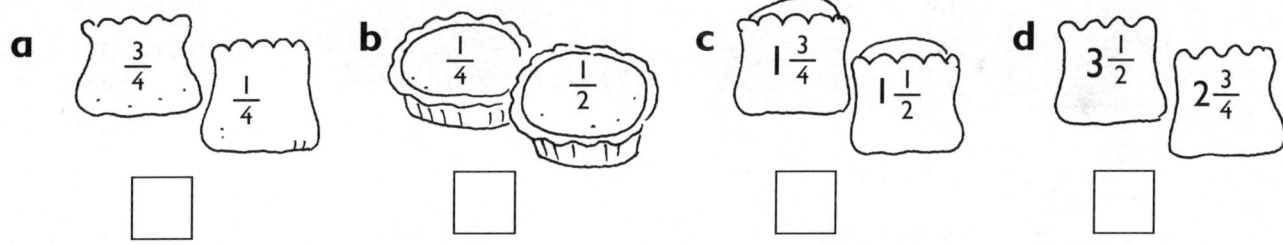

a $\frac{3}{4}$ $\frac{1}{4}$ ☐   b $\frac{1}{4}$ $\frac{1}{2}$ ☐   c $1\frac{3}{4}$ $1\frac{1}{2}$ ☐   d $3\frac{1}{2}$ $2\frac{3}{4}$ ☐

2 Write any number that lies between each of the following.

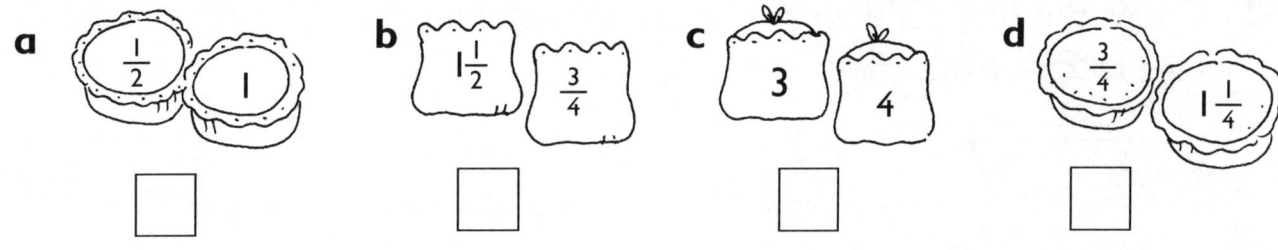

a $\frac{1}{2}$ 1 ☐   b $1\frac{1}{2}$ $\frac{3}{4}$ ☐   c 3 4 ☐   d $\frac{3}{4}$ $1\frac{1}{4}$ ☐

Write down the number that lies halfway between each of the following.

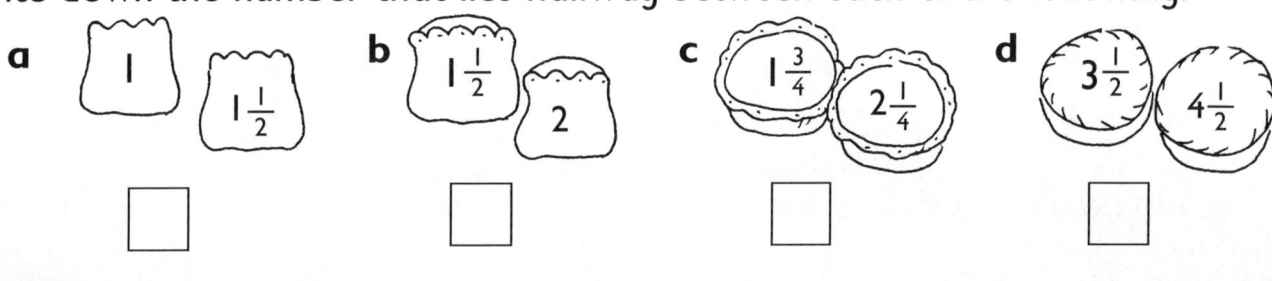

a 1 $1\frac{1}{2}$ ☐   b $1\frac{1}{2}$ 2 ☐   c $1\frac{3}{4}$ $2\frac{1}{4}$ ☐   d $3\frac{1}{2}$ $4\frac{1}{2}$ ☐

Builders' estimates

- **Identify and estimate fractions**

■ Estimate the number of screws in each box.
The number shows how many are in a full box.

| **a** | **b** | **c** | **d** |

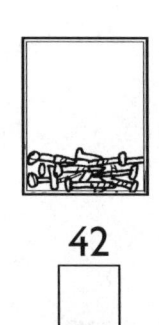 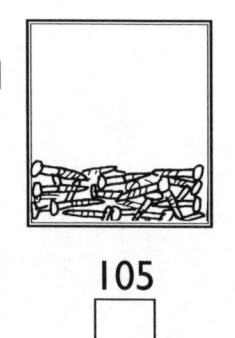

87   58   42   105

● 1 Estimate how many nails are in each bag.
The number shows how many are in a full bag.

a   **b**   **c**   **d**

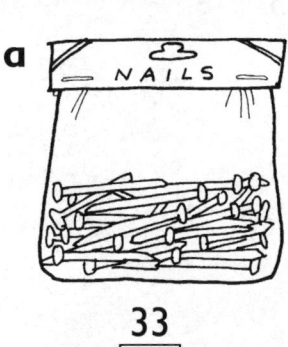 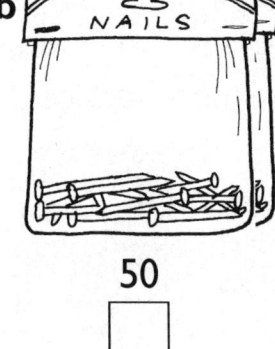 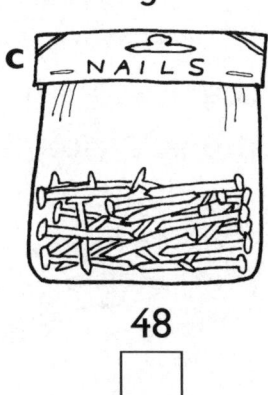 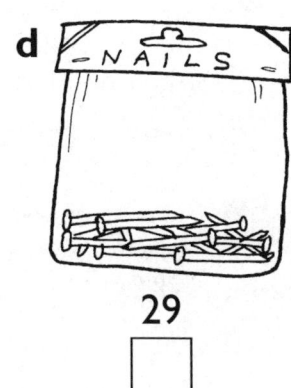

33   50   48   29

2 Count the tiles on the roof. Estimate the number of
tiles to cover the roof.

a 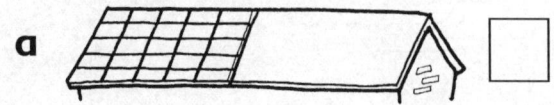   **b**

c    **d**

 Explain how you worked out your answer for question **1a** in the ● activity.

Name _____ Date _____

Multiplying two-digit numbers

- **Multiply a two-digit number by a one-digit number**

Write a one-digit number greater than 2 in each grey box. Then multiply the two numbers together. Be sure to estimate your answer first.

a 14 × ⬜ = ⬜

b 16 × ⬜ = ⬜

c 23 × ⬜ = ⬜

a 57 × ⬜ = ⬜

b 63 × ⬜ = ⬜

c 48 × ⬜ = ⬜

d 76 × ⬜ = ⬜

e 89 × ⬜ = ⬜

f 94 × ⬜ = ⬜

a 116 × ⬜ = ⬜

b 154 × ⬜ = ⬜

c 163 × ⬜ = ⬜

Collins
New
Primary
Maths

Name _____   Date _____

Dividing two-digit numbers

- **Divide a two-digit number by a one-digit number**

■ Write a one-digit number greater than 2 in each grey box. Then divide the two-digit number by the one-digit number. Be sure to estimate your answer first.

a $14 \div \boxed{} = \boxed{}$

b $32 \div \boxed{} = \boxed{}$

c $58 \div \boxed{} = \boxed{}$

● **a** $63 \div \boxed{} = \boxed{}$

b $79 \div \boxed{} = \boxed{}$

c $86 \div \boxed{} = \boxed{}$

d $97 \div \boxed{} = \boxed{}$

e $68 \div \boxed{} = \boxed{}$

f $83 \div \boxed{} = \boxed{}$

▲ **a** $114 \div \boxed{} = \boxed{}$

b $122 \div \boxed{} = \boxed{}$

c $126 \div \boxed{} = \boxed{}$

Your Life
KS4 Co-ordinator's File

The whole-school solution for Citizenship and PSHE

John Foster

Contents

Introduction

This book provides teachers with suggestions how to use the *Your Life 4* and *Your Life 5* student books in the form of lesson plans and with additional materials, presented as copymasters.

Planning the course

The *Your Life 4* and *Your Life 5* Student Books together provide a course that meets the requirements for Personal, Social, Health and Economic Education (PSHEE) and for Citizenship at Key Stage 4. Using the Your Life books as the core of a course, therefore, ensures that a school is not only covering the statutory requirement for Citizenship, but also the non-statutory guidelines for Personal wellbeing and Economic wellbeing and financial capability. Specific units included in the Keeping Healthy strand of the course also provide appropriate sex and relationship education that can be incorporated into a school's own sex education policy. Similarly, there are units in the Economic wellbeing and financial capability strand designed to develop students' awareness of themselves and their aptitudes, as part of the school's careers and guidance programme.

As the units in each of the books are divided into four strands – Developing as a citizen; Personal wellbeing – understanding yourself and handling relationships; Personal wellbeing – keeping healthy; and Economic wellbeing and financial capability – it is possible to plan to deliver the course strand by strand. This arrangement may suit schools in which the course is being delivered by a team of teachers with expertise in different areas. However, the units within each strand are free-standing and can, therefore, be delivered in any order. Schools can either use the units in any sequence they choose, or they can follow the order in which they appear in the books. Whatever the school decides, there is sufficient material in each book to provide the basis for a full year's course.

Planning a unit

Each of the units in *Your Life 4* or *Your Life 5* covers a specific area of either the PSHEE or the Citizenship curriculum in two to three lessons. The lessons within a unit are planned so that there is a clear progression in the way that a student's knowledge and understanding of the topic is developed. Thus in Unit 5 (Crime and punishment), the first lesson examines youth crime, focusing on criminal responsibility and anti-social behaviour, the second lesson explores the youth justice system and youth courts, and the third lesson explores the kinds of sentencing available to the courts and prison as a form of punishment. Similarly, in Unit 7 (It's your council), the first lesson explains what local government is and how it functions, the second lesson examines how local government could be reformed, and the third lesson explores what devolution is.

It is important that the course co-ordinator draws the attention of the teachers in their team to these links between lessons at the start of a unit. Therefore, it is suggested that the lesson plans are distributed to teachers unit-by-unit rather than lesson-by-lesson.

Using the lesson plans

Each lesson plan is presented on a separate sheet, so that it can be duplicated easily and distributed to teachers. The lesson plans all have the same structure so that they are easy to follow:

1 The learning **aim** is stated, so that it can be made clear to the students. It can be written up on the board and explained at the beginning, and referred to during the lesson. If it is the second, or third lesson of a unit, the ways in which the learning aim follows on from the previous lesson(s) and links to subsequent lesson(s) can be explained.

2 Details are given of any **preparation** that is required for the activities. The resources are mainly optional. Often the only resource needed is one of the copymasters that are available and that is only if the teacher decides to incorporate one of the suggested extension activities into the main lesson.

3 A short **starter** activity is suggested as a way into the topic and these take a variety of forms. In some instances, the starter activity involves asking students to do a brainstorm, e.g. to suggest what human rights are; the teacher lists their ideas on the board, prior to a detailed exploration of the question during the main part of the lesson. Another type of starter activity involves asking them what they already know about a topic, e.g. elections. Other activities involve the explanation of key terms, such as 'devolution', and writing definitions of them on the board. Often, it is possible to incorporate the explanation of the learning objective as part of the starter activity. The length of time allocated to the starter activity will obviously vary depending on the activity, but typically it is expected to occupy approximately five minutes of the lesson.

4 **Suggested activities** are designed for the main part of the lesson. These vary according to the topic. Many of the activities require students to study an article prior to discussing it in pairs or groups, then sharing their ideas in a class discussion. Others present a number of statements expressing different opinions on a controversial issue for students to debate. There are also suggestions for writing activities ranging from making lists and writing e-mails to designing leaflets and posters.

There are sufficient suggestions to fill an hour's lesson. However, the length of a lesson varies from school to school, and in many cases may be less than an hour. When planning the lesson, therefore, teachers may have to decide which of the suggested activities to include. Obviously, the more activities that are completed, the more comprehensively a topic will be covered. However, in the majority of the lessons, it is not essential for all the activities to be done in order for the learning objective to be achieved.

5 There is a **plenary** activity that is designed to round off the lesson by drawing attention to what has been learned. This is usually an oral activity, for example, in which the teacher summarises the main points of the lesson in some way. The aim of the plenary activity is to review and reinforce the learning that has taken place is the main body of the lesson.

6 For each lesson, there are a number of **extension activities**. These can be done either within the main lesson as additional activities or can be set as follow-up work. This section includes the activities that can be developed using the copymasters provided in the Teacher's Resources. It also contains suggestions for activities that require more time than a single lesson to complete (for example, preparing and carrying out a survey). There are also research activities encouraging the students to use the Internet in order to find out more information on the topic.

7 **Further resources** are listed where appropriate. These take the form of details of websites and are designed to allow students to research the topic further, for follow-up project work and personal interest.

The copymasters

There are either two or three copymasters per unit, depending on the number of lessons within that unit. Each copymaster provides additional material that can be either incorporated within the main lesson or used as an extension activity. At least one of the copymasters in each unit provides an activity that can be used to assess the students' knowledge and understanding of the topic. Many of these assessment copymasters contain some form of writing activity: filling in a word puzzle; answering a multiple-choice quiz; deciding whether a series of statements are true or false. They are designed so that they can be done individually or in pairs, and students are often encouraged to check their own answers by referring to the relevant pages of the Student Book.

The other copymasters range from questionnaires and ranking activities to writing replies for letters sent to an agony aunt. Several of them contain further material for which space could not be found in the Student Book. Thus, one of the copymasters for Unit 5 (Crime and punishment) focuses in detail on knife crime, one for Unit 6 (It's your government) provides detailed arguments for and against giving 16 year olds the vote, and one for Unit 14 (Safer sex and contraception) presents information and views on the subject of abortion.

The overall aim of the copymasters is to provide a range of flexible materials that teachers can use, as appropriate, either to assess students' grasp of a topic or to extend and develop further investigation of that topic.

CD-ROM

The enclosed CD-ROM contains PDF files of all the lesson plans and copymasters, so you can either print them or photocopy them – whichever is easier. In order to use these files you must have Acrobat Reader installed. Put the CD-ROM into your CD-ROM drive and, if you are using a PC, double-click on the CD-ROM drive icon inside My Computer. Or, if you are using a Mac, double-click on the CD-ROM icon on your desktop. Then double-click on the file you want to use.

How *Your Life 4* and *5* meet the requirements of the Key Stage 4 National Curriculum for Citizenship

The National Curriculum for Citizenship at Key Stage 4 stresses the importance of effective citizenship education and that citizenship should develop social and moral responsibility, community involvement and political literacy. The particular units of *Your Life 4* and *5* that meet the specific requirements of the Citizenship curriculum are detailed below.

1. Key concepts

1.1 Democracy and justice		
1.1a Participating actively in different kinds of decision-making and voting in order to influence public life.		
Your Life 4	Unit 6	It's your government
	Unit 7	It's your council
	Unit 8	Working for change
1.1b Weighing up what is fair and unfair in different situations, understanding that justice is fundamental to a democratic society and exploring the role of law in maintaining order and resolving conflict.		
Your Life 4	Unit 4	The law of the land
	Unit 5	Crime and punishment
1.1c Considering how democracy, justice, diversity, toleration, respect and freedom are valued by people with different beliefs, backgrounds and traditions within a changing democratic society.		
Your Life 4	Unit 13	Challenging offensive behaviour
1.1d Understanding and exploring the roles of citizens and parliament in holding government and those in power to account.		
Your Life 4	Unit 6	It's your government
	Unit 7	It's your council
1.2 Rights and responsibilities		
1.2a Exploring different kinds of rights and obligations and how these affect both individuals and communities.		
Your Life 4	Unit 2	Human rights
	Unit 3	Rights and responsibilities
	Unit 13	Challenging offensive behaviour
Your Life 5	Unit 2	Human rights
1.2b Understanding that individuals, organisations and governments have responsibilities to ensure that rights are balanced, supported and protected.		
Your Life 4	Unit 2	Human rights
	Unit 3	Rights and responsibilities
	Unit 13	Challenging offensive behaviour
Your Life 5	Unit 2	Human rights

1.2c	Investigating ways in which rights can compete and conflict, and understanding that hard decisions have to be made to try to balance these.		
	Your Life 4	Unit 2	Human rights
	Your Life 5	Unit 2	Human rights

1.3 Identities and diversity: living together in the UK			
1.3a	Appreciating that identities are complex, can change over time and are informed by different understandings of what it means to be a citizen in the UK.		
	Your Life 4	Unit 1	Britain: a diverse society
1.3b	Exploring the diverse national, regional, ethnic and religious cultures, groups and communities in the UK and the connections between them.		
	Your Life 4	Unit 1	Britain: a diverse society
1.3c	Considering the interconnections between the UK and the rest of Europe and the wider world.		
	Your Life 4	Unit 1	Britain: a diverse society
1.3d	Exploring community cohesion and the different forces that bring about change in communities over time.		
	Your Life 4	Unit 1	Britain: a diverse society

2. Key processes

2.1 Critical thinking and enquiry			
2.1a	Be able to question and reflect on different ideas, opinions, beliefs and values when exploring topical and controversial issues and problems.		
	Your Life 4	Unit 1	Britain: a diverse society
		Unit 2	Human rights
		Unit 3	Rights and responsibilities
		Unit 4	The law of the land
		Unit 5	Crime and punishment
		Unit 6	It's your government
		Unit 7	It's your council
		Unit 13	Challenging offensive behaviour
	Your Life 5	Unit 1	The UK and its relations with the rest of the world
		Unit 2	Human rights
		Unit 3	Media matters
		Unit 4	Global challenges – wars, weapons and terrorism
		Unit 5	Global challenges – environmental issues
		Unit 6	Global challenges – poverty, education and health
		Unit 7	Working for change
		Unit 8	Co-operating on a community project
		Unit 9	Developing your own values
		Unit 20	The UK economy
		Unit 21	The global economy

2.1b Be able to research, plan and undertake enquiries into issues and problems using a range of information, sources and methods.

Your Life 4	Unit 1	Britain: a diverse society
	Unit 2	Human rights
	Unit 3	Rights and responsibilities
	Unit 5	Crime and punishment
Your Life 5	Unit 1	The UK and its relations with the rest of the world
	Unit 3	Media matters
	Unit 4	Global challenges – wars, weapons and terrorism
	Unit 5	Global challenges – environmental issues
	Unit 6	Global challenges – poverty, education and health
	Unit 9	Developing your own values
	Unit 20	The UK economy
	Unit 21	The global economy

2.1c Be able to interpret and analyse critically sources used, identifying different values, ideas and viewpoints and recognising bias.

Your Life 4	Unit 1	Britain: a diverse society
	Unit 2	Human rights
	Unit 3	Rights and responsibilities
Your Life 5	Unit 1	The UK and its relations with the rest of the world
	Unit 3	Media matters
	Unit 4	Global challenges – wars, weapons and terrorism
	Unit 5	Global challenges – environmental issues

2.1d Be able to evaluate different viewpoints, exploring connections and relationships between viewpoints and actions in different contexts (from local to global).

Your Life 4	Unit 7	It's your council
Your Life 5	Unit 3	Media matters
	Unit 4	Global challenges – wars, weapons and terrorism
	Unit 5	Global challenges – environmental issues

2.2 Advocacy and representation

2.2a Be able to evaluate critically different ideas and viewpoints including those with which they do not necessarily agree.

Your Life 4	Unit 5	Crime and punishment
Your Life 5	Unit 2	Human rights
	Unit 3	Media matters

2.2b Be able to explain their viewpoint, drawing conclusions from what they have learnt through research, discussion and actions, including formal debates and votes.

Your Life 4	Unit 5	Crime and punishment
Your Life 5	Unit 2	Human rights
	Unit 3	Media matters

2.2c Be able to present a convincing argument that takes account of, and represents, different viewpoints, to try to persuade others to think again, change or support them.

Your Life 4	Unit 5	Crime and punishment
Your Life 5	Unit 2	Human rights
	Unit 3	Media matters

2.3 Taking informed and responsible action

2.3a Be able to explore creative approaches to taking action on problems and issues to achieve intended purposes.

Your Life 4	Unit 8	Working for change
Your Life 5	Unit 7	Working for change
	Unit 8	Co-operating on a community project

2.3b Be able to research, initiate and plan action to address citizenship issues, working individually and with others.

Your Life 4	Unit 8	Working for change
Your Life 5	Unit 8	Co-operating on a community project

2.3c Be able to negotiate, decide on and take action to try to influence others, bring about change or resist unwanted change, managing time and resources appropriately.

Your Life 4	Unit 8	Working for change
Your Life 5	Unit 8	Co-operating on a community project

2.3d Be able to assess critically the impact of their actions on communities and the wider world, now and in the future, and make recommendations to others for future action.

Your Life 4	Unit 8	Working for change
Your Life 5	Unit 8	Co-operating on a community project

2.3e Be able to reflect on the progress they have made, evaluating what they have learned from the intended and unintended consequences of action, and the contributions of others as well as themselves.

Your Life 4	Unit 8	Working for change
Your Life 5	Unit 8	Co-operating on a community project

3. Range and content

3a Political, legal and human rights and freedoms in a range of contexts from local to global.

Your Life 4	Unit 2	Human rights
Your Life 5	Unit 2	Human rights
	Unit 3	Media matters

3b The roles and operations of civil and criminal law and the justice system.

Your Life 4	Unit 4	The law of the land
	Unit 5	Crime and punishment

3c	How laws are made and shaped by people and processes, including the work of parliament, government and the courts.		
	Your Life 4	Unit 4	The law of the land
		Unit 5	Crime and punishment
		Unit 6	It's your government
3d	Actions citizens can take in democratic and electoral processes to influence decisions, locally, nationally and beyond.		
	Your Life 4	Unit 6	It's your government
		Unit 7	It's your council
		Unit 8	Working for change
3e	The operation of parliamentary democracy within the UK and of other forms of government, both democratic and non-democratic, beyond the UK.		
	Your Life 4	Unit 6	It's your government
3f	The development of, and struggle for, different kinds of rights and freedoms (speech, opinion, association and the vote) in the UK.		
	Your Life 4	Unit 2	Human rights
3g	How information is used in public debate and policy formation, including information from the media and from pressure and interest groups.		
	Your Life 4	Unit 8	Working for change
	Your Life 5	Unit 3	Media matters
		Unit 7	Working for change
3h	The impact and consequences of individual and collective actions on communities, including the work of the voluntary sector.		
	Your Life 4	Unit 8	Working for change
	Your Life 5	Unit 8	Co-operating on a community project
3i	Policies and practices for sustainable development and their impact on the environment.		
	Your Life 5	Unit 5	Global challenges – environmental issues
3j	The economy in relation to citizenship, including decisions about the collection and allocation of public money.		
	Your Life 5	Unit 20	The UK economy
		Unit 21	The global economy
3k	The rights and responsibilities of consumers, employers and employees.		
	Your Life 4	Unit 3	Rights and responsibilities
3l	The origins and implications of diversity and the changing nature of society in the UK, including the perspectives and values that are shared or common, and the impact of migration and integration on identities, groups and communities.		
	Your Life 4	Unit 1	Britain: a diverse society
	Your Life 5	Unit 2	Human rights

3m The UK's role in the world, including Europe, the European Union, the Commonwealth, the United Nations.		
Your Life 5	Unit 1	The UK and its relations with the rest of the world

3n The challenges facing the global community, including international disagreements and conflict, and debates about inequalities, sustainability and use of the world's resources.		
Your Life 5	Unit 2	Human rights
	Unit 4	Global challenges – wars, weapons and terrorism
	Unit 5	Global challenges – environmental issues
	Unit 6	Global challenges – poverty, education and health
	Unit 21	The global economy

4. Curriculum opportunities

4a To debate, in groups and whole-class discussions, topical and controversial issues, including those of concern to young people and their communities.		
Your Life 4	Unit 6	It's your government
	Unit 7	It's your council
	Unit 8	Working for change
	Unit 13	Challenging offensive behaviour
Your Life 5	Unit 3	Media matters
	Unit 4	Global challenges – wars, weapons and terrorism
	Unit 5	Global challenges – environmental issues
	Unit 6	Global challenges – poverty, education and health
	Unit 9	Developing your own values
	Unit 21	The global economy

4b To develop citizenship knowledge and understanding while using and applying citizenship skills.		
Your Life 4	Unit 7	It's your council
	Unit 8	Working for change

4c To work individually and in groups, taking on different roles and responsibilities.		
Your Life 4	Unit 8	Working for change
Your Life 5	Unit 8	Co-operating on a community project

4d To participate in both school-based and community-based citizenship activities and reflect on their participation.		
Your Life 4	Unit 8	Working for change
Your Life 5	Unit 8	Co-operating on a community project

4e To participate in different forms of individual and collective action, including decision-making and campaigning.		
Your Life 4	Unit 8	Working for change
Your Life 5	Unit 6	Global challenges – poverty, education and health
	Unit 7	Working for change
	Unit 8	Co-operating on a community project

4f	To work with a range of community partners and organisations to address issues and problems in communities.	
Your Life 5	Unit 8	Co-operating on a community project

4g	To take into account legal, moral, economic, environmental, historical and social dimensions of different political problems and issues.	
Your Life 5	Unit 2	Human rights
	Unit 4	Global challenges – wars, weapons and terrorism
	Unit 5	Global challenges – environmental issues
	Unit 6	Global challenges – poverty, education and health

4h	To take into account a range of contexts, such as school, neighbourhood, local, regional, national, European, international and global, as relevant to different topics.	
Your Life 5	Unit 2	Human rights
	Unit 6	Global challenges – poverty, education and health

4i	To use and interpret different media and ICT both as sources of information and as a means of communicating ideas.	
Your Life 5	Unit 3	Media matters

4j	To make links between citizenship and work in other subjects and areas of the curriculum.	
Your Life 4	Unit 1	Britain: a diverse society
Your Life 5	Unit 5	Global challenges – environmental issues

How *Your Life 4* and *5* meet the requirements of the National Curriculum non-statutory content for Personal wellbeing at Key Stage 4

The National Curriculum stresses the importance of personal wellbeing in helping young people to embrace change, feel positive about who they are and enjoy healthy, safe, responsible and fulfilled lives. Personal wellbeing also makes a major contribution to the promotion of personal development. The particular units of *Your Life 4* and *5* that meet the specific aspects of the non-statutory content for Personal wellbeing are detailed below.

1. Key concepts

1.1 Personal identities

1.1a Understanding that identity is affected by a range of factors, including a positive sense of self

Your Life 4	Unit 9	Developing your identity and image

1.1b Recognising that the way in which personal qualities, attitudes, skills and achievements are evaluated affects confidence and self-esteem

Your Life 4	Unit 9	Developing your identity and image
Your Life 5	Unit 9	Developing your own values

1.1c Understanding that self-esteem can change with personal circumstances, such as those associated with family and friendships, achievements and employment

Your Life 4	Unit 11	Changing relationships

1.2 Healthy lifestyles

1.2a Recognising that healthy lifestyles, and the wellbeing of self and others, depend on information and making responsible choices

Your Life 4	Unit 9	Developing your identity and image
	Unit 12	Coping with crises
	Unit 14	Healthy eating
	Unit 15	Safer sex and contraception
	Unit 16	Drinking and smoking
	Unit 17	Health matters
Your Life 5	Unit 15	Safer sex
	Unit 16	Drugs and drugtaking

1.2b Understanding that physical, mental, sexual and emotional health affect our ability to lead fulfilling lives, and that there is help and support available when they are threatened

Your Life 4	Unit 14	Healthy eating
	Unit 15	Safer sex and contraception
	Unit 16	Drinking and smoking
	Unit 17	Health matters
Your Life 5	Unit 14	Managing stress and dealing with depression
	Unit 15	Safer sex

1.2c Dealing with growth and change as normal parts of growing up

Your Life 4	Unit 9	Developing your identity and image

1.3	Risk

1.3a Understanding risk in both positive and negative terms and understanding that individuals need to manage risk to themselves and others in a range of situations

Your Life 4	Unit 12	Coping with crises
	Unit 15	Safer sex and contraception
	Unit 16	Drinking and smoking
	Unit 17	Health matters

Your Life 5	Unit 15	Safer sex
	Unit 16	Drugs and drugtaking

1.3b Appreciating that pressure can be used positively or negatively to influence others in situations involving risk

Your Life 4	Unit 16	Drinking and smoking

1.3c Developing the confidence to try new ideas and face challenges safely, individually and in groups

Your Life 4	Unit 15	Safer sex and contraception

1.4	Relationships

1.4a Understanding that relationships affect everything we do in our lives and that relationship skills have to be learned and practised

Your Life 4	Unit 10	Managing your emotions and moods
	Unit 11	Changing relationships

Your Life 5	Unit 11	Marriage and commitment

1.4b Understanding that people have multiple roles and responsibilities in society and that making positive relationships and contributing to groups, teams and communities is important

Your Life 5	Unit 8	Co-operating on a community project

1.4c Understanding that relationships can cause strong feelings and emotions

Your Life 4	Unit 10	Managing your emotions and moods
	Unit 11	Changing relationships

1.5	Diversity

1.5a Appreciating that, in our communities, there are similarities as well as differences between people of different race, religion, culture, ability or disability, gender, age or sexual orientation

Your Life 4	Unit 1	Britain: a diverse society
	Unit 13	Challenging offensive behaviour

Your Life 5	Unit 13	Challenging offensive behaviour

1.5b Understanding that all forms of prejudice and discrimination must be challenged at every level in our lives

Your Life 4	Unit 13	Challenging offensive behaviour

Your Life 5	Unit 13	Challenging offensive behaviour

2. Key processes

2.1 Critical reflection			

2.1a Be able to reflect critically on their own and others' values and change their behaviour accordingly

Your Life 4	Unit 9	Developing your identity and image
	Unit 13	Challenging offensive behaviour
Your Life 5	Unit 9	Developing your own values
	Unit 13	Challenging offensive behaviour

2.1b Be able to reflect on their own and others' strengths and achievements, give and receive constructive praise and criticism, and learn from success and failure

Your Life 4	Unit 10	Managing your emotions and moods

2.1c Be able to identify and use strategies for setting and meeting personal targets and challenges in order to increase motivation, reflect on their effectiveness and implement and monitor strategies for achieving goals

Your Life 5	Unit 10	Managing your time and studies

2.1d Be able to reflect on feelings and identify positive ways of understanding, managing and expressing strong emotions and challenging behaviour, acting positively on them

Your Life 4	Unit 10	Managing your emotions and moods
	Unit 11	Changing relationships
	Unit 12	Coping with crises
Your Life 5	Unit 14	Managing stress and dealing with depression

2.1e Be able to develop self-awareness by reflecting critically on their behaviour and its impact on others

Your Life 4	Unit 10	Managing your emotions and moods
	Unit 11	Changing relationships

2.2 Decision-making and managing risk			

2.2a Be able to use knowledge and understanding to make informed choices about safety, health and wellbeing, evaluating personal choices and making changes if necessary

Your Life 4	Unit 12	Coping with crises
	Unit 14	Healthy eating
	Unit 15	Safer sex and contraception
	Unit 16	Drinking and smoking
	Unit 17	Health matters
Your Life 5	Unit 15	Safer sex
	Unit 16	Drugs and drugtaking

2.2b Be able to find and evaluate information, advice and support from a variety of sources and be able to support others in doing so

Your Life 4	Unit 15	Safer sex and contraception
	Unit 16	Drinking and smoking
	Unit 17	Health matters

2.2c Be able to assess and manage the element of risk in personal choices and situations and demonstrate how to help others do so

| Your Life 4 | Unit 15 | Safer sex and contraception |
| | Unit 16 | Drinking and smoking |

| Your Life 5 | Unit 15 | Safer sex |
| | Unit 16 | Drugs and drugtaking |

2.2d Be able to use strategies for resisting unhelpful peer influence and pressure, assessing when to use them and when and how to get help

| Your Life 4 | Unit 16 | Drinking and smoking |

2.2e Be able to identify how managing feelings and emotions effectively supports decision-making and risk management

| Your Life 4 | Unit 10 | Managing your emotions and moods |

2.3 Developing relationships and working with others

2.3a Be able to use social skills to build and maintain a range of positive relationships, reflect on what makes these successful and apply this to new situations

| Your Life 4 | Unit 10 | Managing your emotions and moods |
| | Unit 11 | Changing relationships |

2.3b Be able to use the social skill of negotiation within relationships, recognising their rights and responsibilities and that their actions have consequences

| Your Life 4 | Unit 10 | Managing your emotions and moods |
| | Unit 11 | Changing relationships |

2.3c Be able to work individually, together and in teams for specific purposes, making use of the social skills of communication, negotiation, assertiveness and collaboration

| Your Life 5 | Unit 8 | Co-operating on a community project |

2.3d Be able to demonstrate respect for and acceptance of the differences between people, and challenge offensive behaviour, prejudice and discrimination assertively and safely

| Your Life 4 | Unit 13 | Challenging offensive behaviour |

| Your Life 5 | Unit 13 | Challenging offensive behaviour |

2.3e Be able to explore feelings and emotions related to changing relationships and develop skills to cope with loss and bereavement

| Your Life 4 | Unit 12 | Coping with crises |

3. Range and content

The study of personal wellbeing should include:
3a the effect of diverse and conflicting values on individuals, families and communities and ways of responding to them

| Your Life 4 | Unit 13 | Challenging offensive behaviour |

| Your Life 5 | Unit 13 | Challenging offensive behaviour |

3b	how the media portrays young people, body image and health issues		
	Your Life 4	Unit 14	Healthy eating

3c	the characteristics of emotional and mental health, and the causes, symptoms and treatments of some mental and emotional health disorders		
	Your Life 5	Unit 14	Managing stress and dealing with depression

3d	the benefits and risks of health and lifestyle choices, including choices relating to sexual activity and substance use and misuse, and the short and long-term consequences for the health and mental and emotional wellbeing of individuals, families and communities		
	Your Life 4	Unit 14	Healthy eating
		Unit 15	Safer sex and contraception
		Unit 16	Drinking and smoking
		Unit 17	Health matters
	Your Life 5	Unit 15	Safer sex
		Unit 16	Drugs and drugtaking

3e	where and how to obtain health information, how to recognise and follow health and safety procedures, ways of reducing risk and minimising harm in risky situations, how to find sources of emergency help and how to use basic and emergency first aid		
	Your Life 4	Unit 15	Safer sex and contraception
		Unit 16	Drinking and smoking
		Unit 17	Health matters
	Your Life 5	Unit 17	Emergency first aid

3f	the characteristics of positive relationships and awareness of exploitation in relationships and of statutory and voluntary organisations that support relationships in crisis		
	Your Life 4	Unit 11	Changing relationships
	Your Life 5	Unit 11	Marriage and commitment

3g	the roles and responsibilities of parents, carers, children and other family members		
	Your Life 4	Unit 11	Changing relationships
	Your Life 5	Unit 12	Parenthood and parenting

3h	parenting skills and qualities and qualities and their central importance to family life		
	Your Life 5	Unit 12	Parenthood and parenting

3i	the impact of separation, divorce and bereavement on families and the need to adapt to changing circumstances		
	Your Life 4	Unit 12	Coping with crises

3j	the diversity of ethnic and cultural groups, the power of prejudice, bullying, discrimination and racism, and the need to take the initiative in challenging this and other offensive behaviours and in giving support to victims of abuse		
	Your Life 4	Unit 13	Challenging offensive behaviour
	Your Life 5	Unit 13	Challenging offensive behaviour

4. Curriculum opportunities

The curriculum should provide opportunities for pupils to:

4a make real choices and decisions based on accurate information obtained through their own research using a range of sources, including the Internet, other media sources and visits and visitors to or from the wider community

| Your Life 4 | Unit 8 | Working for change |
| Your Life 5 | Unit 8 | Co-operating on a community project |

4b form opinions and express viewpoints confidently to a range of audiences

| Your Life 5 | Unit 16 | Drugs and drugtaking |

4c meet and work with people from the wider community both in school and through external visits

| Your Life 4 | Unit 8 | Working for change |

4d use case studies, simulations, scenarios and drama to explore personal and social issues and have time to reflect on them in relation to their own lives and behaviour

| Your Life 5 | Unit 13 | Challenging offensive behaviour |

4e take part in individual and group discussion to consider personal, social and moral dilemmas and the choices and decisions relating to them

| Your Life 5 | Unit 9 | Developing your own values |
| | Unit 16 | Drugs and drugtaking |

4f work as members of groups and teams for specific purposes, taking on different roles and responsibilities and identifying the range of skills and attributes needed for teamwork

| Your Life 4 | Unit 21 | Enterprise challenge |

4g evaluate their own personal development and learning, set realistic targets and goals for future life choices and develop strategies for meeting them

| Your Life 4 | Unit 18 | Thinking ahead – planning your future |
| Your Life 5 | Unit 18 | Thinking ahead – planning your future |

4h identify sources of help, support and accurate information and take responsibility for providing accurate information to others in a range of situations

| Your Life 4 | Unit 17 | Health matters |

4i make links between personal wellbeing and work in other subjects and areas of the curriculum and out-of-school activities

How *Your Life 4* and *5* meet the requirements of the National Curriculum non-statutory content for Economic wellbeing and financial capability at Key Stage 4

The particular units of *Your Life 4–5* that meet the requirements of the non-statutory content for Economic wellbeing and financial capability are detailed below.

1. Key concepts

1.1 Career
1.1a Understanding that everyone has a career
Your Life 4 — Unit 18 — Thinking ahead – planning your future
Your Life 5 — Unit 18 — Thinking ahead – planning your future
1.1b Developing a sense of personal identity for career progression
Your Life 4 — Unit 18 — Thinking ahead – planning your future
Your Life 5 — Unit 18 — Thinking ahead – planning your future
1.1c Understanding the qualities, attitudes and skills needed for employability
Your Life 4 — Unit 18 — Thinking ahead – planning your future
Your Life 5 — Unit 18 — Thinking ahead – planning your future
1.2 Capability
1.2a Exploring what it means to be enterprising
Your Life 4 — Unit 21 — Enterprise challenge
1.2b Learning how to manage money and personal finances
Your Life 4 — Unit 19 — Managing your money
Your Life 5 — Unit 19 — Managing your money
1.2c Understanding how to make creative and realistic plans for transition
Your Life 5 — Unit 18 — Thinking ahead – planning your future
1.2d Becoming critical consumers of goods and services
Your Life 4 — Unit 3 — Rights and responsibilities
1.3 Risk
1.3a Understanding risk in both positive and negative terms
Your Life 4 — Unit 20 — Financing businesses
1.3b Understanding the need to manage risk in the context of financial and career choices
Your Life 4 — Unit 20 — Financing businesses
Your Life 5 — Unit 19 — Managing your money
1.3c Taking risks and learning from mistakes
Your Life 4 — Unit 21 — Enterprise challenge

1.4 Economic understanding			
1.4a Understanding the economic and business environment			
	Your Life 4	Unit 20	Financing businesses
		Unit 21	Enterprise challenge
	Your Life 5	Unit 20	The UK economy
		Unit 21	The global economy
1.4b Understanding the functions and use of money			
	Your Life 4	Unit 20	Financing businesses
	Your Life 5	Unit 20	The UK economy
		Unit 21	The global economy

2. Key processes

2.1 Self-development			
2.1a Be able to develop and maintain their self-esteem and envisage a positive future for themselves in work			
	Your Life 4	Unit 18	Thinking ahead – planning your future
2.1b Be able to identify major life roles and ways of managing the relationships between them			
	Your Life 4	Unit 18	Thinking ahead – planning your future
2.1c Be able to assess their needs, interests, values, skills, abilities and attitudes in relation to options in learning, work and enterprise			
	Your Life 4	Unit 18	Thinking ahead – planning your future
	Your Life 5	Unit 18	Thinking ahead – planning your future
2.1d Be able to assess the importance of their experiences and achievements in relation to their future plans			
	Your Life 4	Unit 18	Thinking ahead – planning your future
	Your Life 5	Unit 18	Thinking ahead – planning your future
2.2 Exploration			
2.2a Be able to identify, select and use a variety of information sources to research, clarify and review options and choices in career and financial contexts relevant to their needs			
	Your Life 4	Unit 18	Thinking ahead – planning your future
	Your Life 5	Unit 18	Thinking ahead – planning your future
		Unit 19	Managing your money
2.2b Be able to recognise bias and inaccuracies in information about learning pathways, work and enterprise			
	Your Life 5	Unit 18	Thinking ahead – planning your future
2.2c Be able to investigate the main trends in employment and relate these to their career plans			
	Your Life 5	Unit 18	Thinking ahead – planning your future

2.3 Enterprise	
2.3a Be able to identify the main qualities and skills needed to enter and thrive in the working world	
	Your Life 4 Unit 18 Thinking ahead – planning your future
2.3b Be able to assess, undertake and manage risk	
	Your Life 5 Unit 18 Thinking ahead – planning your future
2.3c Be able to take action to improve their chances in their career	
	Your Life 4 Unit 18 Thinking ahead – planning your future
	Your Life 5 Unit 18 Thinking ahead – planning your future
2.3d Be able to manage change and transition	
	Your Life 5 Unit 18 Thinking ahead – planning your future
2.3e Be able to show drive and self-reliance when working on work-related tasks	
	Your Life 4 Unit 18 Thinking ahead – planning your future
2.3f Be able to develop approaches to working with others, problem-solving and action planning	
	Your Life 4 Unit 21 Enterprise challenge
2.3g Be able to understand the key attitudes for enterprise, including self-reliance, open-mindedness, respect for evidence, pragmatism and commitment to making a difference	
	Your Life 4 Unit 21 Enterprise challenge
2.3h Be able to demonstrate and apply skills and qualities for enterprise	
	Your Life 4 Unit 21 Enterprise challenge
2.3i Be able to demonstrate and apply understanding of economic ideas	
	Your Life 4 Unit 20 Financing businesses
2.4 Financial capability	
2.4a Be able to manage their money	
	Your Life 4 Unit 19 Managing your money
	Your Life 5 Unit 19 Managing your money
2.4b Be able to understand financial risk and reward	
	Your Life 4 Unit 19 Managing your money
	Your Life 5 Unit 19 Managing your money
2.4c Be able to explain financial terms and products	
	Your Life 4 Unit 19 Managing your money
	Your Life 5 Unit 19 Managing your money
2.4d Be able to identify how finance will play an important part in their lives and in achieving their aspirations	
	Your Life 4 Unit 19 Managing your money

3. Range and content

The study of economic wellbeing and financial capability should include:

3a different types of work including employment, self-employment and voluntary work

| Your Life 4 | Unit 3 | Rights and responsibilities |
| Your Life 5 | Unit 8 | Co-operating on a community project |

3b the organisation and structure of different types of business, and work roles and identities

| Your Life 4 | Unit 20 | Financing businesses |

3c rights and responsibilities at work and attitudes and values in relation to work and enterprise

| Your Life 4 | Unit 3 | Rights and responsibilities |
| | Unit 18 | Thinking ahead – planning your future |

3d the range of opportunities in learning and work and changing patterns of employment (local, national, European and global)

| Your Life 5 | Unit 18 | Thinking ahead – planning your future |

3e the personal review and planning process

| Your Life 4 | Unit 18 | Thinking ahead – planning your future |

3f skills and qualities in relation to employers' needs

| Your Life 4 | Unit 18 | Thinking ahead – planning your future |
| Your Life 5 | Unit 18 | Thinking ahead – planning your future |

3g a range of economic and business terms, including the connections between markets, competition, price and profit

Your Life 4	Unit 20	Financing businesses
	Unit 21	Enterprise challenge
Your Life 5	Unit 20	The UK economy
	Unit 21	The global economy

3h personal budgeting, wages, taxes, money management, credit, debt and a range of financial products and services

| Your Life 4 | Unit 19 | Managing your money |
| Your Life 5 | Unit 19 | Managing your money |

3i risk and reward, and how money can make money through savings, investment and trade

| Your Life 4 | Unit 20 | Financing businesses |

3j how and why businesses use finance

| Your Life 4 | Unit 20 | Financing businesses |

3k social and moral dilemmas about the use of money

| Your Life 5 | Unit 20 | The UK economy |
| | Unit 21 | The global economy |

4. Curriculum opportunities

The curriculum should provide opportunities to:

4a use case studies, simulations, scenarios, role play and drama to explore work and enterprise issues

Your Life 4	Unit 8	Working for change
	Unit 18	Thinking ahead – planning your future
	Unit 20	Financing businesses
	Unit 21	Enterprise challenge
Your Life 5	Unit 19	Managing your money

4b use their experiences of work to extend their understanding of work

Your Life 4	Unit 18	Thinking ahead – planning your future

4c recognise, develop and apply their skills for enterprise and employability

Your Life 4	Unit 18	Thinking ahead – planning your future
	Unit 21	Enterprise challenge

4d have direct and indirect contact with people from business

Your Life 4	Unit 18	Thinking ahead – planning your future

4e research options and progression routes in learning and work

Your Life 5	Unit 18	Thinking ahead – planning your future

4f have contact with information, advice and guidance specialists

Your Life 4	Unit 18	Thinking ahead – planning your future

4g engage with ideas, challenges and applications from the business world

Your Life 4	Unit 20	Financing businesses
	Unit 21	Enterprise challenge

4h explore sources of information and ideas about work and enterprise

Your Life 4	Unit 18	Thinking ahead – planning your future
	Unit 21	Enterprise challenge

4i discuss contemporary issues in work

Your Life 5	Unit 20	The UK economy

4j review and update a personal statement and make an individual learning and career plan for their transition into the post-16 phase

Your Life 5	Unit 18	Thinking ahead – planning your future

4k make links between economic wellbeing and financial capability and other subjects and areas of the curriculum

Your Life 5	Unit 20	The UK economy
	Unit 21	The global economy

Introduction

How *Your Life 4* and *5* fit within the Every Child Matters outcomes framework

Many of the units on the Your Life course lead to the outcomes set in Every Child Matters. Examples of particular units that fit the five outcomes of the Every Child Matters framework are given below.

Be healthy

1 Physically healthy e.g. *Your Life 4* Unit 14 Healthy eating

2 Mentally and emotionally healthy e.g. *Your Life 5* Unit 14 Managing stress and dealing with depression

3 Sexually healthy e.g. *Your Life 4* Unit 15 Safer sex and contraception

4 Healthy lifestyles e.g. *Your Life 4* Unit 16 Drinking and smoking

5 Choose not to take illegal drugs e.g. *Your Life 5* Unit 16 Drugs and drugtaking

Stay safe

6 Safe from accidental injury and death e.g. *Your Life 5* Unit 17 Emergency first aid

7 Safe from bullying and discrimination e.g. *Your Life 4* Unit 13 Challenging offensive behaviour

8 Safe from crime and anti-social behaviour – in and out of school e.g. *Your Life 4* Unit 5 Crime and punishment

9 Have security, stability and are cared for e.g. *Your Life 5* Unit 12 Parenthood and parenting

Enjoy and achieve

10 Achieve personal and social development and enjoy recreation e.g. *Your Life 4* Unit 9 Developing your identity and image

11 Achieve stretching national educational standards at secondary level e.g. *Your Life 4* Unit 22 Reviewing and recording your learning

Making a positive contribution

12 Engage in decision-making and support the community and environment e.g. *Your Life 5* Unit 8 Co-operating on a community project

13 Engage in law-abiding and positive behaviour both in and out of school e.g. *Your Life 4* Unit 8 Working for change

14 Develop positive relationships and choose not to bully and discriminate e.g. *Your Life 5* Unit 13 Challenging offensive behaviour

15 Develop self-confidence and successfully deal with life changes and challenges e.g. *Your Life 4* Unit 12 Coping with crises

16 Develop enterprising behaviour e.g. *Your Life 4* Unit 21 Enterprise challenge

Achieve economic wellbeing

17 Ready for employment e.g. *Your Life 4* Unit 11 Thinking ahead – planning your future

How *Your Life* 4 and 5 provide opportunities to develop Personal Learning and Thinking Skills (PLTS)

The topics and issues explored in the *Your Life* course provide learning experiences that lead to the development of the skills in the National Curriculum framework for Personal Learning and Thinking Skills. Examples of units that contain activities which develop the six skills are given below.

Independent enquirers

The skills of independent enquirers are developed throughout the course by presenting the students with issues and problems to explore and information to analyse and evaluate. There are also opportunities to plan and carry out research, prior to the writing suggested in the 'For your file' activities and in the extension activities in the Teacher's Resources.

Examples of particular units in which there are activities specifically designed to develop these skills include:

- Researching the jobs of people in the law e.g. solicitors, barristers, judges, magistrates and producing a leaflet about their roles in *Your Life 4* Unit 4 The law of the land
- Researching and writing an article on a global environmental issue in *Your Life 5* Unit 5 Global challenges: Environmental issues.

Creative thinkers

There are many opportunities during the course for students to think creatively, exploring ideas, suggesting ways to resolve problems and working with others to find solutions.

Examples of particular units in which there are activities that develop these skills include:

- An enterprise activity in *Your Life 4* Unit 21 Enterprise challenge
- Organising a petition for a skate park in *Your Life 5* Unit 8 Co-operating on a community project.

Reflective learners

Students identifying their strengths and limitations, setting themselves targets and monitoring their own performance and progress form an integral part of the *Your Life* course. Both the students' books for Key Stage 4 have a final unit in which students are encouraged to record their achievements and review their progress.

In addition, *Your Life 4* and *Your Life 5* each include a careers unit in which the students are encouraged to reflect on their abilities when thinking ahead and planning for the future.

Team workers

There are numerous group discussion activities in the *Your Life* course providing students with opportunities to work effectively with others, listening to different views and learning how to form collaborative relationships to reach agreed outcomes.

Particular activities which involve students working in teams include:

- Setting up a pressure group in *Your Life 4* Unit 8 Working for change
- Exploring local environmental issues in *Your Life 5* Unit 5 Global challenges: Environmental issues.

Self-managers

Underlying objectives of the *Your Life* course are to develop each student's ability to take responsibility for their own learning and behaviour, to learn how to manage their time and how to handle their emotions.

Your Life 4 and *Your Life 5* each contain a unit on managing your money and there is also a unit in *Your Life 5* on managing your time and studies. *Your Life 5* Unit 17 Health matters also includes a section on looking after your own health.

There are also specific units focusing on managing their emotions:

- *Your Life 4* Unit 10 Managing your emotions and moods
- *Your Life 4* Unit 12 Coping with crises
- *Your Life 5* Unit 14 Managing stress and dealing with depression.

Effective participants

The *Your Life* course encourages students to engage with issues that affect them and those around them and to play a full part in school and community affairs.

Examples of activities in which students are given the opportunity to participate in local affairs include:

- becoming members of a youth council in *Your Life 4* Unit 7 It's your council
- setting up a pressure group in your local area in *Your Life 4* Unit 8 Working for change
- getting involved in a community project in *Your Life 5* Unit 8 Co-operating on a community project.

How *Your Life 4* and *5* contribute to the learning of the social and emotional skills identified in SEAL (Social and Emotional Aspects of Learning for secondary schools)

Examples of particular units of *Your Life 4* and *Your Life 5* that contribute to the learning outcomes of SEAL are given below:

Self-awareness

Knowing myself (outcomes 1–7)		
Your Life 4	Unit 9	Developing your identity and image
	Unit 17	Health matters
	Unit 18	Thinking ahead -planning your future
Your Life 5	Unit 9	Developing your own values
	Unit 18	Thinking ahead – planning your future
Understanding my feelings (outcomes 8–12)		
Your Life 4	Unit 10	Managing your emotions and moods
	Unit 11	Changing relationships
	Unit 12	Coping with crises
Your Life 5	Unit 14	Managing stress and dealing with depression

Managing my feelings

Managing my expression of emotions (outcomes 13–15)		
Your Life 4	Unit 10	Managing your emotions and moods
	Unit 11	Changing relationships
	Unit 12	Coping with crises
Your Life 5	Unit 14	Managing stress and depression
Changing uncomfortable feelings and increasing pleasant feelings (outcomes 16–18)		
Your Life 4	Unit 9	Developing your identity and image
	Unit 12	Coping with crises
	Unit 14	Healthy eating
Your Life 5	Unit 14	Managing stress and depression

Motivation

Working towards goals (outcomes 19–24)		
Your Life 4	Unit 18	Thinking ahead – planning your future
	Unit 19	Managing your money
	Unit 22	Reviewing and recording your learning
Your Life 5	Unit 18	Thinking ahead – planning your future
	Unit 19	Managing your money
	Unit 22	Reviewing and recording your learning

Persistence, resilience and optimism (outcomes 25–27)		
Your Life 4	Unit 10	Managing your emotions and moods
	Unit 21	Enterprise challenge
Your Life 5	Unit 10	Managing your time and studies

Evaluation and review (outcomes 28–30)		
Your Life 4	Unit 18	Thinking ahead – planning your future
	Unit 22	Reviewing and recording your learning
Your Life 5	Unit 18	Thinking ahead – planning your future
	Unit 22	Reviewing and recording your learning

Empathy

Understanding the thoughts and feelings of others (outcomes 31–33)		
Your Life 4	Unit 1	Britain – A diverse society
	Unit 12	Changing relationships
Your Life 5	Unit 11	Marriage and commitment

Valuing and supporting others (outcomes 34–38)		
Your Life 4	Unit 2	Human rights
	Unit 13	Challenging offensive behaviour
Your Life 5	Unit 2	Human rights
	Unit 13	Challenging offensive behaviour

Social skills

Building and maintaining relationships (outcomes 39–42)		
Your Life 4	Unit 10	Managing your emotions and moods
	Unit 11	Changing relationships
	Unit 15	Safer sex and contraception
Your Life 5	Unit 11	Marriage and commitment
	Unit 15	Safer sex

Belonging to groups (outcomes 43–46)		
Your Life 4	Unit 3	Rights and responsibilities
	Unit 8	Working for change
	Unit 21	Enterprise challenge
Your Life 5	Unit 7	Campaigning for change
	Unit 8	Co-operating on a community project

Solving problems, including interpersonal ones (outcomes 47–50)		
Your Life 4	Unit 9	Developing your identity and image
	Unit 11	Changing relationships
	Unit 12	Coping with crises
	Unit 13	Challenging offensive behaviour
Your Life 5	Unit 13	Challenging offensive behaviour

UNIT 1 Britain: A diverse society

Aim: To explore the origins of Britain as a multicultural and multiethnic society, and the benefits that this has brought.

Preparation

Make copies of copymaster 1 (Migration into Britain) for each pair.

Starter

Put the terms 'immigrant', 'refugee' and 'asylum seeker' on the board and ask students in groups to come up with a definition of each, then feed this back to the class and discuss.

Suggested activities

- Students read the articles 'Culture club' and 'Britain's benefit' in groups and discuss the questions given. Ask selected groups to feed back their responses to the class. It will help to fix details in the students' minds if they construct a migration map, using the template on copymaster 1. Less able students may like to construct a diagram of a 'melting pot' (explain the term first) and add labels of all the ethnic groups who are part of Britain's melting pot, with some dates/comments if they can.

- Pairs study the timeline to learn in more detail about immigration into Britain in the last 60 years. Ask them to work together to extend the timeline backwards 40 000 years.

Plenary

Ask students to write one or two sentences stating if this lesson has changed their attitude to immigration, and giving reasons. Ask four or five students to feed back their statements. Allow students to hold on to their opinions whatever the majority view, though they should be backed up by good reasons and evidence.

Extension activities

- Students log on to www.traceit.com and enter their family name. Ask them what they discover about the history of their family name, and what this might mean about their roots.

- Research the cultural roots of class members and construct a class family tree to represent this diversity.

- Students research one of the immigrant groups in more detail, with a focus on what they contributed to Britain's history, economy and culture (see Further resources).

- Students can add items to their timeline to show what difficulties immigrant groups have had to contend with over the centuries.

Further resources

'Race for opportunity', a PDF file, giving details of migration to the UK since World War Two and immigrants' contributions to the British economy can be found at www.bitc.org.uk

COPYMASTER

Migration into Britain

Create a migration map to show where different groups of people have come from to make up today's Great Britain. Add a date and a short comment, as in the example given. Add groups from outside Europe in the margins. You may like to use different colours to indicate different ethnic groups, or different eras.

1 c.700 BC Celts come from Europe. They bring use of iron.

UNIT 1 Britain: A diverse society

Your Life 4/Year 10

Lesson 2 *Your Life 4*, pages 8–9
Citizenship 1.3a, 1.3b, 2.1a, 2.1b 2.1c, 3l; Personal wellbeing 1.5a

Aim: To explore the meaning of national identity and culture.

Preparation
Make copies of copymaster 2 (Ethnic minorities fact check) for each student.

Starter
Read the statements in 'What does 'being British' mean?'. Ask groups to discuss how they would define 'being British'. Point out that this is a complex question, and that there is no one correct answer – the group's aim is to canvas views on what being British means to each member, and to prepare a short presentation giving the various approaches to the answer. Ask two or three groups to present and open it up to a full class discussion.

Suggested activities
- Students read the information on 'The British citizenship test' and 'The citizenship ceremony'. Discuss with the class why the tests have been introduced and invite them to share their views on them. Then ask individuals to write a short statement saying whether they think the tests are a good idea.

- Students read the article 'Roots and branches' and discuss the questions before feeding back to the class. List on the board what the class considers to be the benefits and drawbacks of belonging to more than one culture.

- Focus on what the three young people say about their identity. In pairs, discuss their statements and invite each of them to draft a statement about their own identity. Encourage some of them to share their statements in a class discussion about identity.

Plenary
Ask students to write one or two sentences stating whether this lesson has changed their attitude to what being British means. Recap the various different ways of defining what being British means.

Extension activities
- Give copymaster 2 to individuals or pairs. The answers are: 1. False – at the end of 2007 it was 10.3%; 2. False – the largest is Indian; 3. True – London is often cited as the most ethnically diverse city in the world; 4. True; 5. True; 6. False – the largest come from Europe; 7. True; 8. False – the number was 2.5 million; 9. True; 10. False – there were only 15; 11. True; 12 True.

- Ask 'Is the Union Jack a good representation of the United Kingdom?' If not, describe or design a different flag.

- Discuss the statement: 'People are more alike than different' (Maya Angelou).

2 Ethnic minorities fact check

○ On your own

Decide whether the following statements are true or false. Then compare your answers with a partner before being given the right answers by your teacher

		True	False
A	20% of Britain's population are from ethnic minorities.	☐	☐
B	The largest ethnic minority group in the UK is Pakistani.	☐	☐
C	In London, 35% of the population is non-white.	☐	☐
D	There has been a continuous black population in the UK since the 1500s.	☐	☐
E	Nearly 10% of children under 16 live in a family with heritages from more than one ethnic group.	☐	☐
F	The largest number of people living in Britain but born elsewhere come from the Indian sub-continent.	☐	☐
G	Islam is the second largest religion in the UK with over 1.6 million followers.	☐	☐
H	Half a million Indian soldiers served for Britain in the Second World War.	☐	☐
I.	About 60% of British families with a Pakistani or Bangladeshi background are living in low-income households.	☐	☐
J.	In 2009, 37 out of the 646 MPs were non-white.	☐	☐
K.	Less than 1% of Britain's 20,000 local councillors are women from ethnic minority communities.	☐	☐
L	Every year over 100,000 people from other countries apply for the right to stay in Britain permanently.	☐	☐

UNIT 2 Human rights

Your Life 4/Year 10

Lesson 1 *Your Life 4*, pages 10–11
Citizenship 1.2a, 1.2b, 1.2c, 2.1a, 2.1b, 2.1c, 3a, 3f

Aim: To discuss what human rights are, and which rights are most important.

Preparation

Make a copy of copymaster 3 (Are some human rights more important than others?) for each student.

Starter

Write the phrase 'Human rights' on the board. Explain what it means. Ask the students to brainstorm different rights they think they are entitled to and make a list on the board. Then read 'What are human rights'?

Suggested activities

- Ask the students to look at the photo, and discuss in pairs what rights and responsibilities the protesters in the photo have. Draw together these ideas as a class.

- Read 'Where did human rights come from?' Explain how the modern views of human rights developed and what the Universal Declaration of Human Rights is. Point out that the European Convention of Human Rights gives a legal framework for human rights in the UK and explain that the rights of UK citizens are protected by the Human Rights Act of 1998.

- Ask groups to read and discuss 'Human rights issues', then to share their views on assisted suicide and the death penalty with the rest of the class.

- Discuss the newer human rights included in the European Charter of Fundamental Rights. Ask the students in groups to discuss the laws they would introduce to enforce a new human right. Then ask them to write a short statement saying what new human rights law they would pass, and why.

Plenary

Ask the students which they consider to be the most important human rights, and why.

Extension activities

- Invite individuals to study copymaster 3 and to rank the rights according to how important they think each one is. Students should then share their views in a group discussion.

- Ask groups to discuss how well rights are being met in the UK compared to a less economically developed country in Africa or Asia. Should the international community be doing more to help protect rights in less economically developed countries? (See copymaster 3.)

- Ask students to write an e-mail to their local MP or local councillor. Students should ask them what they are doing to help promote human rights in their area. Invite them to come and speak on the subject at your school.

Further resources

A full copy of the 30 articles of the Universal Declaration of Human Rights can be found at www.amnesty.org.uk

3   Are some human rights more important than others?

Look at the following list of rights. Which ones do you think are the most important? Rank them on a scale of 1–5 according to how important each one is (1 = most important). Then compare your answers in groups. Give reasons for your views.

❶ The right to move freely within your own country.

❷ The right to a free primary and secondary education.

❸ The right to life.

❹ The right to take part in free and fair elections.

❺ The right to say what you like or freedom of expression.

❻ The right to wear religious symbols anywhere you like.

❼ The right to have paid holidays with any job.

❽ The right to a private life.

❾ The right to have access to clean drinking water.

❿ The right to own property.

⓫ The right to be treated the same as everyone else without discrimination, whoever you are.

⓬ The right to be presumed innocent until proven guilty.

Are there any other rights that you think are important that are not on your list?

⣿ In groups

Think about the UK, and a less economically developed country in Africa or Asia.

● Which of these rights do you think are being met in the UK?

● Which of these rights are not being met in a less developed country?

● Are there any rights where the international community should be doing more to help less economically developed countries?

UNIT 2 Human rights

Your Life 4/Year 10

Lesson 2 *Your Life 4*, pages 12–13
Citizenship 1.2a, 1.2b, 1.2c, 2.1a, 2.1b, 2.1c, 3a, 3f

Aim: To discuss what responsibilities are, and how they relate to human rights.

Preparation

Make a copy of copymaster 4 (What do you know about human rights?) for each student.

Starter

Write the term 'responsibility' on the board. Ask the students what they think behaving responsibly means in terms of other people's rights. Explain that whenever we have rights, we have responsibilities that go with them.

Suggested activities

- Read 'What are responsibilities?' and study 'How rights become responsibilities'. Discuss which are the most important. Ask the students to draw their own chart consisting of two columns: one a list of rights, the other a list of the responsibilities that go with each right.

- Ask the groups to read 'Freedom of speech – a conflict of rights' and to discuss their views on whether Nick Griffin and the BNP should have the right to freedom of speech. Then share the groups' views in a class discussion.

- Read 'Disability rights in the UK'. Ask the students in groups to discuss the statements, then to think about your school, or local shopping centre. Make a list of all the things they think need changing to make sure people with disabilities are not discriminated against or denied any of their rights. Ask them to compare their ideas with other groups, then to write an e-mail to the local newspaper with their suggestions. They could copy their e-mails to the local council, and ask them what action they will be taking as a result.

Plenary

Ask the students what they have learnt about their responsibilities towards other people's rights. In particular, what responsibilities do they have towards people with disabilities?

Extension activities

- Use copymaster 4 to assess students' knowledge and understanding of human rights by getting them individually to complete the quiz, then to check their answers. Answers are: 1, True; 2, False (1948); 3, True; 4, True; 5, False; 6, True; 7, False; 8, False; 9, True; 10, False; 11, False; 12, False.

- The students could invite a person with a disability to give a talk to the class. Suggest groups prepare for the visit by drafting a list of questions to ask, e.g. to find out what living with a disability is like, whether they feel discriminated against and whether society does enough to ensure they are not denied their rights.

- Design a poster promoting rights and responsibilities to be displayed in the school.

Your Life 4/Year 10

What do you know about human rights?

◯ On your own

Study these statements about human rights. Decide whether you think they are true or false.
Compare your answers with a partner, then check them by looking at pages 10–13 of *Your Life 4*.

		TRUE	FALSE
1	Everyone is entitled to human rights.	☐	☐
2	The Universal Declaration of Human Rights was created in 1988.	☐	☐
3	Since 1998, complaints about human rights can now be heard in a UK court.	☐	☐
4	The European Union is proposing a new set of human rights, such as the right to data protection.	☐	☐
5	Everyone in the UK has the right to a well-paid job.	☐	☐
6	Many human rights were violated in World War II.	☐	☐
7	The UK Government never restricts anyone's human rights.	☐	☐
8	People with disabilities no longer face discrimination in the UK.	☐	☐
9	We all have responsibilities to consider other people's human rights.	☐	☐
10	We have the same human rights laws as the USA.	☐	☐
11	It is illegal to join the BNP because it campaigns against human rights.	☐	☐
12	Abortion is illegal in the UK as it violates the right to life.	☐	☐

◌ In pairs

Look at pages 10–13 of *Your Life 4* on Human Rights. Write three more statements that are true
or false about human rights. Take it in turns with other pairs to test each other's knowledge.

UNIT 3 Rights and responsibilities

Your Life 4/Year 10

Lesson 1 *Your Life 4*, pages 14–15
Citizenship 1.2a, 1.2b, 2.1a, 2.1b

Aim: To explore the rights and responsibilities of people at home and at school.

Preparation

Bring in copies of the home-school contract or agreement of your school. Make copies of copymaster 5 (At what age?)

Starter

Write 'Drinking' on the board, above two columns headed 'rights' and 'responsibilities'. Ask students to supply the rights, and write them on the board (you may need to prompt, e.g. 'When can you be given alcohol in your home?'). The relevant rights are: to be given alcohol in your home – from age 5; to go to a bar (but not drink alcohol) – from age 14; to drink beer or cider in a restaurant – from age 16; to buy alcohol – from age 18. Then get students in groups to discuss what responsibilities young people have regarding drinking. Add their feedback to the right-hand column. Explain how, as in this case, rights are balanced by responsibilities.

Suggested activities

- Groups read the article 'Parental responsibility', and discuss the questions. Ask groups to note down a summary of their views and feed back to the class.

- Pairs read 'Growing up under the law' and complete the activities outlined. The 'For your file' activity can be set for homework. Give out copies of copymaster 5 to help with this activity.

Plenary

Students write down two rights that children have, and then two responsibilities that go with these rights. Ask three or four individuals to read out their lists, and invite the class to comment. Refer back to the starter activity if necessary to emphasise that rights and responsibilities are two sides of the same coin.

Extension activities

- Give out copies of the home-school agreement to pairs. Students should read the section on 'Rights and responsibilities at school'. Ask pairs to study the home-school agreement and to make notes of the rights and responsibilities of the school, parents and students. Invite several pairs to feed back their findings to the class, and encourage the class to comment.

- Students use the Internet to research parental rights and responsibilities. Do mothers automatically have parental rights and responsibility? What rights and responsibility do fathers have? Report their findings in a class discussion.

- Ask students to draw up a list of the rights and responsibilities that they have in their families then to share this list with a partner. Is the list of rights or responsibilities longer? Why?

Further resources

- The NSPCC's leaflet 'Is it legal?' discusses the law as it applies to parents and children. It is downloadable from the Internet on www.familyandparenting.org

- 'Young Citizen's Passport' edited by Tony Thorpe (Hodder 2009) is a useful guide to legal rights and responsibilities in England and Wales.

At what age?

Here is a list of some of the activities that young people are allowed to do when they reach certain ages. Keep this for your reference, and answer the questions underneath.

12	You can watch a '12A' film in a cinema without an adult with you. You may rent or buy a '12' rated DVD. You can buy a pet.
13	You can get a part-time job, subject to certain restrictions, e.g. you can work for a maximum of 2 hours per day.
14	You can go to a bar, as long as you have a soft drink.
15	You can rent or buy DVDs and watch films with a '15' certificate.
16	You can legally consent to have sex. You can marry with your parents' permission (England and Wales only). You can leave school and work full time. You can drive a moped. You can buy a lottery ticket
17	You can drive a motorbike or car. You can leave home without your parents' consent.
18	You can vote. You can serve on a jury. You can buy alcohol. You can buy cigarettes and tobacco. You can have a tattoo. You can get married without your parents' consent. You can stand to be a Member of Parliament.

❶ Choose one of these rights, and explain why you think the law states that you have to be that age to do it.

_____

_____

❷ What responsibilities go along with this right?

_____

_____

❸ Is there a law that you disagree with in this list? Give your reasons.

_____

_____

UNIT 3 Rights and responsibilities

Your Life 4/Year 10

Lesson 2 *Your Life 4*, pages 16–17
Citizenship 1.2a, 1.2b, 2.1a, 2.1b, 2.1c, 3k; Economic wellbeing and financial capability 3a, 3c

Aim: To explore the rights and responsibilities of people at work.

Preparation

Make copies of copymaster 6 (Breaking employment laws) and cut into cards, one set for each group.

Starter

Brainstorm the word 'work', putting students' words on the board. Elicit examples of part-time and voluntary work if necessary. Then ask groups to discuss which are the three examples of work that are the most valuable for society. Which three pay the most? Do these lists coincide, and if not, why not? (What about unpaid work in the home? What do students feel about footballers and film stars being paid thousands of pounds a week?) Ask 2–3 groups to feed back their findings and invite the class to comment.

Suggested activities

- Students read the section 'Starting work' and complete the writing activity on their own.

- In groups of five, students read 'The law at work'. Give each group the cards on copymaster 6; they should read the case studies on the cards and decide which law the employer was breaking in each case.

- Groups then discuss which law they think is the most important, and prepare a presentation as part of a class debate on which is the most important law to protect workers. Alternatively, you can allocate a law to each group, to ensure that all are covered in the debate.

- Pairs role play a scene in which one of them has been the victim of discrimination and asks the other for advice on what to do. They then discuss the view that there are too many laws about employment and discrimination.

Plenary

Recap what the main laws are which protect employees' rights and take a vote to determine which law the class believes is the most important.

Extension activities

- Students read 'Tribunals', then search the Internet to find other examples of cases of discrimination which have been taken to employment tribunals, before writing a brief statement about discrimination in the workplace.

- Why do unions exist? Research trade unions, and write one paragraph on their history, and one detailing the benefits that unions provide to workers.

Further resources

www.adviceguide.org.uk is the Citizens Advice Bureau website which provides information on employment rights, among others.

Breaking employment laws

❶ Dawn was working as a cleaner for a cleaning services firm for £4.00 an hour. After eight months she discovered that she was earning 60p less per hour than a man who worked as a cleaner for the same company. When she raised it with her supervisor she was told that a woman would never earn £4.60. Her employer later told her that the reason for the difference was that she was not trained to use certain pieces of machinery that the male cleaners used. A tribunal ordered the firm to pay Dawn £2,540 in compensation.

❷ Gary, 18, worked in a butcher's and was cutting meat when his hand slipped and he cut off the top of two fingers. His boss had often told him to use a special guard, but most people at work, including Gary, ignored this. Gary was awarded damages in court because his employer did not make sure that he was working in the right way, but they were reduced by a third because he hadn't followed the safety instructions.

❸ Susan, a train driver on the London Underground, was forced to hand in her notice when new shift arrangements meant that she could not work and look after her three-year-old child. An employment tribunal decided that the new working arrangements indirectly discriminated against women because more women were single parents.

❹ Eugene suffered constant racist taunts from other workers on the building site where he worked, and the management did little to stop it. They said that 'black bastard' and 'nigger' were words often used on sites. The tribunal decided that Eugene had been directly discriminated against. He was awarded £2000 damages.

❺ Ms N works as a check-out operator in a large supermarket. Because she has epilepsy, she needs to take an average of one day per month off work. Apart from these disability-related absences, Ms N rarely has any time off work for sickness. However, she was disciplined for this by her employer, and told that her bonus would be affected if her sick leave remained so high. Eventually the Disability Rights Commission advised Ms N to take out a grievance against her employer, who agreed that any absences taken by Ms N due to her epilepsy would not be classed as sick leave.

UNIT 3 Rights and responsibilities

Your Life 4/Year 10

Lesson 3 *Your Life 4*, pages 18–19
Citizenship 1.2a, 1.2b, 2.1a, 2.1b, 3k; Economic wellbeing and financial capability 1.2d

Aim: To explore your rights and responsibilities as a consumer.

Preparation

Make a copy of copymaster 7 (What are their rights?) for each group.

Starter

Write the word 'consumer' on the board and ask class what it means. Repeat with 'goods' and 'services'. Invite groups to discuss any examples where the students or their families have had to complain about goods or services. What happened? Can they work out what their rights were from these examples? Ask groups to feed back to the class.

Suggested activities

- The class finds out about the rights proposed in the starter activity by reading the articles 'Your rights when shopping' and 'When you have a complaint'. Pairs discuss what they have learned about their rights under the Sale of Goods Act and draw up two lists – one stating when they are entitled to a refund or an exchange and one stating when they are not entitled to a refund.

- Discuss with the class their rights under the Sale of Goods and Services Act.

- Give each student a copy of copymaster 7. Ask groups to discuss what the person's rights are and what advice they would give in each case.

Plenary

Ask students to write down one main feature of the Sale of Goods Act, and one main feature of the Supply of Goods and Services Act. Ask several students to read out what they have written and invite the class to comment.

Extension activities

- Students design and write a short leaflet for consumers outlining their rights when shopping.

- Invite groups to plan a role play of a radio phone-in consumer affairs programme, using the examples of consumer rights on the copymaster and/or others of their own devising. Ask one or two groups to perform their role play in front of the class, then open the discussion to the 'studio audience'.

- Discuss with the class what the term 'ethical consumer' means. Ask: Do consumers have responsibilities as well as rights? How could the following factors affect whether you buy a product – the human rights of producers? environmental concerns? animal welfare? Encourage them to visit the Ethical Consumer website and to investigate and write about one of the companies that is listed (see 'For your file', page 18).

Further resources

- www.tradingstandards.gov.uk/schools/smartshoppersguide/ is a course for students on consumer rights, with lesson plans and teacher's notes.

- www.oft.gov.uk is the Office of Fair Trading's website. It lists consumers' rights and details how to make a complaint.

What are their rights?

Look at the following case studies. What are the rights of these young people? What would you advise them to do in each case?

1 Raj hired some powerful speakers so that he could put on a disco at school. He paid £50 deposit. When he got them home, he couldn't get them to work properly. The manager of the music shop claimed that he had broken the speakers and refused to return the deposit.

2 Anita bought a jacket that was reduced in a sale from £49 to £29. When she got home, her mother pointed out a mark on one of the arms. She assumed that the jacket was reduced because it was damaged, and thought she would not get a refund because she had bought it in a sale.

3 Leo's guitar needed repairing before a gig the following week so he took it to the local music shop. They gave him an estimate of £36 for the repair and said it would be ready in time for the gig. It wasn't, as it took an extra two days, and the repair turned out to be £42.

4 In October, Monica bought an expensive sports bag as a gift for her sister. When she opened it on Christmas day, her sister found that the zip was faulty. Helen had kept the receipt, but when she took it back to the shop the manager refused to exchange or refund it. He said she must have broken the zip herself some time in the last two months.

UNIT 4 The law of the land

Aim: To understand what the law is and how laws are made.

Preparation

Make copies of copymaster 8 (Which type of law?) and cut out the cards, one set for each pair.

Starter

Supply five or six common human activities on the board, e.g. travelling, eating, shopping, sex, playing music, working. Pick one of these activities, then brainstorm all the rules and regulations that students think relate to that area of life. After two minutes, ask groups to categorize these into 'laws', 'customs', 'morality', and 'rules and regulations' (you may want to define these areas first). Then invite groups to pick one other activity in the list and do the same activity. Ask two or three groups to feed back their findings. In the class discussion, emphasise (a) how these rules act as a framework for our rights and duties, and (b) how many different kinds of rule apply.

Suggested activities

- Groups read the articles 'What is the law?' and 'Making the law' and discuss the questions. You may need to explain that 'state' is the term used to refer to the highest political bodies in the land that can exercise power – in Britain, this is mainly Parliament, the army, the police, the civil service and local government. Ask two or three groups to feed back their findings and invite the class to comment. (Some advantages of judge-based law: consistency, as similar decisions are made in similar cases; experience, as judges make decisions based on hundreds of other cases. Some disadvantages: inflexibility, as bad decisions in the past can be repeated; complexity, as there are nearly half a million reported cases. Statute law is exposed to democratic scrutiny, but MPs often vote on party lines rather than as their constituents wish.)

- Cut out the cards on copymaster 8 and put 15 strips of paper into an envelope. Make enough envelopes for each group to have one. Students should categorize them as features of the different types of law without referring to the Students Book (the category cards are in capitals).

Plenary

Ask two or three groups to feed back their results, explaining why they have grouped the cards as they have.

Extension activities

- Students write an entry on 'Law' for an encyclopedia for teenagers (see 'For your file', page 21).

- Students use the Internet to research Sharia law. Then, as a class, ask them to discuss the arguments for and against incorporating aspects of Sharia law into UK law.

Further resources

www.learn.co.uk/citizen/legal/ has a scheme of work for rights and responsibilities under the law.

www.bbc.co.uk/religion/religions/islam/beliefs/sharia/_1.shtml has information on sharia law.

Which type of law?

COMMON LAW

Made by judges

Custom & tradition

Precedent

Unwritten law

STATUTE LAW

House of Commons

Bill

House of Lords

Act of Parliament

EUROPEAN LAW

European Parliament

Directive

Regulation

Supremacy over
national law

UNIT 4 The law of the land

Aim: To explore the two main branches of national law, as well as the court system and the different professions involved in the law.

Preparation

Make a copy of copymaster 9 (The sad story of Solomon Grundy) for each student.

Starter

Read the panels on civil law and criminal law to the class and make sure they understand the difference between the two. Test their understanding by giving examples of different kinds of laws, e.g. 'A couple want to change their will' or 'A man is accused of forging someone's signature on a will' and asking them if each example relates to civil or criminal law.

Suggested activities

- Study 'The court system' and ensure that students understand the difference between civil and criminal law. Then put students into pairs to discuss what they have read so far and ask them to compose a quiz for their partner.

- Prompt groups to discuss the news summaries and write down the answers to the questions. Ask some of the groups for their answers and check these with the rest of the class.

- Ask groups of students to choose one of the situations listed and prepare a presentation to explain the workings of the law. Tell students to assume that the cases are not settled out of court.

Plenary

Choose three pairs to present their scenarios in front of the class and invite class comment.

Extension activities

- Give a copy of copymaster 9 to each student. Students annotate the story of Solomon Grundy with respect to the ways in which the law intervened in his life (and death). Students can add as much detail as they wish, extending the scenarios as they imagine.

- Students research the jobs of solicitors, barristers, judges and magistrates, and write a short leaflet 'People in the law'. Alternatively, ask students to work in groups, each researching one of these occupations to go into a class leaflet.

The sad story of Solomon Grundy

Make notes on the story of Solomon Grundy to show where and how the law came into his life. Give as much detail as you can about the law in each case. The notes have been started for you.

The law says you have to be in full-time education until 16

His birth must be registered by law

The sad story of Solomon Grundy

Solomon Grundy was born in 1959. He attended local schools from 1964 to 1975, then worked as a mechanic in a garage. He lost two fingers in an accident at work in 1977, which he blamed on faulty equipment. The compensation money allowed him to buy his own car.

Solomon married Frieda in 1979 and they had one child. But Frieda left him for another man two years later. In his distress, he turned to crime. He was eventually convicted of robbery and sent to prison for 6 months. There he wrote a book about his experiences, but a fellow prisoner stole the material and published it under his own name. It became a best seller. Solomon eventually sued him.

He bought a house with the settlement money, and started his own business selling cars, but he died of food poisoning after a meal at a local restaurant in 2004.

UNIT 5 Crime and punishment

Your Life 4/Year 10

Lesson 1 *Your Life 4*, pages 24–25
Citizenship 1.1b, 2.1a, 2.1b, 2.2a, 2.2b, 2.2c, 3b, 3c

Aim: To explore how crime relates to young people, focusing on anti-social behaviour.

Preparation

Make a copy of copymaster 10 (Focus on knife crime) for each student.

Starter

Ask the class at what age they think people are really responsible for their crimes, giving their reasons. Then read the section on criminal responsibility to the class and prompt groups to discuss the questions and feed back. Has anyone's view changed as a result of this discussion? Note that the age of criminal responsibility varies from country to country: Luxembourg, 18; Spain, 16; Denmark, 15; Holland, 13; England, Wales and Northern Ireland, 10; Scotland, 8. You could ask the groups if their views differ when they hear these statistics. Note also that, although in England, Wales and Northern Ireland you can't be charged until you are 10, you can be put into care.

Suggested activities

- Read the information on anti-social behaviour and invite students to discuss the questions in pairs. Then ask students to join up with another pair to role-play being members of a local committee tackling anti-social behaviour. Ask two or three groups to present their ideas to the class.

- Students read the information on knife crime (copymaster 10), and discuss the questions in groups. Then invite individuals to write a short statement on 'knife crime and how to tackle it' to put in their files.

Plenary

Ask some of the students to share what they have written in a class discussion.

Extension activities

- Students could set up a Youth Action Group. Information on Youth Action Groups can be obtained from www.crimeconcern.org.uk

- Students can research joyriding, focusing on the roles and viewpoints of one of the following in dealing with joyriding: the Police, the fire service, the ambulance service, Victim Support, magistrates, Youth Offending Teams (YOTs). They can then present their findings to the class.

Further resources

- www.ukcjweblog.org.uk/categories/youngoffenders has links to news articles on youth crime and young offenders.

- Further information about knife crime can be found at talkaboutknives.direct.gov.uk and www.droptheweapons.org

10 Focus on knife crime

Young people and knife crime

- A survey on gun and knife crime found that:
  - 63% of young people believe image is directly linked to gun and knife crime
  - 61% think gun and knife crime is about revenge and reprisals
  - 63% believe peer pressure is a main reason for gun and knife crime.

- The most commonly given reason for carrying a knife is 'for protection'.

- Other reasons include 'in case there's a fight' and 'for use in crimes'

Source: adapted from talkaboutknives.direct.gov.uk

Know the facts: Carrying knives

- If you carry a knife you could go to prison for four years.

- You could serve a life sentence if found guilty of murder.

- The law is clear and unforgiving – you don't have to have your hand on the knife to be convicted for murder. If you are with someone who uses a knife, you too could be found guilty of the killing.

- The law places a heavy burden on young people in groups. You need to ask yourself constantly who is in a group. Are they carrying weapons and what might they do with those weapons?

Source: www.droptheweapons.org

Knife crime – Tackling the problem

A number of ways of tackling knife crime have been suggested. These include:
- An automatic prison sentence for anyone convicted of carrying a knife.
- Tougher penalties for people who sell knives to anyone under 16.
- Banning the sale of knives on the Internet.
- Introducing more knife amnesties, which encourage people to hand in knives without fear of prosecution.
- Random sweeps by police in which they set up metal detectors at places such as stations and schools.
- The regular use of metal detectors in schools.
- Showing graphic pictures of real-life stab wounds to young people convicted of carrying a knife.
- Arranging for young offenders to meet the victims of knife crime.
- Encouraging young people to anonymously report anyone they see with a knife.
- More publicity about knife crime, such as DVDs which include accounts of the effects of a stabbing on the personal lives of both the victim and the offender.

⚇ In groups

Read the information above and discuss these questions:

1 What do you think are the causes of knife crime? What part do a) image b) revenge/reprisal c) peer pressure play in knife crimes?

2 What are the reasons why some young people carry knives?

3 What can be the consequences if you are a) found to be carrying a knife b) present when a member of the group you are with carries out a stabbing?

4 Discuss the suggestions for tackling knife crime and rank them in order of effectiveness, starting with which of them you think would be the most effective. Can you suggest any other ways of tackling knife crime?

UNIT 5 Crime and punishment

Your Life 4/Year 10

Lesson 2 *Your Life 4*, pages 26–27
Citizenship 1.1b, 2.1a, 2.1b, 2.2a, 2.2b, 2.2c, 3b, 4a

Aim: To explore the youth justice system and what happens in youth courts.

Preparation

Make a copy of copymaster 11 (Stop and search) for each student.

Starter

Explain that young offenders are treated differently from adult offenders and that the youth justice system deals with young people up to the age of 17. Prompt the students to suggest the reasons why there is a separate system for young offenders. Ask: What should the aims of the youth justice system be?

Suggested activities

- Read the information about 'Youth courts'. Ask groups to discuss the questions, then invite individuals to write an article for a teenage magazine – 'Ten things you need to know about youth courts'.

- In groups, students read the case study, then discuss whether or not the names of young offenders should be made public.

- Study the information on crown courts and juries. Ask students, in groups, to discuss the three statements about jury trials and to share their views on whether trial by jury should be restricted to certain serious cases.

Plenary

Ask students to write down three key facts about youth courts that they have learnt from this lesson. Ask several students to read out what they have written. You could collect them in and invite one or two students to use them as the basis for a class factsheet about youth courts.

Extension activities

Students write a short encyclopedia article on the system of trial by jury (see 'For your file', page 27).

Further resources

- An interactive virtual tour of the criminal justice system is given at www.cjsonline.gov.uk/victim/walkthrough/index.html.

- Details of the Youth Justice Board which oversees the youth justice system in England and Wales can be found at www.yjb.gov.uk

- Police powers to stop and search are explained at homeoffice.gov.uk/police/powers/stop-and-search

Your Life 4/Year 10

11 Stop and search

The police have the power to stop and search someone if they have reasonable grounds to think you may be carrying illegal drugs, stolen goods, weapons or anything that might be used for theft or burglary.

Even if they have no reason to believe you are carrying any of these things, the police can stop and search you if you are travelling to a sports stadium or if you are in an area where incidents involving serious violence may take place.

The police also have the powers to stop and search people when there is a terrorist threat or a threat to public order. In such instances, they do not need to have reasonable grounds to suspect anyone before stopping and searching them.

However, stop and search powers are controversial, as the following report shows.

When being black and driving a Jaguar makes you a criminal

Senior newspaper executive Michael Eboda was returning home from a weekend away with his girlfriend. Suddenly they were confronted by armed police. Their crime? Having a nice car.

Four officers appeared, two on either side of my car. All were armed. They told us to get out of the vehicle and turn off the engine. We were then shocked to see down the road, behind us, at least 30 more police officers, who had come in vans and cars, some with dogs, others with more weapons. We were frisked and I was asked what I did for a living.

Stop and search has been a major issue of contention between black people and the police for as long as I can remember. Basically if, like me, you are black, you are eight times more likely to be stopped and searched by the cops than if you are white, despite the fact that the average black person is no more likely to commit a crime than the average white person.

Source: *The Observer*

Stop and search – for or against?

Possible advantages	Possible disadvantages
● It leads to fewer crimes	● It is too random
● It helps police deter crimes	● It makes the innocent feel like criminals
● Police have strict rules which restrict when and who they can stop and search	● It allows the police to pick on certain types of people, e.g. the young or ethnic minorities
● If you have nothing to hide, you don't need to worry about being stopped	● It infringes basic rights not to be harassed

In groups

Read the article on the police powers of stop and search and discuss the advantages and disadvantages of these powers.

UNIT 5 Crime and punishment

Your Life 4/Year 10

Lesson 3 *Your Life 4*, pages 28–29
Citizenship 1.1a, 2.1a, 2.1b, 2.2a, 2.2b, 2.2c, 3b, 3c

Aim: To explore the kinds of sentencing available to the courts, focusing especially on the use of prisons.

Preparation

Make a copy of copymaster 12 (Match the sentences) for each student.

Starter

Write the question 'Why do we punish criminals?' on the board. Brainstorm immediate responses and discuss. Introduce the ideas of protection of society, deterrence, retribution, helping to reform offenders and helping the community.

Suggested activities

- Read the article 'Sentencing' with the class. Get them to discuss this in pairs and list the pros and cons of custodial and alternative types of sentencing. They may come up with the following responses:
  - alternative sentences – can be better at reducing reoffending;
  - cost the taxpayer less; offer offenders a chance to pay back to society;
  - do not create 'colleges of crime';
  - are less disruptive to offenders and their families.

  On the other hand, alternative sentences are not as immediate or easily understood; are riskier; are less harsh; are not as shameful; are less high profile.

- Give copies of the copymaster (Match the sentences) and invite groups to match the four cases to possible sentences. Ask groups to explain their choices, and deal with any discrepancies by opening up a class discussion. (The actual sentences given in the case studies are: 1C, 2A, 3D, 4B.)

- Read the articles 'Barring the way' and 'Prison worked for me' with the class. Groups discuss the articles and come to a consensus on the value of prisons as a punishment. Ask two or three groups to feed back the results of their discussion and elicit class comment.

Plenary

Recap the five reasons for giving different types of sentences. Discuss the view that the main purpose when choosing an appropriate sentence should be to try to help the offender from committing further crimes.

Extension activity

'Imprisonment is the best way of taking criminals off the streets and protecting society.' Students write two paragraphs saying whether they agree or disagree with this statement, quoting evidence from these pages to support their answers.

Further resources

- www.nacro.org.uk is the website of the National Association for the Care and Rehabilitation of Offenders, which works to reduce crime by assisting ex-prisoners to rebuild their lives and to reduce the unnecessary use of custody.

- Details of organisations that campaign for reform of prisons and the penal system can be found at www.prisonreformtrust.org.uk and www.howardleague.org

- Guardian Unlimited, a useful website, has a special report on prisons at www.guardian.co.uk/prisons

 **12** Match the sentences

Match the crimes with the sentences given by the judge in each case. (Each is based on a real case.)

THE CRIMES

Case 1

Clive, 23 and unemployed, was found guilty of causing criminal damage by smashing a shop window in the early hours of the morning. He said he was very sorry and the judge believed that he meant it. It was Clive's first offence.

Case 2

Paul, 25, was part of a gang of football supporters that ran riot in a pub. Three people were injured. No one actually saw Paul attack the individuals. Paul was found guilty of 'causing an affray'. The judge was told that Paul had three previous convictions for violence at football matches.

Case 3

Laurence, 12, admitted stealing property worth £3,000. Another 78 offences were 'taken into account'. He was thought to have stolen about £10,000 worth of goods, passing them on to adults.

Case 4

Three 16-year-old girls attacked a woman, injured her, and stole her bag and watch. None of the girls had a previous conviction. The judge said he wanted to make them think twice before doing anything like it again.

THE SENTENCES

A Six years in prison

B Conditional discharge (if offender commits another offence within a certain time, they go back to court to be sentenced for both offences)

C A fine and an order to pay compensation

D Being taken into the care of the local authority

In groups

1 Which of the sentences would you give to Clive, Paul, Lawrence and the three girls?

2 If you could, would you give an entirely different sentence?

3 What are your reasons for choosing the sentences? What do you hope they will achieve?

UNIT 6 It's your government

Aim: To understand what the UK Parliament is and what it does.

Preparation

Make a copy of copymaster 13 (Understanding Parliament) for each student.

Starter

Explain that the UK government is made up of three parts known as the executive, the legislature and the judiciary. Read what their function is and who carries out that function in the UK.

Suggested activities

- Read the rest of the section 'How the UK government works' including the part explaining how the US system is different. Discuss with the class the difference between a fusion of powers and a separation of powers and which gives the government more power.

- Study 'The Cabinet and the Opposition'. Discuss what they do, then ask students, in groups, to name as many members of the Cabinet and Shadow Cabinet as they can. Invite them to draw up lists of posts and names and to use the Internet to extend their lists and fill in gaps.

- Read 'What Parliament does' and discuss its functions and the importance of each function. Then, read 'The House of Commons' and then 'The House of Lords.' Consolidate the students' understanding by asking them comprehension questions. Then put them in groups to discuss the importance of the House of Lords and their views on life peers and how they are appointed.

Plenary

Ask students to summarise what they have learnt about Parliament. What do they think the most important points they have learnt are? Was there anything that surprised them about Parliament?

Extension activities

- Test their knowledge of the information about Parliament given on these two pages by getting them to complete the multiple choice quiz on copymaster 13 'Understanding Parliament' The answers are 1c, 2b, 3c, 4b, 5b, 6c, 7b, 8b, 9b, 10c.

- Ask students to imagine they were MPs. How would they divide up their time? Give them a choice between sorting out local people's problems, attending debates in the House of Commons, or campaigning for their party. Which of these do they think is the most important? Why? Ask for reasons for their views.

- Ask students to imagine they had to design our parliamentary system from scratch. How many chambers would they have? How would they be elected? How would they operate? In groups, students write up proposals, and then present them to the class.

- Students use the Internet to research proposals for further reform of the House of Lords, then organize a debate on the motion 'This house believes that the House of Lords should be replaced by an elected House of Representatives'.

Further resources

www.parliament.uk/education includes an online resource 'Parliament explained' which covers what Parliament does and the difference between Parliament and Government.

Your Life 4/Year 10

Understanding parliament

Copy out these sentences choosing the correct ending from those in the brackets.

❶ The most powerful of the three parts of Parliament is:
a) the monarch
b) the House of Lords
c) the House of Commons

❷ A general election has to be called if Parliament has lasted for:
a) 3 years   b) 5 years   c) 7 years

❸ The number of MPs in the House of Commons is:
a) 378   b) 523   c) 659

❹ In 2005, the number of women MPs elected was:
a) 47   b) 128   c) 261

❺ After a debate, MPs vote:
a) electronically
b) by a show of hands
c) by walking though one of two corridors

❻ The number of hereditary peers in the House of Lords in 2009 was:
a) 0   b) 92   c) 150

❼ The majority of members of the House of Lords are:
a) hereditary peers
b) life peers
c) public nominees

❽ The Law Lords are:
a) the people who make the rules governing the House of Lords
b) 12 judges who also sit as the highest court in the land
c) appointed by lawyers to represent their interests in the House of Lords

❾ Members of the House of Lords who are not affiliated to a political party are known as:
a) floating peers
b) cross-benchers
c) non-conformists

❿ A break when Parliament is not sitting is known as:
a) remission
b) vacation
c) adjournment

▦ In groups

Imagine you had to design your own Parliament for the UK. How big would it be? Where would it be located? What powers would it have? Who would sit in Parliament? How would its members be elected? Compare their ideas with other groups.

Notes:

UNIT 6 It's your government

Lesson 2 *Your Life 4*, pages 32–33
Citizenship 1.1a, 1.1d, 2.1a, 3c, 3d, 3e, 4a

> **Aim:** To understand how Parliament is elected, to explore different systems of election and to discuss what can be done to improve voter turnout.

Preparation

Make a copy of copymaster 14 (Should 16 year olds have the vote?) for each student.

Starter

Introduce the topic of elections by asking the class what they already know about elections. Ask students if they know how to vote. Then write the word 'constituency' on the board and explain what it means.

Suggested activities

- Study the information on 'First past the post' and 'Proportional Representation' in the section 'You and your vote – elections'. Ask groups to consider the different viewpoints and to decide which system of election they prefer and why. Conclude the activity with a class discussion of their views.

- Ask groups to discuss what voter apathy is and what they think the causes are. Read the statements in 'Is it worth voting?' Ask: Which of the statements do they agree with? Would they vote at a general election?

- Split the class into two groups. One group should list all the reasons they can think of for why people should vote. The other group should list all the reasons for not voting. Then role play a TV studio debate in which some people argue that you should always vote, and others argue that people have the right to choose not to vote.

- Read 'Get out the vote'. Discuss suggestions for increasing the turnout at elections. Students research these and other ideas on the Internet, then prepare a presentation to give to the rest of the class saying which you would introduce and why.

- Ask students to write an article for the local paper, stating why they would or wouldn't vote in a general election, and explaining the reasons.

- Give out copies of copymaster 14 'Should 16-year-olds have the vote?' Ask the students to read the arguments and to discuss whether they believe they should be able to vote at 16. Then students should write a letter stating their own views.

Plenary

Recap the suggestions for overcoming voter apathy. Ask: What are the arguments in favour of making voting compulsory and fining people who do not vote? What are the arguments against? Conclude by asking for a show of hands – who is in favour of compulsory voting?

Extension activities

- Students design a leaflet encouraging young people to vote. They should decide what key messages to include on their leaflets.

- Students use the Internet to research previous local and national elections in their area. They should look at the percentage of votes that were cast, and the percentage of seats that were won. Do they think the results are fair?

Further resources

www.electoral-reform.org.uk gives details of the campaigns for the reform of the voting system run by the Electoral Reform Society.

Should 16-year-olds have the vote?

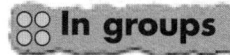
In groups

Study these articles from the Daily Telegraph. What points do the writers make for and against votes at 16? Which do you agree with? Give reasons for your views, then share them in a class discussion

It's not right to give 16-year-olds the vote

There are strong signs that the Government is planning to lower the voting age from 18 to 16. We wonder why it should wish to do so. We have noticed no great public demand for such a change. It would right no obvious wrong. Yet the idea has been floated in Labour's 'Big Conversation' policy document. And now the schools minister, David Miliband, has told a conference of A-level students that it is 'illogical' to prevent 16-year-olds from voting, while they are allowed to get married and work.

That argument itself is as illogical as it would be to say that since people aged 16–18 are not allowed to vote, it must be wrong that they are allowed to marry or work. It confuses two entirely unrelated issues. It is another example of the woolly thinking of a government that lowered the age of homosexual consent to 16, in this era of Aids, while on the very same day it increased to 18 the age at which teenagers were allowed to buy tobacco.

The arguments against giving the vote to 16-year-olds should be clear to anybody who has had direct experience of the average British teenager. We are aware that some 16-year-olds are reading these very words this morning. All credit to them, and to their curiosity. If some system could be devised whereby they could be given the vote, while their contemporaries were denied it, we would be all in favour of it.

But we know, and they know, that they are a very small minority. Most 16-year-olds in Britain – more than 70 per cent – are still in full-time education and completely dependent on their parents for all their needs. They pay no taxes. They are much more interested in video games than in the rights and wrongs of foundation hospitals or trial by jury. If they have political opinions at all, these are mostly second-hand and ill-thought-out.

It would be quite wrong to give these teenagers a say in the choice of the next government.

Re: Old enough to die for their country
Date: 9 February 2004

Sir – Having worked and lived with teenagers for 40 years, my daily direct experience demonstrates the entitlement of 16-year-olds to participate in choosing their representatives.

The compulsory citizenship education pioneered by Community Service Volunteers has taught them about the rights and duties of citizens, how the nation works, and the value of trial by jury. The rights and wrongs of foundation hospitals are familiar to them; they will

be affected for longer than most. Very many young people have jobs and are all too familiar with paying taxes. At school they have identified community problems, worked out solutions and implemented them. Bus shelters have been repaired, crime reduced, playgrounds refurbished and derelict sites transformed.

Many 16-year-olds are recruited into the Army. If they are old enough to die for their country, surely they are old enough to vote first.

From: Dame Elisabeth Hoodless, Executive Director CSV (Community Service Volunteers), London N1

On your own

Write your views either for or against giving 16-year-olds the vote.

UNIT 6 It's your government

Aim: To understand different forms of government and what the key characteristics are of the UK's political system.

Preparation

Make a copy of copymaster 15 (Systems of Government – the UK and the USA) for each student.

Starter

Ask students what a democracy is. Explain that it is a system of government where all the citizens share power. Talk about how it would be impractical for all the adults in Britain to get together to make decisions, so they elect representatives to do so on their behalf. Then read the first paragraph of 'Democracy and the UK political system.'

Suggested activities

- Read the rest of 'Democracy and the UK political system'. Discuss the views expressed in the two statements and the ways in which politicians try to keep in touch with the people they represent. Ask: How can the public be more involved in policy making? Conclude the activity by asking the students, in pairs, to list what they think the main advantages and disadvantages of representative democracy are.

- Study 'Different political systems', then ask the students, in groups, to discuss the similarities and differences between the four systems. Share their views in a class discussion and talk about how living in countries which have these systems would be different from living in the UK.

Plenary

Students debate the view that a representative democracy is the fairest system of government, then write a short statement saying whether or not they agree with that view.

Extension activities

- Use copymaster 15 to help the students understand the difference between the USA's system of government and the UK system. Gapfill answers: Cabinet; Prime Minister; Parliament; Judiciary; interpret.

- In pairs, students choose one of the following countries – Cuba (communist), Saudi Arabia (dictatorship by absolute monarchy), India (democracy) – and use the Internet to find out as much as possible about that country's system of government. Then they prepare a report, and present it to the class.

Further resources

Plans for a lesson on types of government can be found at www.parliament.uk/education

Systems of government – the UK and the USA

 **In pairs**

Study the diagram that shows the different parts of the UK Government. Look at pages 34–5 of *Your Life 4*, and fill in the gaps. Then study the diagram of the USA Government. What are the main differences between the Government in the UK and the Government in the USA?

The UK:

The Executive
Head: Prime Minister
Bodies: The _____ made up of government Ministers.
Functions: Takes day to day decisions.
How appointed: The head of the largest party in the legislature becomes Prime Minister.

The Legislature
Head: _____
Bodies: The Houses of _____
Functions: Makes the law.
How appointed: Elected in the House of Commons, appointed in the House of Lords by the Prime Minister.

The _____
Head: The Lord Chancellor
Bodies: The House of Lords when sitting as the highest court in the land, other judges.
Functions: To _____ the law.
How appointed: Appointed by the Lord Chancellor, a member of the Executive AND legislature.

The USA:

The Executive
Head: The President, directly elected by the voters.
Bodies: The Cabinet, appointed by the President.
Functions: Takes day-to-day decisions.
How appointed: Elected by voters in a presidential election.

The Legislature
Head: The Heads of Congress
Bodies: The House of Representatives and the Senate.
Functions: Makes the law.
How appointed: Elected by voters in elections.

The Judiciary
Head: The US Supreme Court
Bodies: The Supreme Court, other courts.
Functions: Interprets the law.
How appointed: Appointed for life by the President to remain independent, but approval of Congress required.

UNIT 7 It's your council

Lesson 1 *Your Life 4*, pages 36–37
Citizenship 1.1a, 2.1a, 3d, 4a, 4b

Aim: To understand what local government is, and how it functions.

Preparation

Make a copy of copymaster 16 (Your local council) for each student.

Starter

Write the phrase 'Local Government' on the board. Elicit from the students what they already know about local government (eg: what their council is called, who runs their council, who is their local councillor etc).

Suggested activities

- Ask students in pairs to study 'What is local government' and 'Different types of local government.' Then consolidate class knowledge of local government with comprehension questions. Build up a chart on the board showing the various types of council and what services they are responsible for.

- Read 'Local councillors – who are they, and what do they do?' Ask students visit the local council's website to research who their local councilors are, which party they belong to and what areas of responsibility they have.

- Ask the class, in pairs, to think about what problems they would like their local councillor to sort out in their ward. Students choose a problem and draft an e-mail to send to a local councilor requesting their help with the matter.

- Read 'Standing to be a local councillor' In groups, students consider whether or not councillors should be full-time politicians. Ask: What are the arguments for and against people being able to stand for the council at 16 rather than 18? Students then share their views in a class discussion.

- Explain that you need planning permission from the local council to do any new building, whether it's a major development like a new supermarket or a minor one, such as putting an extension on your house. Read 'Case study – planning decisions'. Put students in groups to discuss local planning decisions. Invite them to role play being councillors discussing what they would demand from a developer in return for planning permission to build 100 flats on a derelict site (see 'Planning applications' page 37)

Plenary

Recap on all the services that are provided by local councils and discuss the importance of having local matters dealt with by local people rather than by central government.

Extension activities

- Ask students to fill in copymaster 16 by researching information about what sort of council it is, how many members it has, how often it has elections, which party (if any) is in control, and what the council is responsible for. Web links to local councils can be found at www.direct.gov.uk

- Encourage students to find out about local issues by looking in the local newspapers. What sort of issues, especially planning applications, has the local council been dealing with recently? Ask students to make notes and discuss the issues with the rest of the class.

Your local council

Fill in this sheet with details of your local council.

1 Name of Council: _____

2 Type of Council (tick one):

County council ☐   District council ☐   Metropolitan council/unitary authority ☐

3 How many councillors are there on the council? ☐

4 How many councillors does each party have?

Conservative ☐   Labour ☐   Liberal Democrat ☐

Independent ☐   Other party (please specify) ☐ _____

5 Does any one party have a majority on the council? Yes ☐   No ☐

6 Is there either:

a) A directly elected mayor for your council?

(If yes, write the name of the directly elected Mayor here ☐

_____).

b) A Cabinet system which controls your council?

(If yes, write the leader of the Council who chairs the Cabinet here ☐

_____).

7 What is the name of the local council ward in which you live? _____

8 How many councillors represent your ward? _____

9 **a)** How often do elections for the local council take place? _____

b) When is the next local council election? _____

10 How often do meetings of the full council take place? _____

11 Write down three controversial issues the council has dealt with over the last year.

1 _____

2 _____

3 _____

UNIT 7 It's your council

Lesson 2 *Your Life 4*, pages 38–39
Citizenship 1.1a, 2.1a, 3d, 4a, 4b

Aim: To examine how local government could be reformed in order to reduce the democratic deficit that exists in UK politics.

Preparation

Make a copy of copymaster 17 (Local government – fact-check) for each student.

Starter

Explain that some people argue that there is a lack of democracy in local government and that this is called a democratic deficit. For example, many people choose not to vote in local elections due to lack of interest. Read 'What is the democratic deficit?'. Ask for a show of hands for: "Would you vote in a local election if you had the right do so?" Ask students to explain their reasons.

Suggested activities

- Read 'Changes within local government.' Ask students, in groups, to decide which statements they agree or disagree with, and why.

- Ask students to read 'Involving local people', then to discuss, in groups, which of these ways of getting people involved they think is the most effective. Compare their conclusions as a class.

- Read 'Involving young people'. Students in groups then discuss how they think young people could be more involved in making decisions in their local area.

Plenary

Ask groups to share their ideas about how young people could be more involved in local affairs.

Extension activities

- Test knowledge and understanding of local government by asking students to complete the multiple choice quiz on copymaster 17. The answers are: 1c, 2a, 3c, 4b, 5d, 6d, 7a, 8b, 9d, 10a.

- Encourage students to conduct a survey amongst young people in the area, finding out what they would like to see the local council doing in their area, and to present a report to the class. They can then send the report to their local councillor, with a covering letter asking them how young people can currently get involved in local politics.

- In groups, students imagine that they could hold a local referendum, but only on one issue. Which issue would they choose? Why? Students should give reasons for their views.

Further resources

What the UK Youth Parliament is and how students can get involved can be found at www.ukyouthparliament.org

Local government – fact-check

○ **On your own**

Complete this quiz. Then compare your answers in pairs, before being given the correct answers by your teacher.

1 What type of council has the most powers?

   a) A district council

   b) A county council

   c) A unitary authority

   d) None of the above

2 What is the area a local councillor represents known as?

   a) A ward

   b) A constituency

   c) A village

   d) A council

3 How old do you have to be in order to become a councillor?

   a) 16   **b)** 18   **c)** 21   **d)** 25

4 What sort of councils have the power to make planning decisions?

   a) District councils

   b) District councils and Unitary authorities

   c) County councils

   d) County councils and Unitary authorities

5 What is devolution?

   a) Making councils work together

   b) Making councils work with the government

   c) Taking power from councils and giving it to the government

   d) Taking power from the government and giving more power to local people

6 Which of the following areas doesn't have devolution?

   a) Wales   **b)** London

   c) Scotland   **d)** Liverpool

7 Which of the following is not part of a local council?

   a) Residents' associations

   b) Neighbourhood management

   c) Scrutiny committees

   d) Directly elected mayors

8 Local councillors have certain entitlements. Which of the following is not one of their entitlements?

   a) Time off work to fulfill council duties

   b) Free accommodation in a council-owned property

   c) An allowance to compensate them from time off work

   d) Expenses for travelling to meetings

9 Which of the following is a district council responsible for?

   a) Education

   b) Social Services

   c) Local transport

   d) Rubbish collection

10 Which of the following people are not allowed to become councillors?

   a) People who have been bankrupt in the last five years

   b) People who have been councillors for more than 10 years

   c) Members of Parliament

   d) People who own businesses in the local area.

UNIT 7 It's your council

Your Life 4/Year 10

Lesson 3 *Your Life 4*, pages 40–41
Citizenship 1.1a, 2.1a, 2.1d, 3d, 4a, 4b

Aim: To understand what devolution is, and how it is changing UK politics – nationally and locally.

Preparation

Make a copy of copymaster 18 (Going local: making a difference) for each student.

Starter

Introduce the term 'devolution' and explain what this means by reading the first paragraph of 'What is devolution?' and drawing a diagram on the board which shows the UK Parliament > Regional Assemblies > Local Councils > Neighbourhood Management.

Suggested activities

- Read 'Case study – The Scottish Parliament'and discuss with the class 'Where is there devolution nationally?' Ask students what arguments Conservatives use against devolution? Why are Labour and the Liberal Democrats for devolution?" Then ask students for their views of devolution, and for reasons for these views. Students should share their opinions in a class discussion.

- Look at the 'Case study – the Scottish Parliament'. Students use the Internet to research what powers the Scottish Parliament has and report their findings in a class discussion. Then discuss whether it was right for the Scottish Parliament to decide to release the Lockerbie bomber or whether the UK government should have made the decision.

- Study 'Case study – The Welsh Assembly'. Prompt students to discuss how the Welsh Assembly differs from the Scottish Parliament.

- 'Does devolution really matter?' Ask students in pairs or groups to decide whether they agree or disagree with the statements, and why.

Plenary

Recap on how the Welsh Assembly differs from the Scottish Parliament.

Extension activities

- Read copymaster 18. Point out that these are examples of how people can have decisions devolved to them at a local level. In pairs, ask students to imagine they are either residents on the Welsh Farm estate, discussing what a difference having an area caretaker has made, or residents of Erdington discussing what their town centre manager has achieved.

- If your area has devolution, invite a member of the regional government in your area to come to your school, and give a talk about what they do. If your area doesn't have devolution, students could draw up a survey on whether people would like devolution in your area. They should try to interview 10 people. Students then compare their results with other groups, and present them to the class.

Further resources

Information about how devolution was set up and how it is working can be found at the following sites www.scottish.parliament.uk, www.wales.gov.uk and education.niassembly.gov.uk

Your Life 4/Year 10

Going local: making a difference

Read 'Susan takes good care of us' and 'Erdington - What a difference a year makes', which describe two examples of Birmingham's 'Going Local' initiative to involve local people in making decisions about their own areas. What do you learn about how devolution is making a difference on the Welsh Farm estate and in Erdington?

What elements of these projects do you think would work in your local area? Why? Give reasons for your views.

'Susan takes good care of us':

Susan Allen is the city's first area caretaker – and she's already making a difference. Based on the Welsh House Farm estate, she has a broad remit. This is decided by local people and the Welsh House Farm Residents' Action Group.

She's already making valuable improvements to the estate's appearance, carrying out odd jobs for vulnerable or older people, and increasing awareness of environmental issues. So far, she has:

- resolved a longstanding problem when sewage entered a stream.
- cleared rubbish and organised special collections.
- cut back overgrown shrubbery
- had abandoned cars removed
- met with local groups and agencies to promote a healthy, clean environment.

Susan says 'Our steering group meets each month with local people and outside experts. It amazing how we can overcome obstacles and achieve our goals by working together.'

Source: Birmingham City Council

Erdington – 'What a difference a year makes':

Erdington town centre manager Nigel Godfrey has had a busy first year in the post. Projects completed include linking retailers' two-way radio system to the CCTV control centre, which has helped to achieve a cut in crime of up to 25 per cent.

Hanging baskets have been introduced in the High Street, and graffiti and fly posters removed. In October, there was a joint project with the local Co-op to bring artwork depicting Erdington's history to the High Street.

Events such as the St Patrick's Day Festival and St George's Day celebrations have raised Erdington's profile, boosted further by the launch of a town brochure and web site in November.

Nigel said, 'This works as a kind of early devolution, with lots of local people, teachers, businesses and council workers genuinely feeling that they are stakeholders. Joint working has helped secure these achievements, and a better Erdington town centre.'

Source: Birmingham City Council

UNIT 8 Working for change

Aim: To discuss pressure groups and campaigning in your town or local area.

Preparation

Make a copy of copymaster 19 (Understanding pressure groups) for each student.

Starter

Write the phrase 'Pressure Groups' on the board. Elicit from the students what this means. Ask the students to name examples of any pressure groups they can think of.

Suggested activities

- Read 'What are pressure groups?' and 'Case study: Heathrow Airport'. Students, in groups, discuss the action taken by Plane Stupid and whether or not breaking the law in order to protest can ever be justified.

- Students research the arguments for and against a new runway being built at Heathrow, then, in groups, perform the role play (see page 42).

- Ask students to think about their town. Explain that a pressure group often focuses on a single, particular issue. Are there any 'single issue' pressure groups that they think need setting up? Which issues do they think are the most important? Why?

- In groups, students read 'Setting up a pressure group' Then ask them to imagine they are setting up a pressure group either in favour of or against the building of a new by-pass around Oldtown. Students should follow the step-by-step guidelines and draw up plans for their pressure group, then compare them with those of the rest of the class.

- Ask the students which of the different methods suggested in 'Getting things done' they think are the most effective and why. A short, brisk class debate may be an interesting way to pinpoint the best methods.

Plenary

Discuss with the class what they have learned about pressure groups, how to set up a pressure group and how pressure groups campaign.

Extension activities

- Prompt the students, in groups, to design a website for their campaign for or against the new by-pass around Oldtown.

- Ask the students to complete the word puzzle on copymaster 19. The answers are: 1, fundraising; 2, influence; 3, single; 4, sectional; 5, trade union; 6, support; 7, illegal; 8, campaign; 9, residents; 10, network; 11, public; 12, petition; 13, stunt.

- Ask the students to write a short report on what pressure group they would join locally, and why.

- Contact a local pressure group to invite a representative to come into the school and give a talk about what they do. Give the students time to prepare their questions and encourage them to take notes. They could then write a report of the visit for the school newspaper.

Your Life 4/Year 10

19 Understanding pressure groups

Use the clues below to help you to complete the word puzzle.

❶ Activities that increase the amount of money available to your group (11)

❷ To affect the way someone is making a decision (9)

❸ A group that campaigns on only one issue is called a _____ issue pressure group (6)

❹ A pressure group that campaigns on behalf of one group of people, but a variety of issues (9)

❺ A pressure group that campaigns on behalf of employees to get better working conditions from employers (5)

❻ To show that you agree with someone (7)

❼ An action that is against the law (7)

❽ A plan of action to get your message across and achieve your aims (8)

❾ People who live in the local area, who may form an association to represent their view (9)

❿ To meet lots of other people and to make lots of good contacts (7)

⓫ The group of ordinary people whose opinions can influence decisions (6)

⓬ A list where people sign their name to say what they support (8)

⓭ Doing something different or crazy, to get attention from the media (5)

UNIT 8 Working for change

Aim: To discuss what pressure groups exist nationally, and how they campaign.

Preparation

Make a copy of copymaster 20 (Campaigning for older people – Age UK) for each student.

Starter

Ask the students to think of two issues each that they believe everybody in the country should be concerned about, e.g. nuclear weapons, treatment of animals, older people and their problems, or an environmental issue. List the issues on the board and explain that in many cases, because other people share their concerns, there are national pressure groups campaigning on the issue, e.g. CND, RSPCA, AgeUK, Friends of the Earth.

Suggested activities

- Explain that national pressure groups differ from local pressure groups in a number of ways. Read 'Single issue pressure groups' and 'Sectional pressure groups' and discuss the differences with the class.

- Invite students to imagine they are setting up a Students' Union at their school. What local and national issues would they want to campaign on? Why? Ask them to rank the issues in order of priority.

- Study 'New social movements'. Discuss with the class what they are and what they campaign on. Encourage students to use the Internet to find out more about the anti-globalisation movement.

- Read 'Lobbying' and ask pairs to discuss their views on lobbying, then to share them in a class discussion.

Plenary

Ask students to imagine that a relative has offered to pay an annual subscription so that they can become a member of a national pressure group. Get them to discuss this, saying which pressure group they would join and why.

Extension activities

- Study copymaster 20. Ask students what it tells them about Age UK. In pairs, ask students to discuss what Age UK does, then to research its current campaigns, before choosing one of them and drafting an e-mail asking their MP to put pressure on the government to take action on the issue.

- Hold a class discussion. Ask students why membership of pressure groups is increasing while that of political parties is declining? Do students think pressure groups are more important than political parties in the UK today? Do they think this is a good or a bad thing?

- Ask students if there are any pressure groups that they think should exist nationally, but don't? What are they? What sort of issues should they be campaigning on?

Your Life 4/Year 10

Campaigning for older people – age UK

Age UK is the new force combining Age Concern and Help the Aged which joined together in 2009.

Age UK believes that:
✦ Older people should have access to the same opportunities as everyone else.
✦ Older people should be able to live with dignity.
✦ The contributions of older people should be valued.
✦ Older people should have a voice in decisions affecting their lives.
Therefore, Age UK campaigns for the fair treatment of older people and against all forms of ageism.

Priorities

Age UK's priorities are:

✦ *To prevent poverty and maximize income in retirement.*
Age UK provides older people with information to enable them to claim the benefits to which they are entitled. One estimate suggests that up to £4.6 billion of income-related benefits go unclaimed by older people.

✦ *To promote age equality and enable older people to make full contributions to our economy, society and neigbourhoods.*
Ageism, also known as age discrimination, exists in many areas. For example, it may lead to a person losing their job because of their age, or a doctor deciding not to refer a patient to a consultant because the patient is 'too old'.
In 2006, a new age discrimination law came into force providing protection against age discrimination in employment, training and adult education for people of all ages. Age UK offers older people information and advice on their rights.

✦ *To maximize healthy life expectancy and promote health, independence and wellbeing for older people.*
Over two million older people live in housing that does not meet the Government's Decent Homes Standard.

✦ *To achieve greater social inclusion of the most disadvantaged older people and challenge the causes of exclusion.*
Twelve per cent of older people (over 1.1 million) feel trapped in their own homes.

✦ *To have a greater focus on older people as contributors to all that we do.*
Only 30% of those aged over 75 have Internet access, compared to the national average of 72%.

Source: Age Concern and Help the Aged websites

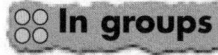 **In groups**

Study the article. What do you learn from it about why Age UK campaigns on behalf of older people? What issues does it campaign on?

Get involved. Research what issues Age UK is currently focusing on by visiting www.ageuk.org. Choose one of its current campaigns and draft an e-mail to your local MP expressing your concerns about the matter, stating what you think the government should do and urging them to put pressure on the government to take action.

UNIT 8 Working for change

Your Life 4/Year 10

Lesson 3 *Your Life 4*, pages 46–47
Citizenship 2.3a, 2.3b, 2.3c, 2.3d, 2.3e, 4a, 4b, 4c, 4d, 4e; Economic wellbeing and financial capability 4a

Aim: To understand what Youth Funds are and to draw up an application, including a budget.

Preparation

Make a copy of copymaster 21 (Youth funds application) for each group.

Starter

Explain that Youth Funds consist of money provided by the government to fund projects proposed by teenagers that will be of benefit to teenagers and the local community. Local councils have each been given a share of £173 million to spend.

Suggested activities

- Read 'Applying for youth funds to improve local facilities'. Ensure that the class understands what youth funds are for and that any application must explain how the proposed project relates to the five outcomes set out by the government. Then discuss the examples of youth funds in action and how each project meets the requirements of one or more of the five outcomes.

- Students, in groups, list their ideas for a project, then, as a class, vote to choose one of the ideas, because it would benefit the most people.

- Read 'Planning a budget for your project'. In groups, students list all the costs that the project will involve. Compare their lists in a class discussion and prompt them to agree on a list of all the costs to be included on a budget sheet to accompany an application.

- Give out a copy of copymaster 21 to each group and invite them to draft an application for funding for their project.

Plenary

Read 'Joining a youth panel' and discuss what the three teenagers say about being members of a youth panel. Make a list of the benefits of serving on a youth panel and, in pairs, invite them to say whether they would volunteer to be a member.

Extension activities

- Invite the local Youth Funds co-ordinator to give a talk explaining what funds are available and what projects have so far received grants. Ask for their advice on your project. After their visit, decide whether or not to go ahead with making an application to fund your project.

- Encourage students to write a letter to the local MP explaining their views on the Youth Funds scheme and saying whether they think it should be extended beyond 2011.

21 Youth funds application

❶ Title of project

_____

_____

❷ Description of project (Give details e.g. Who? What? When? Where?)

_____

_____

❸ How many young people will benefit from this project?

_____

_____

❹ How will the project benefit young people? (e.g. make them feel safer, healthier, more knowledgeable, more secure, more skilled)

_____

_____

❺ What is the timetable for the project? (When will any preliminary work commence? When will it be completed? When will the project start? When will it finish?)

_____

_____

❻ What is the total cost of the project?

_____

_____

❼ How much funding do you require from Youth Funds?

_____

_____

❽ How will you spend the grant? (Give full details of estimated costs)

_____

_____

Amount

Description of goods (e.g. materials)
and services (e.g. hire of premises)

Total

❾ How will you measure the success of the project?

_____

_____

UNIT 9 Developing your identity and image

Your Life 4/Year 10

Lesson 1 *Your Life 4*, pages 48–49
Personal wellbeing 1.1a, 1.1b, 1.2a, 1.2c, 2.1a

> **Aim:** To explore your sense of identity, and your feelings about image and becoming an adult.

Preparation

Make a copy of copymaster 22 (Enough to make a grown man weep) for each student.

Starter

Read the article 'What kind of adult?' and invite students to draw up a list of the qualities they want to have (and not have) as adults. Alternatively, introduce this topic orally without reference to the book, and model the start of a possible list on the board, before reading the article. Pairs then compare and discuss the questions under the article and feed back to the class. Students may also like to consider, in a whole class discussion or in groups, whether the lists made by young men differ significantly from those of young women, and if so, why.

Suggested activities

- Read the article 'Self image' and ask groups to discuss how important the way you look is to your self-image and self-esteem. Do they agree that the media create unrealistic expectations? Invite them to list what they can do to protect themselves from the negative influence of the media, then to feed back their suggestions to the class.

- Encourage the same groups to read the article 'Designer clothes' and discuss the questions given. Ask two or three groups to feed back their findings to the class.

Plenary

Ask students to consider whether or not their sense of identity has altered at all as a result of this lesson. Can they write down one aspect of their identity that has become clearer, and one that has become less clear? Invite two or three volunteers to share what they have written.

Extension activities

- Give each student a copy of copymaster 21 and read the article with the class. Groups discuss the questions and feed back.

- Individuals complete the personal statement in 'For your file'.

22 Enough to make a grown man weep

Enough to make a grown man weep

Should men dissolve into tears? An independent panel considers the psychology of misty-eyed males

'It's unattractive and undignified'
Terence Blacker, author

Frankly, I'm embarrassed by how damp-eyed and trembly-lipped men have recently become. It is an unattractive and undignified trend and it is time for us all to snap out of it. I should confess that I can well up at the slightest excuse – winning, losing, loving, the sound of children, virtually any film … but at least I have the decency to be ashamed of myself and try to do it alone or in the dark.

But if for a man to cry in private is embarrassing, doing it in public is far worse.

'Look how sensitive I am,' these public tears are saying. 'I'm a caring, vulnerable guy in touch with my feelings.' It's the worst kind of emotional flashing. Handkerchiefs away, chaps. It's time for manliness to make a comeback.

'The stiff upper lip is long gone'
Virginia Ironside, agony aunt

These days men cry just as much as women, if not more. The stiff-upper lip idea went out with my father's generation, when 'blubbing' was though to be so unspeakably wet that any man caught with red eyes was expected to go into a nearby wood and do the decent thing with a gun.

But that's all changed. For the past 30 years, men have been busy showing their humanity, and it's not difficult. Because underneath a thin veneer, most men are far, far more sentimental than us, the more realistic and more pragmatic sex.

'No tears is a lousy deal for men'
Susie Orbach, psychotherapist

Men have come to rely on macho behaviours to bolster a sense of maleness and adequacy. But appearing untouched, gritting one's teeth, managing difficulty by relying on an internal voice that cautions the individual man not to cry – this has not only hurt the individual man, it has often injured those around him. If you can't cry when you are hurt, you might hurt another instead. The ban on boys and men crying mean that aggression, relying on competition and denying one's need for another are the usual routes to masculinity. It's a lousy deal for men and it is a lousy deal for women.

Source: *The Independent*

In groups

1 Read the article 'Enough to make a grown man weep' and discuss the views on men and crying.

2 Do you agree with Terence Blacker that manliness should make comeback? What is manliness?

3 Do you agree with Virginia Ironside that men are more sentimental than women?

4 What does Susie Orbach mean when she says 'No tears is a lousy deal for men'? Why does she say it is a lousy deal for women as well?

UNIT 9 Developing your identity and image

Lesson 2 *Your Life 4*, pages 50–51
Personal wellbeing 1.1a, 1.1b, 1.2a, 1.2c, 2.1a

Aim: To explore the influences on your behaviour and self-image.

Preparation

Make a copy of copymaster 23 (Influences on your behaviour and your self-image) for each student.

Starter

Talk about role models and how they influence behaviour. Brainstorm the different role models that young people may have e.g. parents / grandparents, family friends, people who have particular skills that they want to develop, media personalities and celebrities, people with characteristics they admire, such as bravery or care and compassion. List the categories they suggest on the board.

Suggested activities

- Read the two newspaper articles about celebrities and young people. Ask: How much do celebrities influence young people? Invite groups to discuss who their role models are and what qualities they have which make them role models.

- Study 'The importance of parents'. Discuss with the class what Jessica Howie says about how parents' influence changes as they grow up and the importance of this change.

- Invite students individually to make a list of all the different influences on their behaviour in order of importance and to add an example of the kind of influence that each category has had. Ask volunteers to share their views with the rest of the class.

- Read the magazine article on labels to the class and encourage pairs to discuss the questions and feed back to the class.

Plenary

Ask students to write a paragraph on what makes a good role model. Prompt two or three students to read out their paragraphs and answer any questions from the rest of the class.

Extension activities

- Groups read the article 'Airbrushed models make women feel inadequate' (copymaster 23) and discuss the questions.

- Pairs read 'Celebrity role models' (copymaster 23), then carry out the ranking activity, before sharing their views in a class discussion.

23 Influences on your behaviour and your self-image

What influences your self-image?
Airbrushed models make women feel inadequate

Women are suffering from poor self-esteem because of advertising campaigns which feature airbrushed models to portray 'unattainable perfection', a survey has claimed.

More than 1,000 women were questioned by the beauty brand Dove. They said the advertising campaigns were having a negative impact on their lives.

A total of 96% of women questioned said they felt the models used in beauty advertising were not a realistic representation of women today.

Over 40% said the advertising made them feel self-conscious about their appearance, 28% said they were left feeling inadequate and 20% said they were less confident in their daily lives as a result of such images.

Katie Adams, Dove's senior brand manager, said: 'Our research shows that women want to see more realistic representations of beauty in the media and advertising campaigns.'

Source: *The Daily Telegraph*

In groups

Discuss the results of the survey. Do media images of beauty make women feel inadequate? What about media images of manliness? Do they have a similar effect on men?

Who influences your behaviour?
Celebrity role models

A study carried out by researchers from Leicester and Coventry Universities suggests that celebrities are becoming more influential to young people than their parents, teachers and even their friends. Young people today look up to the pop stars, actors and sporting heroes they see on TV and read about in magazines as role models, and are influenced by them accordingly. Previously, say the researchers, parents, teachers and friends have been the key influence on children.

In groups

1 Who has more influence on your behaviour – family and friends, school and teachers or celebrity role models?
2 Study the list (below) and rank each one on a scale of 1 (no influence at all) to 10 (extremely influential):

- TV celebrities
- Pop stars
- Sports personalities
- Fashion models
- Film stars
- Parents

- Relatives (grandparents etc.)
- Friends (of your own age)
- Family friends (of your parents)
- Teachers
- Community leaders
- Members of your religious community

UNIT 10 Managing your emotions and moods

Your Life 4/Year 10

Lesson 1 *Your Life 4*, pages 52–53
Personal wellbeing 1.4a, 1.4c, 2.1b, 2.1d, 2.1e, 2.3a

Aim: To explore how to manage difficult moods and emotions, focusing on anger and disappointment.

Preparation

Make a copy of copymaster 24 (Living with fear) for each student.

Starter

Write 'What makes you angry?' on the board and brainstorm ideas, writing them down. Then add 'How do you deal with your anger?' and brainstorm students' responses, returning to the specific reasons for anger brainstormed earlier. Do not comment too much at this stage, and certainly do not judge, as this is meant as a general introduction to the topic.

Suggested activities

- Read the article 'What is anger?' with the class and encourage groups to discuss the questions. In the feedback, ask if anyone has modified their thoughts on anger and how to deal with it since the start of the lesson, and remind them to give their reasons.

- Give a copy of copymaster 24 to each student. They read the article and complete the quiz on their own. Then in pairs or small groups (preferably friendship groups), students discuss their findings and the advice given in the article. Ask for volunteers to give any feedback to the class on points of interest.

- Pairs read the article 'How do you deal with disappointments?' and discuss the questions. Ask for feedback on what students think about the views and philosophy of the article. Ask volunteers to share any ways in which they could have done things differently when dealing with a failure or disappointment.

Plenary

Students write down the most important thought or feeling that they have taken from this lesson. Ask volunteers to read out what they have written.

Extension activities

Pairs role play a scene 'It's not the end of the world' in which a friend offers advice to someone who has suffered a disappointment or a failure on the best way to deal with it.

Further resources

- Mind has a useful booklet, entitled '*How to deal with anger*' available to download from their website www.mind.org.uk

- Young Minds also has a booklet '*Feeling angry*' available at their website www.youngminds.org

24 Living with fear

Living with fear

Fear is an extremely powerful emotion that can creep into all different aspects of our lives. It controls us and stops us from being free. Free in our self-expression, free in our self-acceptance of ourselves and free in being who we truly are. For example, you might be scared of talking to a new person you've been introduced to, so your fear stops you from meeting new people. Or you might be someone who's scared of singing in front of people, so you miss the chance to be a singer.

How much does fear control you?

Which areas of your life are controlled by fear? Give each issue below a number between 1 and 5 (1 means you're fearless and 5 means you're scared to death).

- speaking aloud in class or a group
- wearing what you want
- fitting in and being liked
- kissing/being physical
- discussing personal issues with family or friends
- being around boys/girls
- talking to new people
- new and unknown experiences
- speaking up when someone has upset you

Facing your fears

Try the following techniques the next time you're faced with fears that stop you from doing something you really want to do – or that you have to do.

1. Focus on your breathing. Take long deep breaths.
2. Remind yourself that you don't have to feel like this. Nothing bad is going to happen to you.
3. Fear is an illusion. When you're feeling fearful, say to your fear, 'You're not going to control me.'
4. Tell someone you're scared. Just by speaking about it you can let go of it.
5. Move around, if you can – shake all your body parts or go for a run.
6. Just do what you can for now. Don't push yourself too much.
7. Don't hide from the fear or you'll never be free.

Add up your total

A score of 0-20: You're fearless
Wow! Nothing gets in your way. You're probably admired by everyone for being so courageous and extrovert. You're not ashamed of who you are and in fact, you probably quite like being you. Beware of trying to prove yourself to be braver than you are.

A score of 21-30: You know what it's like to be scared
You know what it feels like to experience fear. There are quite a few things that scare you, but equally there are many things that don't. Fear doesn't completely rule your life and you've been known to have a go at things even when you've been really scared.

A score above 31: You know fear well
You know exactly what fear feels like and it limits you and the things that you do. It's not a pleasant thing to live with and you often feel really uncomfortable in your body. Don't worry. Just because you feel like this now doesn't mean you always have to. (Read on.)

Source: adapted from *Sisters Unlimited*, by J Howie

 **On your own** **In groups**

Read 'Living with fear' and answer the quiz to see how much room fear has in your life. Then in small groups, discuss your fears and different ways that your friends have of overcoming their fears. Can you add to the list in the article? Which are the best tips for overcoming fear?

UNIT 10 Managing your emotions and moods

Lesson 2 *Your Life 4*, pages 54–55
Personal wellbeing 1.4a, 1.4c, 2.1d, 2.1e, 2.2e, 2.3a, 2.3b

Aim: To explore what assertiveness is, and how to be assertive.

Preparation

Make a copy of copymaster 25 (Self-esteem) for each student.

Starter

Ask the class what 'assertive behaviour' means – ask pairs to come up with a) an example and b) a definition. Invite three or four pairs to share their responses, then read the first part of the article 'How to be assertive without being aggressive' to check the definition.

Suggested activities

- Read the rest of the article 'How to be assertive without being aggressive' with the class, then ask pairs to discuss the questions and perform the role-plays. After class feedback, you may like to expand the discussion by describing passive (or passive aggressive) behaviour as another unhelpful way of responding to a difficult situation. Choose some pairs to perform the role-plays in front of the class. The role-plays can be conducted in two ways; firstly, to show the result of unassertive behaviour, and secondly, to show how assertiveness works. High-ability groups may also be able to introduce passive aggressive responses.

- Read the article 'A quarrel a day…' with the class and encourage groups to discuss the questions. Ask one or two groups to do a presentation to the class on the factors that make an argument successful or unsuccessful.

- Ask students to write a piece for a teenage advice website on 'How to have a good argument' (see 'For your file', page 55). Invite some of the students to read their advice out and invite class comment.

Plenary

Give students a scenario, e.g. someone pushes in front of you in a bus queue, and ask them to write down what would be (a) assertive, (b) aggressive, and (c) passive responses.

Extension activities

Give a copy of copymaster 25 to each student. Groups read the articles on self-esteem and discuss the questions provided. Those who take Poynbee's line should ask themselves if the violent risk-takers in Professor Emler's study really have a high opinion of themselves. (Perhaps two different definitions of self-esteem are being used here?) The ideas and language in these articles is suitable only for higher ability groups.

25 Self-esteem

Self-esteem

Research shows that people who have high self-esteem are most likely to be successful in every aspect of their lives. Psychiatrists say that it is not possible to fully love other people unless we love ourselves.

Self-esteem has been shown to have a bigger effect on how well people do at school and university than the level of intelligence does. Does that surprise you? High self-esteem does not mean thinking that you are perfect and can do no wrong. It means valuing yourself and being kind to yourself, whatever situation you may find yourself in. It means forgiving yourself if you do or say things that you feel are wrong, and being able to forget your mistakes rather than dwelling on them.

People with high self-esteem spend more time thinking about their successes than their failures, and believe that they are basically worthwhile people. Unlike people with a low opinion of themselves, they do not have to put other people down, or bully them, or try to gain power over them, in order to feel better about themselves. Low self-esteem is sadly a very big problem amongst people of all ages. How many people do you know who really like themselves most of the time?

Source: K Dunbar, What's at Issue?' *in Relationships*

At last we can abandon that tosh about low self-esteem

Occasionally a new piece of research demolishes a myth with one fell blow. The accepted view has been that self-esteem – or the lack of it – lies at the root of almost every disorder from delinquency and drug abuse to violence and child abuse. One standard text after another takes this as a given fact without any scientific evidence, repeated as gospel from right to left. More than 2,000 books currently in print offer self-help prescriptions for raising self-esteem. A vast array of expensive social programmes in Europe and the US, designed to solve drug dependency or delinquency, are based on attempts to raise self-esteem. Some have tried to raise the self-esteem of whole schools or even an entire citizenry.

Low self-esteem is the social disease of today. It has many useful attributes: it elevates self-love and sanctifies self-satisfaction. It justifies the introspection of the therapy addict. It excuses bad behaviour, turning perpetrator into victim. For teachers, it makes dealing with bullying, arrogant and disruptive pupils almost impossible, if beneath the insufferable exterior there is supposed to be a whimpering, self-loathing child in need of affirmation and praise.

Professor Emler turns all this on its head in 'Self-Esteem – The Costs and Causes of Low Self-Worth'. Scrutinising all the available research on both sides of the Atlantic, he finds no evidence that low self-esteem causes anti-social behaviour. Quite the reverse. Those who think highly of themselves are the ones most prone to violence and most likely to take risks, believing themselves invulnerable. They are more likely to commit crimes, drive dangerously, risk their health with drugs and alcohol. Exceptionally low self-esteem is indeed damaging – but only to the victim, not to anyone else. Those with low self-esteem are more likely to commit suicide, to be depressed, to become victims of bullying, domestic violence, loneliness and social ostracism.

Source: The Guardian

In groups

Read these two articles on self-esteem and discuss what they say.

1 Do you agree with Katrina Dunbar that it is important to have high self-esteem? Or do you agree with Polly Toynbee that this is just an excuse for bad behaviour?

2 Is it easier to feel good about other people if you feel good about yourself?

3 Are you a confident person? What tips can you share with the group about improving your self-confidence?

UNIT 11 Changing relationships

Lesson 1 *Your Life 4*, pages 56–57
Personal wellbeing 1.1c, 1.4a, 1.4c, 2.1d, 2.1e, 2.3a, 2.3b, 3f, 3g

Aim: To explore your changing relationships with friends and family, and how to deal with these changes.

Preparation

Make a copy of copymaster 26 (Parents and teenagers think differently) for each student.

Starter

Brainstorm what the main difficulties are with (a) friends and (b) family, and write these on the board. Discuss why these difficulties arise and how they are resolved by the students. Do not comment too much at this stage, as this activity is meant to get the ideas flowing.

Suggested activities

- Read the article 'How to get a better deal' with the class and get pairs to discuss the questions. Ask three or four pairs to feed back the results of their discussion and get class to comment. Then invite pairs to perform the role play activity to show how to get what you want and how not to get what you want.

- Read the article 'The trouble with friends' with the class and get groups to discuss the questions provided and feed back.

- Ask pairs to discuss Samantha's letter, then ask individuals to write a reply.

Plenary

Ask two or three students to read out their letters, and invite class comment. How well do the replies show an understanding of the situation? Is Samantha given good advice on how to deal with her friend?

Extension activities

- Give a copy of copymaster 26 to each student and arrange class in groups of three. Groups read the article 'Parents and teenagers think differently', discuss it and do the role-plays. Invite groups to perform their role-plays to the class and to explain what they have learned.

- Groups discuss how recent technological developments, such as mobile phones and social networking sites on the Internet, affect their relationships.

Further resources

www.connexions-direct.com offers advice and information on relationships, including a section on home life.

Parents and teenagers think differently

Parents and teenagers think differently

What is an adult? For parents, it means being responsible and living up to certain standards. For teenagers, it means being independent, being allowed to run their lives the way they want to.

 *She should be more responsible.*

 *I want to be more independent.*

He should choose his friends a bit more carefully.

I'm old enough to choose my own friends.

 *She should spend more time working and less time fooling around.*

 *What I do in my own time is up to me.*

He should be responsible enough to get home at the time we arranged.

Why should I have to get home at the time they said?

 *She's old enough to help around the house a bit more.*

 *I'm tired of them always telling me what to do.*

He's old enough to keep his room tidy without me nagging him.

It's my room. Why can't I keep it the way I want?

 *She should realize that smoking is bad for her health.*

I know smoking is bad for me, but if I want to risk it that's my business.

Unless each understands how the other thinks, there is bound to be trouble. The challenge is to see where the other is coming from and adjust our expectations – and even our behaviour – accordingly.

Source: E Fenwick and T Smith, *Adolescence, the survival guide*

 **In groups**

Read the copymaster 'Parents and teenagers think differently' and discuss what you have learnt. In groups of 3, choose one of the parent/teenage issues presented and choose two members of your group to role-play a particular example of the clash in attitudes. The third member observes the discussion/argument and feeds back what they hear. Together, suggest how the discussion could be more productive, and role-play again.

UNIT 11 Changing relationships

Your Life 4/Year 10

Lesson 2 *Your Life 4*, pages 58–59
Personal wellbeing 1.1c, 1.4a, 1.4c, 2.1d, 2.1e, 2.3a, 2.3b, 3f, 3g

Aim: To explore what love is and how there are different kinds of love.

Preparation

Make a copy of copymaster 27 (Homosexual feelings) for each pair of students.

Starter

Put the question 'What is love?' on the board and brainstorm students' replies. List these on the board without judgment or comment. Then look at the students' definitions of true love on page and open up a discussion about which is the best. Is there a difference between love and true love? Why does 'true love' become an issue at this stage in teenagers' lives?

Suggested activities

- Read the article 'What love wasn't and what love is' with the class and ask groups to discuss the questions and feed back to the class.

- Read the article 'Do you really want a girlfriend?' with the class and invite groups to discuss the questions and feed back to the class.

- Give a copy of copymaster 27 to each pair and prompt them to read the article on same-sex relationships. They discuss the questions and compose an email in reply to someone who has worries about this issue. Ask for volunteers to read out their emails and encourage the class to comment. In this part of the lesson, make it very clear that any homophobic comments are entirely unacceptable.

Plenary

Ask students to write down the most important thing that makes a relationship work, in a single word. Classify the answers. Is there a difference between girls' answers and boys'? Discuss why this may be.

Extension activities

- In pairs or on their own, students design a cartoon strip or write a short play to illustrate the different types of love as shown in the article 'What love wasn't and what love is'.

- Invite groups to role play a TV discussion in which a chairperson asks a number of teenagers to discuss different types of love and to give their definitions of love.

- In same-sex groups, discuss what qualities they would like a boy/girlfriend to have, and write a list. Then they compile a list of what they think boy/girlfriends would look for in them. Students check their findings with groups of the other sex – do young men and women look for the same things? Are their expectations of what the other sex looks for justified?

Further resources

www.childrenfirst.nhs.uk has a section for teenagers on sexuality – 'My sexuality: Am I gay?'

Your Life 4/Year 10

27 Homosexual feelings

Same-sex relationships

The first sexual feelings you have in your teens can be very strong. But they won't necessarily be felt for anyone of the opposite sex. Almost everyone at some time or another in their teens finds themselves attracted to, or having a crush on, someone of their own sex. It's even more likely to happen if you go to a single-sex school and don't meet many people of the opposite sex, or are so shy and self-conscious with them that you try to avoid meeting them.

You can have quite passionate feelings for a friend, but this does not mean that you're gay. Nearly always this is just a 'practice' stage of sexual development, which you grow out of. However, quite a lot of people – it

may be as many as 1 in 10 (rather more men than women) – are gay. For them, homosexual feelings aren't just a stage they are going through. They go on feeling attracted to people of their own sex. People who are gay usually realise this sometime during adolescence. It may not be until you're 19 or 20, however, that you can say with real certainty that you're not going to change and that you're gay.

Don't feel that you have to decide right now whether you're one thing or another. In any case, it's not necessarily an 'either/or' choice. Some people remain attracted to both sexes all their adult lives.

Source: E Fenwick and T Smith, *Adolescence: the Survival Guide*

'I think I might be gay'

If you do realise that you're gay, it might make you feel very unhappy with yourself, especially if you've been brought up in a family where homosexuality is thought of as something dreadful, or you have come across people (and unfortunately there are many) who are prejudiced against gay people. You probably already know it isn't anything you have any choice about or any control over. Being straight or being gay is as much a part of who you are as your height or the colour of your hair.

However, you do have a choice about whether to hide it completely or to suppress your feelings (which can cause a lot of stress and unhappiness), or whether to accept yourself for what you are, and hope that others will too.

Although it may be very difficult telling your parents, it will be an important step in being honest and accepting yourself. If you do decide to tell them:
● Wait until you are sure of your own feelings.
● Show them that you're happy about being gay. If they're reassured about this, they will find your choice much easier to accept and be happy with.

If you're worried about your feelings and haven't got anyone to talk to, phone ChildLine on 0800 400 222 or the Lesbian and Gay Switchboard on 020 7837 7324.

Source: E Fenwick and T Smith, *Adolescence: the Survival Guide*

🔲 In groups

Read the articles 'Same-sex relationships' and 'I think I might be gay' and discuss what you learn about homosexual feelings.

1 How difficult is it for young gay people to 'come out'?

2 A friend has emailed you – they are really worried because they keep having crushes on people of the same sex. Discuss what advice you would give this person, then compose a reply to their email.

UNIT 12 Coping with crises

Lesson 1 *Your Life 4*, pages 60–61
Personal wellbeing 2.1d, 2.3e, 3i

Aim: To explore the effects of family breakdown on young people.

Preparation

Make a copy of copymaster 28 (Children and divorce) for each pair of students. Be sensitive to members of the class who are suffering from recent or ongoing family breakdown.

Starter

Ask the class to imagine that someone's parents are splitting up. How would that person feel? In pairs, students list the various emotions that a young person in that situation might have e.g. anger, shock, guilt, sadness, worry, relief, confusion. Invite students to share their lists in a class discussion.

Suggested activities

- Read the sections 'Dealing with family breakdown' and 'Deciding your future' and invite pairs to discuss the questions provided. Ask two or three pairs to feed back their ideas.

- Read the articles 'Degrees of separation' and 'Children: real victims of every divorce'(copymaster 28) and prompt groups to discuss the questions provided. You may need to explain the term 'adversarial system' with reference to the process of divorce. Ask two or three groups to feed back their ideas. Note that the Leeds University research focused on primary school-aged children (who notoriously suppress their feelings) and that Dr Kraemer's views relate specifically to the battles that children get caught up in, in the courts and elsewhere.

Plenary

Pairs discuss Amy's problem (see 'For your file', page 61), then each student writes their own advice. Ask some of the students to read out their advice and encourage the class to comment. Students should focus in their reply on the over-responsibility of Amy for her mother, and the suppression of her own feelings. She should go to India if she wants to, and tell her mother that she doesn't like her dad being spoken badly of.

Further resources

- www.childline.org.uk has a section dealing with children's worries about stepfamilies
- Advice for teenagers on dealing with divorce can be found at www.teenissues.co.uk

28 Children and divorce

Degrees of separation

Parental break-ups do not always traumatise children

Welfare professionals may over-estimate the significance of parental separation or divorce on many younger children, according to research published this week.

"For some children whose parents had never, or only briefly, lived together, or whose lives were full of violence entailing police and/or social services involvement, divorce could come fairly low down on their list of concerns," says the centre for research on family, kinship and childhood at Leeds University.

"Some were relieved when a violent father left home and their concern would focus more on the qualities of a new stepfather, or whether the mother would start to have more time for them."

Source: *The Guardian*

Children: Real victims of every divorce

Children can be deeply affected by their parents' divorce. Some will remain scarred for life, wary about forming relationships when they reach adulthood and insecure about their ability to make the right choices, according to Dr Sebastian Kraemer, one of Britain's leading child and adolescent psychiatrists.

Dr Kraemer, who practises at the Whittington Hospital in London, is in no doubt that our adversarial system of divorce fuels parental conflict and harms children. "Children become depressed, their school performance falls off, they may start acting up or misbehaving, such as shoplifting," Dr Kraemer says.

The solution, he believes, is to bring parents together early on, and to try to resolve the conflict away from the courts and, crucially, away from the children.

Source: *The Times*

In groups

Read the two newspaper articles about the effects of divorce on children, and discuss these questions:

1 Which report seems to you to be closer to the facts?

2 Do you think younger children are affected in a different way to older children?

3 Do you agree that conflict between parents should be resolved 'away from the children' and 'away from the courts'? Give your reasons.

UNIT 12 Coping with crises

Your Life 4/Year 10

Lesson 2 *Your Life 4*, pages 62–63
Personal wellbeing 2.1d, 2.3e, 3i

Aim: To explore the effects of bereavement and how to cope with them.

Preparation

Make a copy of copymaster 29 (Coping with grief and change) for each student. Awareness and sensitivity are needed in this lesson, as some students may be recently bereaved.

Starter

Write the terms 'bereavement', 'grief' and 'mourning' on the board and ask students, in pairs, to discuss what they mean. (Bereavement is the loss through death of someone close to you. Grief is the emotions you feel as a result of that loss. Mourning is the expression of grief, often in a social ritual such as a memorial service, after someone has died.)

Suggested activities

- Read 'The effects of bereavement' and discuss what the articles say about the emotions people experience and how to cope with grief. Ask students in pairs to discuss what they have learnt and draw up lists ('In Pairs', page 63). Ask for 2 or 3 pairs to present their lists and elicit class comment.

- Read the article 'It happens to us all' with the class and get groups to discuss why they think death is such a taboo subject, and what effect this has.

- Pairs study the reactions to loss and change on copymaster 29 and discuss the questions before writing their thoughts. Note that this copymaster is equally suitable for use in the previous unit on family breakdown.

Plenary

Ask several pairs to share what they have written and get class to comment. In the replies look for a sensitive understanding of why the young person is reacting in this way, as well as suggestions as to how to help.

Extension activities

- Individuals write a reply to Sara (see 'For your file', page 63). Ask several students to read out their replies to Sara, and elicit class comment.

- Students could research how different religions or cultures deal with death, and what their mourning rituals are.

Further resources

- www.childbereavement.org.uk and www.crusebereavementcare.org.uk are both useful websites.

- Winston's Wish has a section for young people who have been bereaved at www.winstonswish.org.uk

Your Life 4/Year 10

29 Coping with grief and change

These young people are all responding to the pain of death, loss or change. Discuss their feelings with a partner, then write a sentence in answer to each of the questions.

Salman has become very withdrawn. All he wants to do is be alone with his thoughts and feelings.

Why is Salman reacting like this? _____

Is it OK? Give your reasons _____

What could you do to help him? _____

_____

Chloe is pretending that nothing has happened. She won't answer any questions about her loss, and has a fixed smile on her face all the time.

Why is Chloe reacting like this? _____

Is it OK? Give your reasons _____

What could you do to help her? _____

_____

Craig has become very angry. He is picking on smaller boys at school, and damaging property.

Why is Craig reacting like this? _____

Is it OK? Give your reasons _____

What could you do to help him? _____

_____

Yasmin is spending all her time and energy helping her parents and her sister get over the loss. She says she is coping fine.

Why is Yasmin reacting like this? _____

Is it OK? Give your reasons _____

What could you do to help her? _____

_____

Ryan is blaming himself for what has happened. He isn't looking after himself, and has thoughts of hurting himself physically.

Why is Ryan reacting like this? _____

Is it OK? Give your reasons _____

What could you do to help him? _____

_____

UNIT 12 Coping with crises

Your Life 4/Year 10

Lesson 3 *Your Life 4*, pages 64–65
Personal wellbeing 1.2a, 1.3a, 2.2a

Aim: To explore the reasons why young people leave home, and what options are available to them.

Preparation

Make a copy of copymaster 30 (Is a roof over your head a home?) for each student.

Starter

Brainstorm the reasons that young people may have for leaving home, and write students' responses on the board. Make suggestions from the list in the 'Why go?' section of the spread if necessary. Then ask students to discuss which are good reasons and which are not, giving their reasons.

Suggested activities

- Read 'Lisa's story' and 'Running away' with the class and ask small groups to discuss what they feel about Lisa's situation. Invite two or three groups to feed back to the class.

- Read the article 'A place of your own' with the class and ask pairs to discuss the advantages and disadvantages of each type of accommodation.

- Students write a short article for a teenage magazine entitled 'Thinking of leaving home?' They can discuss this in pairs first, or even write the article in pairs.

Plenary

Prompt two or three students to read out or present their articles to the class, and invite class comment. What are the main messages that students are giving about leaving home?

Extension activities

- Students design an information leaflet aimed at young people looking for their first place away from home.

- Give copies of copymaster 30 to students, and ask them to consider what a home really means by answering the multiple choice questions. Ask for responses from the class, and discuss any major differences in opinion between students.

Further resources

- www.housemate.org.uk has teacher's resources on the issues of homelessness and leaving home.

- Information about homeless young people can be found at www.centrepoint.org.uk

- www.childline.org.uk has leaflets etc on homelessness and runaways.

Is a roof over your head a home?

Having a home means more than just being in a house or having a roof over your head. For most people, having a home means being able to live in a permanent place that is safe and secure.

Look at the different scenarios below. Decide in each case whether the person is homeless, has a home or you don't know.

❶ A person living in their own house.

Homeless   Has a home   Don't know

❷ A person living in student halls of residence.

Homeless   Has a home   Don't know

❸ A person who is living with a violent partner and wants to leave.

Homeless   Has a home   Don't know

❹ A person who is under 18, living with their granny.

Homeless   Has a home   Don't know

❺ A person living on the floor of a friend's house.

Homeless   Has a home   Don't know

❻ A person living in a bed and breakfast hotel.

Homeless   Has a home   Don't know

❼ A person living in a caravan.

Homeless   Has a home   Don't know

❽ A person living in a bedsit.

Homeless   Has a home   Don't know

❾ A person with their own baby, living at home with their parents.

Homeless   Has a home   Don't know

❿ A person living in accommodation provided as part of their work.

Homeless   Has a home   Don't know

⓫ A person under 18, living with their mum and dad.

Homeless   Has a home   Don't know

⓬ A person living in a council flat.

Homeless   Has a home   Don't know

⓭ A person sleeping rough.

Homeless   Has a home   Don't know

⓮ A person staying in an emergency night shelter.

Homeless   Has a home   Don't know

⓯ A person living in a hostel.

Homeless   Has a home   Don't know

⓰ A person living in a private rented flat.

Homeless   Has a home   Don't know

Source: www.housemate.org.uk

UNIT 13 Challenging offensive behaviour

Your Life 4/Year 10

Lesson 1 *Your Life 4*, pages 66–67
Citizenship 1.1c, 1.2a, 1.2b, 2.1a, 4a; Personal wellbeing 1.5a, 1.5b, 2.1a, 2.3d, 3a, 3j

Aim: To understand what prejudice is, to explore where prejudice comes from, and to discuss how prejudice can lead to discrimination.

Preparation

Make a copy of copymaster 31 (Cases of discrimination?) for each student, and find copies of suitable magazines and newspapers.

Starter

Write the terms 'prejudice' and 'discrimination' on the board, and explain what they mean. Clarify that prejudice is an opinion formed beforehand, especially an unfavourable one based on inadequate facts, and that discrimination is the unfair treatment of a person or group of people as a result of prejudice against them.

Suggested activities

- Read 'What is prejudice?' and look at the case study. Ask students in groups to discuss the questions on the case study.

- Ask students to imagine what prejudices the members of a family group might have that would annoy other members of the family, e.g. that the women should be expected to do all the housework, and men should bring in all the money.

- Ask students to list what groups they belong to and to compare their lists in a class discussion. Then read 'Part of a group or not?'and encourage them to look again at their lists of groups and individually to write down how they think people in each of the groups might generally behave. In pairs, students compare their views and discuss whether any of them are based on prejudice.

- Read 'Where does prejudice come from?' Students then decide in groups what the strongest factors causing prejudice are and share their views in a class discussion.

Plenary

Focus on the section 'Prejudice and discrimination'. Ask groups to discuss these questions: What different types of discrimination are there? Which do you think is the most common?

Extension activities

- Study copymaster 31 and ask pairs to decide which ones are cases of discrimination. The examples of discrimination are: 2, 4, 5, 8 and 9. Hold a class discussion and explain why the others are not examples of discrimination.

- Divide students into groups. Ask each group to look at several magazines or local newspapers. Each group should then look through, and see if they can find any examples of discrimination. Compare the results as a class.

- Students could also conduct an Internet research project on a particular area of discrimination, and find out what the government, the local council, and the local MP think ought to be done about it.

31 Cases of discrimination?

Study the following case studies. Which are examples of discrimination? Why? Give reasons for your views.

❶ A young black student wants to go on a school trip. When he asks, he and other students are all told that the trip is full.

❷ A 12-year-old boy asks if he can play hockey at school. The sports teachers says no, hockey is only a sport for girls.

❸ A 14-year-old girl walks into a shop to buy some cigarettes, but is told she is not old enough. An adult walks into the shop, and is allowed to buy the cigarettes.

❹ A pagan student asks to leave school early one day next month, because it is the Autumn Equinox, an important feast day in her religion. The teacher says 'No'.

❺ A man in a wheelchair isn't allowed into a shop, because he is told he will block other customers from their shopping.

❻ A group of men, stinking of alcohol and shouting and swearing, are not allowed into a pub because they are drunk. Another group, including men and women are allowed into the pub.

❼ An elderly couple are told that they cannot come to swimming classes on Wednesday, as these are for young students. They are told they can come to classes for older people on Thursdays.

❽ A Sikh student is told he is not allowed to wear his headgear at a local scouts meeting.

❾ A student is told they are not allowed to try out for the school football team, because they are partially sighted.

❿ An 18-year-old boy and his 16-year-old sister enter a pub. Both are asked for identification, and the 16-year-old is told that she will only be served with soft drinks.

UNIT 13 Challenging offensive behaviour

Your Life 4/Year 10

Lesson 2 *Your Life 4*, pages 68–69
Citizenship 1.1c, 1.2a, 1.2b, 4a; Personal wellbeing 1.5a, 1.5b, 2.1a, 2.3d,3a, 3j

Aim: To understand that there are laws and equal opportunities policies to combat discrimination and to explore what you can do about discrimination.

Preparation

Make a copy of copymaster 32 (Types of discrimination) for each student.

Starter

Summarise what discrimination is. Ask the students to think of any examples of discrimination that could occur locally.

Suggested activities

- Study 'Discrimination and the law.' Ask groups to look at the statements, and decide which ones they agree or disagree with, and why.

- Read 'Positive discrimination'. Ask students in groups to discuss whether they ever agree with positive discrimination and to compare their ideas in a class discussion.

- Look at 'Taking a stand'. Students share their views of what is the best way to fight discrimination in groups and then in a class discussion.

- Read 'Challenging the myths about asylum seekers'. Hold a class discussion. Ask students what they have learnt about asylum seekers from the report? What does this information tell students about prejudice?

Plenary

Summarise the different types of discrimination and go over how each form of discrimination can be fought.

Extension activities

- Students use copymaster 32 and complete the exercise.

- Ask students to find out if their school, local club, council, or a local employer has an equal opportunities policy. Compare this with other policies locally that other groups have found. Which do students think is the best? Why? Ask for reasons.

- In groups, students imagine they are asylum seekers in this country. How would they cope with the different language, the different people, and the different customs? Do they think these problems would create indirect discrimination? How do they think this discrimination can be fought?

Further resources

Information and guidance on discrimination can be found at the Equality and Human Rights Commission website www.equalityhumanrights.com

Your Life 4/Year 10

32 Types of discrimination

 **In pairs**

In pairs, look at the following lists, which have been mixed up. Correct the lists so that they make sense.

Different types of discrimination:

| Homophobia |
| Racism |
| Ageism |
| Islamaphobia |
| Sexism |

Who they affect:

| Muslims |
| Older people |
| Women |
| Homosexuals |
| Ethnic minorities |

What other forms of discrimination exist? Who do they affect?

Where you discovered the discriminatory behaviour:

| At school |
| At work |
| In a local leisure centre |
| On a TV or radio advertisement |
| In a newspaper |

Who you should report it to:

| The newspaper editor |
| The local council |
| To the Advertising Standards Authority |
| To your teacher or headmaster |
| To your boss, and then to your union |

Think of other places you may encounter discriminatory behaviour. Who do you think such behaviour should be reported to in each case?

UNIT 14 Healthy eating

Your Life 4/Year 10

Lesson 1 *Your Life 4*, pages 70–71
Personal wellbeing 1.2a, 1.2b, 2.2a, 3b, 3d

> **Aim:** To explore attitudes to body shape, eating and dieting and to explain what are healthy eating habits.

Preparation

Make a copy of copymaster 33 (Understanding healthy eating) and copymaster 34 (Good Foods and Bad Foods) for each student.

Starter

Introduce the topic by explaining that we live in a dieting culture. Explain what calories are and that there's more to healthy eating than counting calories. Talk about how bookshops are full of books on dieting, but most of the diets they describe have no scientific evidence to back them up. Explain that diets may be effective but only by cutting down the amount of calories eaten, and that reducing the number of calories you eat can be harmful for growing teenagers, especially if you're missing out on essential nutrients. So why are we so obsessed with dieting?

Suggested activities

- Read 'You and your body image – Be realistic'. Then invite groups to discuss what the article says and to share their views in a class discussion.

- Study 'Develop healthy eating habits' and ask pairs to plan a healthy diet of meals and snacks for a schoolday and a day at the weekend or in the holidays.

- Ask individuals to study the five statements on page 71, to decide whether they agree or disagree with them and to share their views in a group or class discussion. Then ask individuals or pairs to draft a reply to Marvina's letter.

- Read and discuss 'Eating disorders'. Emphasise that while they appear to be about food, what triggers them are a person's feelings about themselves and their situation.

Plenary

Ask some students to read out the letters replying to Marvina and discuss which of them offers the most sound advice and why.

Extension activities

- Use copymaster 33 to assess their knowledge and understanding of healthy eating. The answers are: 1, energy; 2, calories; 3, calcium; 4, vitamins; 5, eight; 6, carbohydrates; 7, exercise; 8, sugar; 9, protein; 10, obesity; 11, anorexia; 12, vegetables.

- Ask groups to read and discuss the article on copymaster 34, listing the key points it makes about healthy eating.

- Ask individuals to use the Internet to research eating disorders and to produce factsheets giving key information about different eating disorders, e.g.: ten things you should know about anorexia nervosa; ten things you should know about bulimia. Useful websites include www.b-eat.co.uk

33 Understanding healthy eating

```
                               H
                   (1) □ □ E □ □ □
                        (2) □ A □ □ □ □ □ □
                   (3) □ □ L □ □ □ □
                   (4) □ □ T □ □ □ □ □ □
               (5) □ □ H □ □
           (6) □ □ □ □ □ Y □ □ □ □ □
               (7) □ □ E □ □ □ □ □
               (8) □ □ A □ □
               (9) □ □ T □ □ □ □ □
           (10) □ □ I □ □ □ □
                   (11) □ □ N □ □ □ □ □ □
               (12) □ □ G □ □ □ □ □ □ □
```

Use the clues (below) to help you to complete the word puzzle.

1 People who do not eat enough food feel tired and weak because they are not getting enough _ _ _ _ _ _ (6)

2 Starving yourself of _ _ _ _ _ _ _ _ is not a smart way to lose weight (8)

3 Dairy products provide you with the _ _ _ _ _ _ _ you need to help build your bones as you grow (7)

4 Fruit and vegetables are packed with _ _ _ _ _ _ _ _, which keep you healthy (8)

5 Your body needs plenty of water, so you should drink at least _ _ _ _ _ glasses a day (5)

6 Cereals, rice and pasta contain _ _ _ _ _ _ _ _ _ _ _ _ _, which give you the energy your body needs (13)

7 Taking _ _ _ _ _ _ _ _ regularly is a better way of keeping your body in shape than dieting (8)

8 Drinking water is better for you than drinking soft or fizzy drinks because they contain _ _ _ _ _ (5)

9 You should eat two portions a day of foods such as meat, chicken, fish, eggs or beans because they contain _ _ _ _ _ _ _, which helps to build and repair cells (7)

10 More people are becoming overweight and suffering from _ _ _ _ _ _ _, because they eat too much and do not take enough exercise (7)

11 A person who avoids eating to keep their weight down below a healthy level has the illness called _ _ _ _ _ _ _ _ nervosa (8)

12 You should eat five portions of fruit and _ _ _ _ _ _ _ _ _ _ a day (10)

34 Good foods and bad foods

Anita Naik explains why labelling some foods as good and others as bad doesn't help you to develop a healthy attitude to eating

'Why are people always saying fat, sugar and salt are bad for you? How are you meant to cut them all out of your diet? I want to eat healthily but it's so confusing.' Tracey, 14

Contrary to popular belief, healthy eating doesn't mean cutting out all your favourite foods, buying more expensive foods, denying yourself what you like, and/or eating the same things over and over. It also doesn't mean feeling hard done by after a meal.

Healthy eating means having a healthy attitude to food, so that your feelings aren't affected by what you eat. If you are obsessed with the food you consume, picky to the point of annoyance, and strict about what you will and won't allow yourself to eat, you're not a healthy eater.

What healthy eating means

According to a Health Education Authority survey, 34% of young adults think that healthy foods are 'too boring'. But healthy eating doesn't mean just eating vegetables and fruit. Healthy eating means eating a balanced diet, including foods you like and not labelling some foods 'bad' and other foods 'good'.

Hundreds of articles are published in the papers every day about healthy eating and what to eat and what not to eat. 'Eat eggs', one paper says, 'No, don't' says another. 'Pasta makes you fat,' claims one, 'Pasta makes you thin,' responds another. Chocolate, junk food, and cheese have all got a bad press too. These reports make us divide foods up into good and bad. The problem with thinking about food like this is that you immediately place yourself in the following vicious circle.

You imagine food to be bad, so you deny yourself it. Then you crave it, so you give in and eat it. Then you imagine you've done something wrong, and so you end up feeling guilty and banning it again.

You also start to imagine a bad food has nothing to offer you. The fact is there are no good and bad foods. Burgers and chips aren't bad, chocolate isn't bad, ice cream isn't bad. It's really a question of how often you eat these things. If you realize that chocolate takes longer to work off than bread, it doesn't mean 'bread' is better and you should deny yourself chocolate. It does, however, mean you

should be aware of what you're eating and educate yourself about how often you should eat certain food.

Moderation is the key here. This means a balanced diet of a little bit of what you like, a little bit of what you should eat and a little bit of vegetables and fruit. By eating a variety of foods like this, you can eat whatever you want, when you want it, and not worry about weight gain. Of course, if you eat loads of junk food, plus all the things that are supposedly good for you, you will gain weight, simply because you have upped your food intake and not balanced out your diet. Below is a run down of some of the foods considered to be 'bad' and why they are not the real enemy.

Junk food

Like it or not, fast food is part of our culture and it isn't going away, so forcing yourself to avoid it is a waste of time. If you eat at fast food places, do so in moderation and it won't hurt your health. Surprisingly, these foods do provide nutrition, especially protein, iron, vitamins and fibre. For example, a burger contains iron, and vitamins essential for growth.

Pasta and bread

Pasta, bread, potatoes and other starches are not fattening and bad for you. If they were, the Health Education Authority wouldn't be recommending that you ate at least six to eight servings a day. Usually it's what you top it with that causes weight gain.

Red meat

The fat content of red meat isn't higher than that of chicken or turkey; it's also a better source of iron, making it a healthy food to eat.

Sugar

Sugar has a bad press but our bodies need a little for energy. Eating it is not only pleasurable but better for you than avoiding it altogether.

Fat

Sure, it's high in calories, but we still need to have fat in our diets. Fat is essential for a variety of functions, including digestion, immunity and hormone production. What's more, fat in food is actually concentrated energy. We need this energy for growth, to keep our bodies working properly and to enable us to do the things we want to do.

Source: *Wise Guides Eating* by Anita Naik

In groups

1 Discuss what Anita Naik says in this article about 'good foods' and 'bad foods'?
2 Explain what you have learnt from the article about healthy eating.

UNIT 14 Healthy eating

Your Life 4/Year 10

Lesson 2 *Your Life 4*, pages 72–73
Personal wellbeing 1.2a, 1.2b, 2.2a, 3b, 3d

Aim: To examine why many teenagers do not eat healthily and to discuss how far junk foods are responsible for making people overweight.

Starter

Read 'Teenagers are getting less fit'. Ask them what they think is the main cause: is it eating habits or a lack of physical exercise? Invite them to decide which they think is the more important by giving a show of hands.

Suggested activities

- Read and discuss the article 'Teenagers 'too idle' to bother with good food.' Do they think the article is fair to teenagers? Conclude the activity with a class discussion of their views.

- Read the news reports on page 73. Ask groups to discuss how far they think junk foods are to blame for increases in the number of overweight people and how effective they think the proposed measures would be. Then ask them to draft their own set of proposals – including any suggested in the reports that they think would be effective – and to present them in a class discussion.

Plenary

Ask students how serious they think the problem of junk foods is. Do they think too much fuss is being made about junk foods? Ask them individually to write 2 or 3 sentences stating their views, then prompt them to share their views in a class discussion.

Extension activities

- Students carry out their own survey of teenagers' eating habits. They report their results to the class and discuss how far they back up the findings of the survey reported on page 72.

- Students draft the letter they would write to Wayne (see 'For your file', page 73).

Further resources

Information and advice for teenagers on healthy eating can be found at www.childrenfirst.nhs.uk

UNIT 15 Safer sex and contraception

Your Life 4/Year 10

Lesson 1 *Your Life 4*, pages 74–75
Personal wellbeing 1.2a, 1.3a, 1.3b, 1.3c, 2.2a, 2.2b, 2.2c, 3d, 3e

> **Aim:** To discuss what you need to consider when deciding whether or not to have sex with someone; to explore attitudes towards sex and how to resist unwanted pressure.

Starter

- Set guidelines for talking about sex and make it quite clear that any personal comments about other people are quite out of order.
- Explain the law about sex – that the age of consent is 16 in the UK. It is illegal for anyone to have sex with a girl under 16 and anyone who does may be taken to court and could be sent to prison and put on the sex offenders register. Women who have sex with under-age boys can be charged with indecent assault.

Suggested activities

- Read 'Sex and you – waiting until the time is right'. Ask the class to study the list of reasons for having sex and hold a class discussion in which they talk about each reason in turn.
- Focus on the first two paragraphs of 'Sex = love?' Discuss what they say with the class, then read and explain the paragraph on 'Protection'. Invite questions and explain that the focus of the next lesson will be on safer sex and contraception.
- Read the section on 'Resisting pressure', then encourage groups to discuss ways of saying 'no' and dealing with pressure.

Plenary

Summarise the main message of the lesson: Don't be pressurised into having sex when you don't want to. Ask groups to report their ideas on how to say 'no' to sex. Conclude by emphasising the importance of weighing up the pros and cons of having sex by discussing them together first and not rushing into doing something that they'll later regret.

Further resources

Advice on teenage relationships can be found at http://www.avert.org/teens-relationships.htm

Articles on all aspects of sex and young people e.g. 'Ready to go all the way?' and 'It's OK to say NO' can be found on the NHS Choices website at www.nhs.uk/Livewell/sexandyoungpeople

UNIT 15 Safer sex and contraception

Your Life 4/Year 10

Lesson 2 *Your Life 4*, pages 76–77
Personal wellbeing 1.2a, 1.3a, 1.3b, 2.2a, 2.2b, 2.2c, 3d, 3e

Aim: To understand methods of contraception and how to practise safer sex, and to discuss unplanned pregnancies.

Preparation

Make a copy of copymaster 35 (Understanding contraception and safer sex) and copymaster 36 (Abortion – facts and opinions) for each student.

Starter

Explain that all sex involves some risk. Introduce the term safer sex, explain why people refer to safer sex rather than safe sex and read the paragraph 'What is safer sex?'

Suggested activities

- Read 'The Lowdown on … Contraception'. Invite questions on the information it contains and discuss it with the class. Then prompt students to discuss who should take responsibility for contraception – the boy or the girl.

- Ask students, in groups, to discuss the statement 'The morning after pill should be available in all schools confidentially to anyone who asks for it, whatever their age.' Students then share their replies in a class discussion.

- Study 'The Lowdown on … Pregnancy'. Students, in groups, discuss their views on the options open to a teenager who gets pregnant, before sharing them in a class discussion. Encourage individuals to write an article for a teenage magazine explaining what the options are for a pregnant teenager.

Plenary

Remind students of the five key pieces of information contained in the lesson:

1 The contraceptive pill protects against unplanned pregnancy but not against STIs.

2 Condoms provide protection against pregnancy and STIs.

3 The Pill only works if taken properly.

4 The emergency contraceptive pill must be taken within 72 hours of having sex.

5 If a girl misses a period and thinks she may be pregnant, she should have a pregnancy test as soon as possible.

Extension activities

- Study copies of copymaster 36. Ask students to share their views on abortion in a group discussion, followed by a class discussion.

- Use copymaster 35 to assess their knowledge and understanding of contraceptive methods and how to practise safer sex. The correct answers are: 1 false; 2 false; 3 true; 4 true; 5 false; 6 false; 7 false; 8 true; 9 true; 10 false.

- Ask students to draft a reply to K's letter (see 'For your file', page 76).

- As individuals or in pairs, encourage students to use the Internet to obtain further information and advice on sex, contraception and abortion. Useful sites to visit include: www.likeitis.org.uk; www.fpa.org.uk; www.mindbodysoul.gov.uk

35 Understanding contraception and safer sex

○ **On your own**

Study these statements about contraception and safer sex. Decide whether you think they are true or false, compare your answers with a partner. Then check them by looking at pages 68–71 of *Your Life 4*.

TRUE FALSE

1 Condoms provide 100% protection against an unwanted pregnancy and catching a sexually transmitted infection.

2 A condom does not have an expiry date.

3 Even high-quality condoms should be used only once.

4 Oil-based products such as Vaseline can damage condoms.

5 Emergency contraception only works if the pill is taken within 18 hours of having sex.

6 Emergency contraceptive pills can only be obtained from a doctor.

7 The Pill protects you against STIs as well as against an unwanted pregnancy.

8 If you have a stomach upset, it may stop the Pill from working.

9 The Pill can ease period pains and stop you from having bad PMS moods.

10 There is no risk of pregnancy if a girl has sex during her period.

36 Abortion – facts and opinions

What is an abortion?

An abortion is when a pregnancy is ended, or terminated. Sometimes a fertilised egg or embryo is lost naturally. This is known as a spontaneous abortion or miscarriage. It happens in about one in five known pregnancies.

An induced abortion (usually just called abortion or termination) happens when a fertilised egg or embryo is removed from the womb, either by taking pills to expel the pregnancy, or by surgery.

Abortion and the law

Abortion is legal in England, Scotland and Wales. A woman who wants an abortion up to the 24th week of her pregnancy will be able to have a safe legal abortion, with the agreement of two doctors. They will need to agree that it is necessary for her mental or physical health.

About 90% of abortions take place very early in pregnancy – in the first 12 weeks (ie: within eight weeks of missing a period).

In Britain, one in five of all known pregnancies are terminated – about 180 000 a year. Women in their 20s account for more than half, teenagers for about a fifth.

Over half of all pregnancies in under 16s end in abortion.

Why women consider having an abortion

Many pregnancies happen without planning. When a woman finds out she is pregnant and it is unplanned, she may decide to keep the baby, have it adopted (though this is not common today), or have an abortion.

Some women know immediately what they want to do. For others it can be a difficult decision.

Here are some of the reasons why a young woman may decide to have an abortion:

- 'I don't want a child until I've finished my education.'
- 'Becoming a parent will change my life. I'm not ready for it.'
- 'I think I am too young to have a baby.'
- 'My boyfriend has left me and I don't think I can cope on my own.'
- 'I'm not in a relationship.'
- 'I don't want anyone to know that I've had sex or that I'm pregnant.'

What about the man?

This may be a difficult time for men, too. Some will want to share in the decisions, others won't want to be involved at all. Many will support their girlfriend's or wife's decision, even if it conflicts with their own feelings. Even where there is no relationship, a man may feel he has a right to be informed.

However, it is up to the woman to decide whether or not to involve the man in her choice. He has no legal right to be informed or involved in her decision.

Abortion – Right or Wrong?

Many people have strong views about unwanted pregnancy. Some say it is the woman's right to choose what to do. Not everyone agrees…

'It's a woman's right to choose.'

'A planned child is a wanted child.'

'The father has a right to decide too!'

'The unborn child has a right to be born.'

'Legal abortion saves lives.'

'Abortion is against my religion.'

'Life begins when a sperm fertilises an egg!'

'Life begins when a baby can survive on its own outside the mother's womb!'

'The fertilised egg possesses a soul that has a right to life!'

'The safety and life of the woman is most important until the foetus can live independently.'

'A pregnant woman is responsible for the life she is carrying.'

'Even when she's been raped?!'

 **In groups**

Discuss your views on abortion. Work together to try to produce a statement that summarizes the different opinions of members of your group. Then choose a spokesperson to present your statement to the rest of the class in a class discussion.

UNIT 16 Drinking and smoking

Your Life 4/Year 10

Lesson 1 *Your Life 4*, pages 78–79
Personal wellbeing 1.2a, 1.3a, 1.3b, 2.2a, 2.2b, 2.2c, 3d, 3e

> **Aim:** To discuss why people drink, to understand the risks of binge-drinking and to explore ways of drinking sensibly.

Preparation

Make a copy of copymaster 37 (Understanding alcohol) for each student.

Starter

Introduce the topic by defining what is meant by 'binge-drinking'. The term 'binge' means a bout of excessive drinking and people who go out binge-drinking do so with the specific aim of drinking enough to get drunk. Explain that the aim of the lesson is to explore the risks of drinking too much and ways of drinking sensibly.

Suggested activities

- Read 'Alcohol – What's the attraction?' and discuss as a class what it says about 'the buzz' and 'the image'.

- Study 'Getting Trashed – the risks'. Then, in groups, students draw up their plans for a video warning of the dangers of binge-drinking and share their ideas in a class discussion.

- Ask groups to discuss the four statements (see 'In groups', page 79) and to share their views with the rest of the class. Then ask them to read Taz's letter (see 'For your file', page 78) and to write a reply to it.

- Read the two newspaper articles on page 79, then get groups to discuss what measures they think would be most effective in cutting down binge-drinking.

- Invite pairs to study the section 'Ways to drink sensibly' and to write down the reasons for each piece of advice.

Plenary

Ask students to report their views on the measures that they think would be most effective in cutting down binge-drinking and then go over the advice given on what to do in order to drink sensibly.

Extension activities

- Use copymaster 37 to assess what students have learned about alcohol from this unit by drafting replies to the six letters.

- Ask students to use the Internet to find out more about alcohol and the problems associated with drinking alcohol and to report three important things they have found out in a class discussion.

37 Understanding alcohol

Here are some letters to an agony aunt asking for information about alcohol. In pairs, discuss each one in turn and draft a reply to it.

Dear Erica

My friend drinks an awful lot. I think she's got a real problem and may be on the verge of becoming an alcoholic. How can I tell if she's in danger? What should I do to try to get her to stop drinking so much?

Cyd

Dear Erica

I'm confused about the laws on alcohol. At what age can you drink it legally? At what age can you go into a pub or a licensed restaurant? At what age can you buy alcohol?

Abi

Dear Erica

I'm worried about damaging my body if I start to drink. What happens when you drink alcohol? What effect does it have on your body? If you drink too much are there quick ways of sobering up – like drinking coffee or splashing your face with cold water? Is it true you can get alcohol poisoning and kill yourself?

Toni

Dear Erica

I've heard it said that women are more vulnerable to the effects of alcohol than men. Is it true that the same amount of alcohol will affect a woman more than a man? Are women more likely to develop liver damage from long-term drinking? If you're on the Pill does it take longer for alcohol to leave your body? And am I right in thinking that you shouldn't drink if you get pregnant?

Shania

Dear Erica

How much alcohol is it safe to drink? Do some people get drunk more easily than others? Does how quickly you get drunk depend on how much you've had to eat and what mood you are in?

Maj

Dear Erica

I'm into sports and I want to keep myself as fit as possible. How much can I drink without it affecting my performance? Should I avoid certain drinks? Should I avoid alcohol altogether?

Jez

UNIT 16 Drinking and smoking

Your Life 4/Year 10

Lesson 2 *Your Life 4*, pages 80–81
Personal wellbeing 1.2a, 1.3a, 1.3b, 2.2a, 2.2b, 2.2c, 2.2d, 3d, 3e

Aim: To understand how smoking and passive smoking can damage your health and to discuss techniques that can be used to resist unhelpful pressure to smoke or drink.

Preparation

Make a copy of copymaster 38 (Smoking fact-check) for each student.

Starter

Ask students why people smoke. Read 'Smoking – What's the attraction?' Discuss with the class the reasons given in the article and ask them to suggest other reasons that people might give.

Suggested activities

- Read the section 'The risks'. Students, in groups, discuss the risks to smokers themselves and to non-smokers from passive smoking.

- Read Erica Stewart's article 'Resisting the pressure to smoke'. In groups, students discuss the advice she gives and share their views on how to say 'No'.

- Students discuss their views of the three statements (see 'In groups' on page 81), then consider the arguments for and against a total ban on the sale of tobacco..

- Groups imagine they are a team of government advisers with the task of drawing up plans for an anti-smoking campaign aimed at teenagers. They take it in turns to present their ideas in a class discussion.

- Ask students in pairs to read Gaby's letter and to draft a reply to it.

Plenary

Recap the facts about passive smoking and hold a vote to determine whether or not they think it is a serious issue. Then summarise ways of saying 'No'. Which do they think is the most effective way?

Extension activities

- Use copymaster 38 to assess what they have learned from this unit about the risks of smoking. The correct answers are: 1d, 2d, 3c, 4d, 5b, 6c, 7d, 8b, 9b, 10c.

- Ask students to find out more information from the Internet on tobacco and its effects by visiting the website of Action on Smoking and Health (ASH) www.ash.org.uk

38 Smoking fact-check

Check your knowledge and understanding of the risks of smoking by doing this fact-check quiz.
Put a circle round what you think is the correct answer.

1 How many adults in the UK smoke?

   a) 4 million   **b)** 8 million   **c)** 12 million   **d)** 16 million

2 How many smokers die each year from illnesses caused by smoking?

   a) 74 000   **b)** 94 000   **c)** 114 000   **d)** 134 000

3 What percentage of deaths from lung cancer are due to smoking?

   a) 10%   **b)** 20%   **c)** 50%   **d)** 90%

4 What percentage of deaths from the lung diseases bronchitis and emphysema are caused by smoking?

   a) 20%   **b)** 40%   **c)** 60%   **d)** 80%

5 How many years earlier than a non-smoker is a smoker likely to die?

   a) 1–3 years   **b)** 3–5 years   **c)** 6–9 years   **d)** 9–10 years

6 How many men under 50 does research suggest are sexually impotent because they smoke?

   a) 20 000   **b)** 40 000   **c)** 80 000   **d)** 120 000

7 How many people are estimated to die each year as a result of diseases caused by passive smoking?

   a) 500   **b)** 1000   **c)** 1500   **d)** 2000

8 How much does the NHS spend annually on treating smoking-related illnesses?

   a) £1 billion   **b)** £1.5 billion   **c)** £2 billion   **d)** £2.5 billion

9 How much does the government earn annually from tobacco duty?

   a) £2 billion   **b)** £4 billion   **c)** £6 billion   **d)** £8 billion

10 What percentage of smokers say they would like to quit?

   a) 20%   **b)** 40%   **c)** 60%   **d)** 80%

UNIT 17 Health matters

Your Life 4/Year 10

Lesson 1 *Your Life 4*, pages 82–83
Personal wellbeing 1.2a, 1.2b, 1.3a, 2.2a, 2.2b, 2.2c, 3e, 4h

Aim: To understand how to take responsibility for your own health.

Preparation

Make a copy of copymaster 39 (Allergies – your questions answered) for each student.

Starter

Talk about how, as young adults, students should be taking more responsibility for their own health – making their own doctor's and dentist's appointments, knowing their own and their family's medical histories and taking responsibility for managing any medical treatments they receive.

Suggested activities

- Read 'Looking after your own health' and 'Immunisations'. Ask students individually to draw two columns on a piece of paper and to label them 'Things I already know about my own health' and 'Things I need to know about my own health'. Ask them to go through the checklist and list the facts they already know and things they need to find out.

- Discuss how important it is to keep yourself fit. In pairs, ask students to design a website page explaining fun ways of taking exercise and keeping fit.

- Read 'NHS Direct' and invite students to use the NHS website to find out about an allergy (see 'For your file', page 83).

- Study 'Dealing with minor ailments', then ask them, in pairs, to discuss how a pharmacy can help them to deal with minor ailments.

Plenary

Go over the things students need to know in order to take responsibility for their own health and talk about other things that it is important to care for, such as eyesight. Recap on how they can obtain advice on health matters from NHS Direct or a pharmacy.

Extension activity

In pairs, ask students to study the information on allergies on copymaster 39. Students then draw up a True or False quiz consisting of ten statements about allergies and give it to another pair to do. Then, get individuals to draft a reply to Hari's letter asking for advice about allergies.

Further resources

The Consumer Health Information Centre website www.chic.org.uk has information and advice on dealing with minor illnesses.

39 Allergies – your questions answered

What is an allergy?

An allergy is an over-reaction of the body's immune system to something that is inhaled, swallowed or comes into contact with the skin or eyes. Any substance that produces an allergic reaction is called an allergen.

How common are allergies?

Eighteen million people in Britain suffer from some kind of allergy. A report in 2003 found that 32% of children aged between 13 and 14 had asthma, 9% had eczema and 40% had allergic rhinitis – a runny nose and eyes – caused by hay fever or another allergic reaction.

What are the symptoms?

Symptoms vary from mild irritation to acute physical discomfort, depending on the allergy and its severity. They can include an itchy, blocked or runny nose, red, itching, watery eyes, skin rashes, nausea or diarrhoea. Some cause difficulty with breathing and can be life-threatening.

Are allergies hereditary?

Allergies tend to run in families. 70% of people with allergic eczema have a close relative with an allergy. If one of your parents has an allergy, you have a 50% chance of having one too. If both parents have allergies, there's an 80% chance.

What causes allergies?

There are many kinds of allergy:

- Airborne allergies: Some people react to airborne allergens, such as pollen, dust, tobacco smoke or traffic fumes.
- Food allergies: All kinds of foods can cause an allergy, ranging from chocolate, eggs, strawberries and mushrooms to shellfish and peanuts.
- Drug allergies: You may get an allergic reaction to a drug prescribed by your doctor e.g. penicillin.
- Stings and bites: About one in ten people suffer an allergic reaction to the sting of a wasp or bee.

- Contact allergies: Your skin may react to certain materials, such as the metal in a bracelet or necklace or the material in the clothes you wear. You may get an allergic reaction to the oils in a particular type of make-up or shampoo.
- Animal allergies: Some people are very sensitive to the skin and hair of certain animals, such as dogs, cats or horses.

How are allergies treated?

Treatment varies according to the allergy.

- Eczema can be treated with creams to get rid of the rash.
- Hay fever can be treated by taking anti-histamine drugs, available over the counter from a pharmacist or on prescription from your doctor.
- Asthma can often be controlled by taking drugs through an inhaler.

If the allergic reaction is severe, producing anaphylactic shock, in which the blood pressure drops suddenly and breathing becomes difficult, a person may require oxygen and a life-saving injection of adrenaline. Someone who knows they are likely to suffer from anaphylactic shock, as a reaction to eating nuts or been stung by a bee, can be given an epi-pen containing adrenaline to carry, so that in an emergency they can inject themselves.

Can I do anything to control the allergy?

The first thing to do is to identify what exactly is causing the allergy. Once you've done that, you can take steps to ensure that you avoid the allergen as much as possible. Then, consult you pharmacist or doctor to find out what treatment is available to relieve the symptoms.

In groups

Draw up a True or False quiz consisting of ten statements about allergies, some of which are true and some of which are false. Then join up with another pair and do each other's quizzes.

On your own

Use the Internet to find out more about allergies, using information from sites such as www.allergyfoundation.com. Then draft a reply to Hari's letter:

> Dear Erica
> My eyes are often itchy and my nose is runny. I think I may have an allergy. How can I tell? What should I do about it?
>
> Hari

UNIT 17 Health matters

Your Life 4/Year 10

Lesson 2 *Your Life 4*, pages 84–85
Personal wellbeing 1.2a, 1.3a, 2.2a, 2.2b, 2.2c, 3d, 4h

Aim: To examine the health risks of sunbathing, tattooing and body piercing.

Preparation

Make a copy of copymaster 40 (How much do you know about skin cancer?) for each student.

Starter

Brainstorm the reasons why some people spend hours lying in the sun in order to get a suntan. List students' suggestions on the board and get them to rank the reasons on a scale of 1–10 (1= very good reason 10 = very poor reason). Then ask for a show of hands on how dangerous they think sunbathing is: very dangerous/quite dangerous/not very dangerous.

Suggested activities

- Read 'Sunbathing – is it worth the risk?'. Ask the students to discuss what they learn from it about the dangers of sunbathing, then individually to design a poster warning of the risks and offering advice on how to sunbathe sensibly. Encourage them to use the Internet to find out more about melanoma at www.melanoma.com

- Study 'Tattoos', then ask pairs to discuss why tattoos are so popular and the health risks from having a permanent tattoo or a temporary tattoo. Why do they think so many people regret having a tattoo? Ask students to share their views about tattooing in a class discussion.

- Ask students to write an article for a teenage magazine 'Think twice before you get a tattoo'.

- Read 'Body piercing'. Then ask students to discuss their views on body piercing in groups and to share their opinions in a class discussion.

Plenary

Summarise the main points made in the lesson by asking students what things they need to take into consideration before a) spending a day lying in the sun b) having a tattoo done c) getting part of their body pierced. List the points they make on the board.

Extension activity

Assess students' knowledge of skin cancer by getting them to complete the true or false quiz on copymaster 40. The answers are: 1, True; 2, True; 3, True; 4, False; 5, True; 6, True; 7, True; 8, True; 9, False; 10, False.

Further resources

The website www.connexions-direct.com has information and advice on a wide range of health issues including safety in the sun and tattoos and piercings.

40 How much do you know about skin cancer?

Study these statements about skin cancer and say whether they are true or false.

	TRUE	FALSE

1 Getting a tan from using a sunbed is less dangerous than getting a tan from lying in the sun.

2 The most dangerous time to sunbathe is between 11am and 3 pm.

3 There are fewer skin cancer deaths in Australia each year than there are in Britain.

4 Melanomas can be surgically removed, but you may be left with a disfiguring scar.

5 People with fair skin are more at risk of developing melanomas than people with dark skin.

6 Getting badly sunburned as a teenager increases the chances of your developing melanomas in middle age.

7 Melanomas are commonest among people who spend most of the year indoors, then take a fortnight's holiday in the sun.

8 To protect yourself from skin damage when sunbathing, you need to use a sunscreen that is factor 15 or over.

9 Younger people have skin that is more at risk to damage from UV radiation than older people.

10 Skin cancer is decreasing because younger people's attitudes towards getting a tan have changed in recent years.

UNIT 18 Thinking ahead: planning your future

Lesson 1 *Your Life 4*, pages 86–87
Economic wellbeing and financial capability 1.1a, 1.1b, 1.1c, 1.2c, 2.1a, 2.1b, 2.1c, 2.1d, 2.2a, 2.3a, 2.3c, 3e, 3f, 4f, 4h

Aim: To begin thinking about careers, based on an assessment of your personal skills.

Preparation

Make a copy of copymaster 41 (Transferable skills) for each student. Collect a selection of job adverts from newspapers.

Starter

Write these statements on the board:

- I'd rather have an interesting job that's badly paid than a boring job that's well paid.
- I don't want to think about my career until I've had the chance to travel and see the world.
- Job security is more important to me than a high level of pay.
- My career comes first, my relationship second.
- I want to get out and start earning money as soon as possible.
- I need to spend more time thinking and studying before committing myself to a career.

Then read 'Which career?' to the class. Prompt students to write down 'Agree', 'Disagree' or 'Don't know' in answer to each statement, then discuss with a partner. What do their answers tell students about their priorities?

Suggested activities

- Students assess their personal qualities, as explained in the article 'Start with yourself'.
- In pairs, students discuss what skills they have that relate to jobs (see 'Skills 4 jobs' and 'Job families'). Ask four or five pairs to feed back what they have discovered.
- Give students a copy of copymaster 41. Emphasise that employers look for evidence of these transferable skills. When students have completed the questionnaire, ask them to share their responses in pairs. Partners can either challenge them to prove their statements or encourage them to find skills which they think are absent. Finally ask students to write some statements for their CV or personal file that show evidence of their skills.

Plenary

Ask students to write down one or two important things that they have discovered about themselves during the lesson. Invite volunteers to share what they have written and how it relates to their future.

Extension activities

- Students look at job adverts and discuss which they would be interested in.
- Students research a particular career that interests them, using the Internet, looking at information in the careers library or talking to people.

Further resources

- www.ideasfactory.com links to a website devoted to careers ideas in the creative industries.

Transferable skills

Schools call them 'key skills', employers call them 'transferable skills' and elsewhere you may hear them described as 'employability skills'. Whatever you call them, there are certain things you can learn that will help you to perform well in school, develop good relationships with people around you, and impress employers.

Identify your transferable skills by ticking the box next to any statement that applies to you.

Communication

I am confident that I can get other people to understand me when I speak to them. ☐

I listen to what other people have to say. ☐

I am happy with my level of written communication. ☐

Application of number

I am confident that I can work out sums in my head. ☐

I can use a calculator to work out percentages and fractions. ☐

I understand that maths is important in everyday life. ☐

Information technology (IT)

I am happy to use a computer to work with documents, spreadsheets and databases. ☐

I have a basic understanding of how the internet works and can use it to research a subject. ☐

I can use email and know how to send attachments. ☐

Working with others

I have worked successfully as part of a team. ☐

I am comfortable taking charge of situations. ☐

I enjoy trying to help other people. ☐

Improving own learning and performance

I understand that you can learn something from every situation. ☐

I know that you can learn a lot from other people. ☐

I am prepared to try new things and have an open mind. ☐

Problem-solving

I can step back from a problem to get a new perspective. ☐

I can think about how a problem can be solved in different ways. ☐

I don't let problems put me off trying something out. ☐

If you have ticked any boxes, well done! You have identified something about yourself that employers will like. Make sure that you show evidence of it on your CV or in your progress file.

UNIT 18 Thinking ahead: planning your future

Your Life 4/Year 10

Lesson 2 *Your Life 4*, pages 88–89
Economic wellbeing and financial capability 1.1a, 1.1b, 1.1c, 2.1c, 2.1d, 2.3a, 2.3c, 3c, 3f, 4a, 4b, 4c, 4d

Aim: To begin thinking about your work placement, and to consider the importance of health and safety at work.

Preparation

Make a copy of copymaster 42 (True Tales of Horrible Happenings) for each pair of students.

Starter

Brainstorm reasons for doing work experience and put suggestions on the board. Then read 'Why bother with work experience?' and see if this can supply any further reasons.

Suggested activities

- Pairs or small groups read the two case studies on page 88 and discuss what Jas and Mark learned from their work experience. Ask several pairs to feed back their responses to the whole class.

- Students on their own write a paragraph on the importance of work experience, to go in their file. This can be incorporated in their letter of application.

- Read the 'Health and safety' section (page 89) to the class. Pairs or groups then discuss the questions, then share their findings in a class discussion.

Plenary

Ask students to list some health and safety issues relating to the four occupations given. Encourage four or five students to share what they have written and ask for class comment.

Extension activities

- Give pairs a copy of copymaster 42 to discuss and complete.

- Students write a paragraph about possible health and safety issues in their own work experience placement.

Further resources

- Details of employers' and employees' responsibilities regarding health and safety at work can be found at http://www.young-worker.co.uk/young/responsibilities.html

- Copies of a booklet on health and safety at work, '*Be Safe*', can be downloaded from the Learning Skills Council's website www.lsc.gov.uk

- Information and advice on health and safety for students on work experience can be found on the Health and Safety Executive website www.hse.gov.uk

42 True Tales of Horrible Happenings

Unfortunately, the stories below really happened. Read each one and answer the questions that follow.

A 16-year-old was employed in the butchery department of a large foodstore. One of his responsibilities was to clean the machines at the end of each day. One Saturday, he was keen to finish work as early as possible. He did not remove the plug of the mincing machine from the wall socket, as he was supposed to do. He did check that the switch on the machine was in the 'off' position, but as he removed the guard and put his hand in the machine to clean it he leant against the 'on/off' switch and his hand was … minced.

Who was to blame for the boy losing his hand?

Is your answer any different if you learn that his employer never taught him how to use the equipment properly?

Helen lived and breathed cars. Her placement was at a small local garage. She turned up on the first day with all the appropriate gear – overalls etc – except for her footwear. Instead of the protective boots that the garage owner had insisted upon, Helen was wearing black trainers which looked like boots. No one noticed the difference. On the first day Helen watched. On the second she was given little bits and pieces to do by herself. On the third day …

Complete this story on the other side of this sheet. Use your imagination, your knowledge and your common sense. Describe what might have happened to Helen and where the fault lay.

Source: adapted from *The Health and Safety Textercise Book*

UNIT 18 Thinking ahead: planning your future

Your Life 4/Year 10

Lesson 3 *Your Life 4*, pages 90–91
Economic wellbeing and financial capability 1.1a, 1.1b, 1.1c, 2.1a, 2.1b, 2.1d, 2.3a, 2.3c, 3c, 3f, 4a, 4b, 4c, 4d

Aim: To prepare yourself in more detail for your work experience placement.

Preparation

Make a copy of copymaster 43 (Use your loaf) for each pair of students.

Starter

Brainstorm 'Things you need to know before you start your work experience'. List the students' suggestions on the board.

Suggested activities

- Small groups read and discuss 'Work experience essentials' and compile a list of the five top tips. Ask spokespersons from each group to present their list and to explain why they have chosen these points.
- Study 'The employer's report' section. Ask pairs to discuss the mock report and to write the overview of Angela's achievements. Ask three or four pairs to feed back their overview and elicit class comment.
- Individually students write a paragraph evaluating their own strengths and weaknesses and expectations of their employer's report.

Plenary

Ask volunteers to share what they have written about themselves and then elicit class comment. Have students correctly assessed their areas of strengths and weaknesses? Can other members of the class make suggestions as to how to improve in certain areas?

Extension activities

Give pairs a copy of copymaster 43. Students discuss what they would do in these situations and note down their responses. The challenge in scenario one is not to become flustered and break down, but prioritise. Students should ask themselves which thing is most important. The friend can be called back later; the person who is angry can be politely transferred to the relevant department; the caller who wants the address can be asked to hold; the person with the appointment could be dealt with next; and the teacher should understand that the student is busy. In scenario two, the student should spend the time filling out his log, thinking about projects associated with the company, reading up about the company, or even doing some school work.

Further resources

- Information and advice on work experience placements for school students can be found at www.direct.gov.uk
- A Work Experience Data Book in which students can record their work experience is available from www.my-work-experience.com

43 Use your loaf

While you are at work, things may happen that you are not sure about. Here are two real-life situations that cropped up on students' work experience placements.

Busy, busy

You have been asked to answer the phones by the supervisor. There are three lines and they all start ringing at once, so you put them all on hold. One of the callers is a friend who wants to know what you are going to do that night. The second caller is really angry about something. The third caller wishes to know the company address. Then a person comes into reception for an appointment with the boss. To cap it all, your teacher walks in to see how you are!

Clock watching

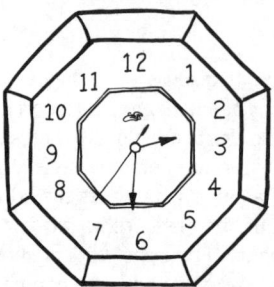

Not much is happening today. Business is really slack. You are quite obviously a 'spare-part'. You have done everything that there is for you to do. Your supervisor has not said anything to you and appears to be very occupied at the moment. It is only 2.30pm and you are not supposed to leave until 5.30pm. No one has said that you can go.

🔡 In groups

Read the situations above and discuss what you would do if these things happened to you. Try to come to an agreement about what is the best thing to do in each case.

UNIT 19 Managing your money

Your Life 4/Year 10

Lesson 1 *Your Life 4*, pages 92–93
Economic wellbeing and financial capability 1.2b, 2.4a, 3h

Aim: To understand the importance of budgeting and how to plan a budget.

Starter

Brainstorm the different thoughts and feelings that the students have about managing their money. Put the worries/negative thoughts on one side of the board and the positive thoughts and feelings on the other. Try to sum up the different feelings and worries that money management elicits in young people.

Suggested activities

- Read the article 'School leavers can't budget' and ask groups to discuss it. What do they think about the results of the research? What will their biggest expenses be when they leave home? (Note that a TV licence costs £142 and a basic fridge costs in the region of £150.)

- Encourage pairs to read and discuss the article on allowances, to draw out the advantages and disadvantages, and to design a questionnaire to find out other students' views on the topic.

- Read 'How to budget' with the class, ensuring students understand the terms 'income' and 'outgoings' and the basic method of creating a budget (including the fact that savings, the third column, are another form of outgoings; the difference is that you hold on to the money until you have enough to spend it). Pairs discuss three other ways in which the teenager could have balanced the budget, e.g. they could have increased their income, spent less on different items, or reduced savings drastically. Ask two or three pairs to feed back their ideas.

- Individuals read Chris's letter (see 'For your file', page 93), then draft a reply. This could be done in pairs for differentiation.

Plenary

Ask two or three students to read out their replies and invite comment from the rest of the class on how good and how well explained the advice is.

Extension activities

- Invite two or three pairs to present their questionnaires on allowances and ask the class to vote on which one is the most useful and interesting. Then duplicate the questionnaire and get students to collate and present the results.

- Individuals complete their own weekly spending record, then bring it back to the class and discuss what they have found out about their spending and budgeting.

Further resources

- The FSA website contains material and resources on budgeting and saving at www.fsa.gov.uk

- http://moneysense.natwest.com has details of the Moneysense programme, which includes the day-to-day management of money and how to open a bank account.

Your Life 4/Year 10

UNIT 19 Managing your money

Your Life 4/Year 10

Lesson 2 *Your Life 4*, pages 94–95
Economic wellbeing and financial capability 1.2b, 2.4a, 2.4b, 2.4c, 2.4d, 3h

> **Aim:** To understand what bank accounts are, what advantages they have and how bank accounts and plastic cards work.

Preparation

Make copies of copymaster 44 (Bank account survey) and copymaster 45 (Cheques and cards) for each student.

Starter

Give students two minutes to write down as many banks and building societies as they can. Write them on the board as they feed back. Are they surprised at the number? Why are there so many? (You may have to explain the difference between banks and building societies, which now is only a matter of ownership.)

Suggested activities

- Read the articles 'Why do I need a bank account?' and 'What kind of bank account should I have?' and invite pairs to discuss the information and issues that arise. Allow any questions to be asked in a whole class discussion before asking the pairs to write definitions of some of the terms, such as current account, savings account, basic account and direct debit. You can illustrate the different parts of a cheque by putting half of copymaster 45 on the whiteboard and filling in the labels. This could act as preparation for lower ability students before they attempt to label the cheque themselves.

- Then read the article 'Plastic – your flexible friend' and invite pairs to study the information carefully and test each other. In a whole class discussion, ask what the advantages and disadvantages of using plastic are. Again, you can label the debit card on copymaster 45 on the whiteboard as before.

- Suggest pairs discuss saving, and jot down different reasons that people might have for saving. Elicit the fact that sometimes you save for things you know you need, sometimes for things you really want, sometimes for things you know will happen, and sometimes in case things happen – all on different timescales. Try to get an example of each category in the feedback.

Plenary

- Ask students to jot down three advantages of bank accounts, and share these with the class.

- Invite students to jot down definitions of three of the basic concepts or terms explored in the lesson, and feed back.

Extension activities

- Ask groups of three to conduct a survey of the bank accounts available to teenagers in their area, by using the form on copymaster 44 This will entail phoning or visiting the banks. Groups present their findings.

- Individuals label the features of the debit card and cheque on copymaster 45. This can be done in pairs for differentiation if necessary.

Further resources

- www.pfeg.org.uk is an excellent website devoted to increasing financial literacy. It has many resources and links to further resources.

- www.moneymatterstome.co.uk has sections covering various aspects of money management including bank accounts.

44 Bank account survey

Use the questionnaire below to find out about different bank accounts available to teenagers.

	Bank account 1	Bank account 2	Bank account 3
Name of bank			
Account name			
Minimum deposit			
Cash card (How much can you withdraw per day?)			
Statement (How often are you sent one?)			
Is interest charged? (Am I allowed to go overdrawn?)			
Other benefits? (Freebies? Welcome pack?)			

Compare your results. Who has found the best deal for teenagers? Should any other factors be taken into account, e.g.

● Is there a branch near by? _____

● Is it friendly? _____

● Are there free cash machines near by? _____

45 Cheques and cards

Cheque

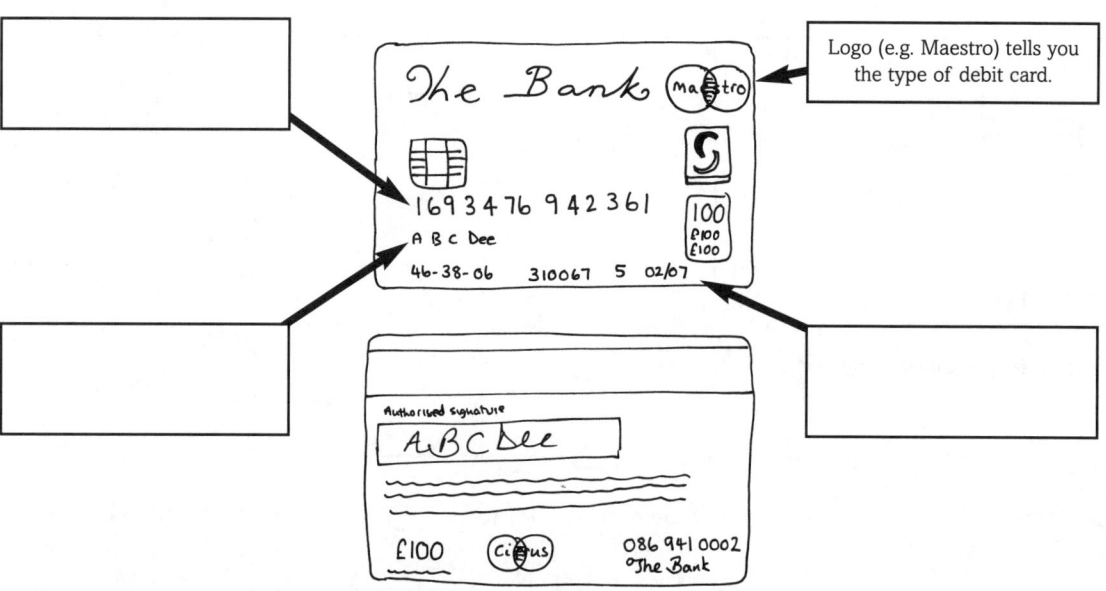

Date

The Bank
1 Bank street
Moneytown

46-38-06
15694 310067

Pay

Date

Account payee

£

A B C Dee

15694   15694   43-3806   310067

Space to write in
the amount to be
paid in words.

Debit card

The Bank (Maestro)

1 6 9 3 4 7 6 9 4 2 3 6 1
A B C Dee
46-38-06   310067   5 02/07

100
£100
£100

Logo (e.g. Maestro) tells you
the type of debit card.

Authorised signature
A B C Dee

£100   (Cirrus)   086 941 0002
°The Bank

88 In groups

Identify each of the features on the cheque and debit card above, and write a brief
explanation of what they are for. The first one has been done for you in each case.
You may need to do some research to fill in all the details.

UNIT 20 Financing businesses

Lesson 1 *Your Life 4*, pages 96–97
Economic wellbeing and financial capability 1.3a, 1.3b, 1.4a, 1.4b, 3g, 3j, 4a, 4g

Aim: To understand why businesses need money and how they obtain it.

Starter

Brainstorm the reasons why businesses need money. Then show how the reasons can be grouped under three headings: To set up a business, To run the business, To expand the business.

Suggested activities

- Read 'Why businesses need money?' and the case study 'Graceful Hair'. Discuss with the class how Grace funded the business. Talk about the difference between private financing and public financing and read the information about them on page 97. Ask groups to discuss the two views on investing in a business and to discuss whether they would be prepared to risk their money by investing it in a business.

- Study the flowchart on page 97. Ask individuals to list the advantages and disadvantages of funding a business a) by a bank loan b) by selling shares. Share their views in a class discussion. Ask: 'If you were setting up a small business, how would you fund it?'

Plenary

Recap what they have learned about why businesses need money and how they can raise it.

Extension activity

Ask students to list the things they would want to know about a business before deciding whether or not to invest in it. Then, draft an e-mail to a friend explaining what you think they should find out about a business before investing in it.

Further resources

An investment managing project for students can be found at www.schoolbiz.org.uk

UNIT 20 Financing businesses

Lesson 2 *Your Life 4*, pages 98–99
Economic wellbeing and financial capability 1.4a, 1.4b, 2.3i, 3g, 3j, 4a, 4g

Aim: To understand that running a business involves costs and that this influences the price charged for goods or services.

Starter

Draw the following diagram on the board: Revenue versus Expenditure

Income > Expenses = Profit

Income < Expenses = Loss

Explain that this is the basic fact that all business people have to remember when making decisions.

Suggested activities

- Read 'Fixed costs and variable costs' and ask pairs to choose a business and to make lists of the two different types of costs, then to compare their lists in groups.

- Read the paragraphs on 'Wages' and discuss how wages may depend not only on the job you do, but on your experience and the amount of responsibility you have. Ask groups to discuss the scenario in which a person is asked to take a wage cut and to report their views in a class discussion.

- Study the information on 'Revenue'. Ask groups to discuss the three statements about prices and to make a list of things you need to consider when setting prices, then to compare their lists.

- Read 'Breaking even' and discuss how the break-even point influences managers' decisions.

- Talk about how businesses pay tax, but not on their expenses. Explain what VAT is and who must register for it. Then read the paragraphs on 'Tax'.

Plenary

Recap the distinction between fixed costs and variable costs. Ask 'What costs would be saved if a company in financial difficulties decided to cut its production to three days per week instead of five?'

Extension activity

Explain that the costs of any business can be affected by fluctuations in the market. Ask pairs to discuss what this means and how it helps to explain why so many businesses failed during the recession.

UNIT 20 Financing businesses

Your Life 4/Year 10

Lesson 3 *Your Life 4*, pages 100–101
Economic wellbeing and financial capability 1.4a, 1.4b, 2.3i, 3g, 3j, 4a, 4g

Aim: To understand budgeting and why businesses draw up budget plans.

Preparation

Make copies of copymaster 46 (Business problems) and copymaster 47 (A Glossary of financial terms) for each student.

Starter

Recap why businesses need money, and explain that a business budget consists of several parts, such as a premises budget, a staffing budget, a production budget, a marketing budget and a sales budget.

Suggested activities

• Read 'Planning a budget' and discuss how the different parts of a budget are interlinked. Ask: 'How does planning a budget help a business to set targets?' Then read 'Making adjustments' and talk about how and why a business may have to adjust its budget plans.

• Study the quarterly budget for Marjorie's Bakery. Ask individuals to calculate her monthly revenue and expenditure and how much profit she made each month.

• Read 'Cashflow problems' and ask individuals to think about Toni's problems and to write a statement saying what they think he should do. Share some of their views in a class discussion.

Plenary

Ask them each to write down the three most important things about financing businesses they have learned from this unit. Compare their opinions in a class discussion.

Extension activities

• Give out copymaster 47 (A glossary of financial terms) for individuals to complete.

• Ask the students in groups to discuss the two problems described on copymaster 46 (Business problems) before sharing their views in a class discussion.

46 Business problems

Case Study 1

Tina runs a babysitting service 'Tash and Tina' with her friend Natasha. Their business is flourishing and the demand for their service is more than they can meet. What should she do? Expand the business by taking on a third person? What would employing somebody else cost? What extra paperwork would it involve? How would they recruit someone they could trust? Or should she turn down the extra work and allow one of her competitors to take it on?

Make a list of everything Tina needs to consider before making her decision. What would you do if you were in Tina's position?

Case Study 2

Jake has cashflow problems. He runs a gardening service and has just bought a new mower, which means he can work more quickly and efficiently. He had to buy the mower on hire purchase. Now he is having difficulty meeting the monthly payments, because one of his customers, for whom he does a lot of work, owes him a considerable sum of money for some fencing work that Jake did for him.

Jake has already asked for payment three times. What can he do to make sure he doesn't fall behind on payments for the mower? Ask the bank for an overdraft on which he'll have to pay interest? Threaten to take the customer to court if he doesn't pay up immediately, with the risk that the customer won't employ him again in the future? Ask his 20-year-old assistant if he'd be prepared to wait a week or two for his next wages? Ask if he can borrow money from a friend to tide him over until the customer pays up?

Discuss the consequences of each action that Jake might take. Can you suggest anything else Jake might do? If you were Jake, what would you do?

47 A glossary of financial terms

Complete this sheet by writing a definition of each term.

assets	
bank loan	
bankrupt	
break-even point	
budget	
cashflow	
fixed cost	
grant	
investment	
profit	
revenue	
shares	
variable cost	
VAT	

UNIT 21 Enterprise challenge

Your Life 4/Year 10

Lesson 1 *Your Life 4*, pages 102–103
Economic wellbeing and financial capability 1.2a, 1.4a, 2.3f, 2.3g, 2.3h, 3g, 4a, 4c, 4g, 4h

Aim: To understand what an enterprise challenge is and to decide on a new business idea.

Preparation

Download details of the current Makeyourmark Enterprise Challenge from www.enterpriseuk.org

Starter

Explain that the term 'enterprise' has more than one meaning. It can mean a company or firm. It can also mean a project, especially one that requires boldness and effort. An enterprise challenge involves you in undertaking a business project in which you will develop particular skills: creating and implementing new ideas, assessing and managing risk and showing the drive necessary to make ideas happen. Write the word 'entrepreneur' on the board and explain that it means the owner or manager of a business enterprise who uses their initiative to try to make a profit.

Suggested activities

- Read 'What is an enterprise challenge?' and discuss what the Makeyourmark Enterprise Challenge and the BiG Challenge are. Explain what this year's Makeyourmark Enterprise Challenge is.

- Groups brainstorm ideas for a new business. See 'Getting Your Big Idea' page 102.

- Read 'Spotting a potential market' and 'Identifying competitors'. Groups discuss which of their 'big ideas' most fills a gap in the market and identify competitors.

Plenary

Read 'The unique selling point'. Groups decide which of their 'big ideas' they are going to develop and identify its u.s.p. In turn, they explain their 'big idea' to the rest of the class.

Extension activity

Write a statement explaining how and why your group chose its 'big idea'. What made it stand out from your other ideas? Why did you choose it and reject the others?

Further resources

- Details of the current BiG challenge can be found at www.thebigwebsite.org.uk

- The NatWest Moneysense for schools website www.moneysense.natwest.com includes an activity 'We're in business' in which students plan and run their own enterprise.

UNIT 21 Enterprise challenge

Lesson 2 *Your Life 4*, page 104
Economic wellbeing and financial capability 1.2a, 1.4a, 2.3f, 2.3g, 2.3h, 3g, 4a, 4c, 4f, 4g, 4h

Aim: To describe your business idea and to draft a questionnaire for a market survey.

Preparation

Make a copy of copymaster 48 (Preparing a market survey) for each student.

Starter

Explain that this is the first of three lessons in which they will be developing and presenting a business plan.

Suggested activities

- Groups draft the first part of their business plan (see 'Description of the product or service' page 104).
- Groups prepare a market research questionnaire, using the guidelines on how to draft a market survey on copymaster 48.

Plenary

Share the drafts of their questionnaires and ask them to offer each other advice on the wording of their questions.

Extension activity

Carry out the survey and analyse the results.

48 Preparing a market survey

Find out whether or not there is a market for your product or service by giving a questionnaire to potential customers. Follow these guidelines as you prepare your questionnaire.

1 Identify your target audience.

For example: 'Is your product or service aimed at a particular age group – young children, teenagers, adults, older people – or a particular type of person (such as a DIY enthusiast)?' Ask questions that are aimed at your target audience.

2 Keep questions short and simple.

For example: 'What price would you be prepared to pay for this product /service?'
£2 / £5 / £10

'How likely would you be to buy this product?' Very likely / Quite likely / Unlikely

3 Use direct questions and avoid indirect questions.

For example, ask: 'Do you think this product fills a gap in the market?' Yes/No

Avoid questions such as 'Where is there a gap in the market for this product?'

4 Do not ask double-barrelled questions.

For example: 'What things appeal to you about our product and how is it different from other similar products?'

5 Avoid leading questions with emotive words.

For example: 'Why do you think our product is brilliant?'

6 Avoid personal questions.

For example: 'Would members of your family be able to afford this product?'

7 Try out your questionnaire.

Give it to one or two people and ask them for their comments on the questions. Can they suggest other questions that you might have asked? Revise the questionnaire in the light of their comments.

UNIT 21 Enterprise challenge

Lesson 3 *Your Life 4*, page 104
Economic wellbeing and financial capability 1.2a, 1.4a, 2.3f, 2.3g, 2.3h, 3g, 4a, 4c, 4g, 4h

Aim: To draft a budget plan for your business.

Starter

Recap what they learned about financing a business in Unit 20.

Suggested activities

- Read 'A budget for the business', then in groups discuss what their start-up costs would be and whether £25 would be a sufficient sum.

- Groups work out what their running costs would be and what price they would need to charge to make a profit. Read 'The price is right?' and ask each group to calculate their rate of return.

- Ask each group to work out a draft budget for their product or service.

Plenary

Invite one or two groups to share their budgets with the rest of the class.

Extension activity

Read 'Quality versus quantity' and discuss the question that follows.

UNIT 21 Enterprise challenge

Your Life 4/Year 10

Lesson 4 *Your Life 4*, page 104
Economic wellbeing and financial capability 1.2a, 1.4a, 2.3f, 2.3g, 2.3h, 3g, 4a, 4c, 4f, 4g, 4h

Aim: To develop a market strategy for your product or service and to prepare a presentation of your business idea.

Preparation

Make a copy of copymaster 49 (Ten things to ask about your business idea) for each student.

Starter

Introduce the concept of a market strategy. Explain that it involves identifying your target audience and outlets for your product. It also involves planning an advertising campaign.

Suggested activities

1. Read 'Developing and marketing your product or service'. Ask groups to identify their target customers and potential outlets for their product or service.
2. Groups plan an advertising campaign, deciding on which media to use.
3. Groups draft a leaflet advertising their product or service.
4. Read 'Expanding your business' and ask groups to discuss ideas for expansion

Plenary

Compare their leaflets. Discuss whose gets the message across most effectively and why.

Extension activity

Groups prepare a five-minute presentation of their business plan, using copymaster 49 (Ten Things To Ask About Your Business Idea) to help to remind them of key points that need to be included in their plan.

 Ten things to ask about your business idea

In your group, consider these questions as you prepare a presentation of your business plan.

- Who is your business idea aimed at? Is it aimed at a particular age group or a particular section of society?

  _____

  _____

- Is your idea practical? For example, could you make the product easily? How easy would it be to provide the service you plan?

  _____

  _____

- How original is the idea? What is its unique selling point?

  _____

  _____

- Does your business idea fill a gap in the market?

  _____

  _____

- Are there any competitors already in business? What does your idea offer that they don't?

  _____

  _____

- How much money would you need to start up your business? Where would you get that money from?

  _____

  _____

- What would be the running costs of your business?

  _____

  _____

- What price would your product or service have to be in order for you to make a profit?

  _____

  _____

- How would you market your product or service?

  _____

  _____

- Who would you consult to ask for advice about how to develop your business idea?

  _____

  _____

UNIT 22 Reviewing and recording your learning

Your Life 4/Year 10

Lesson 1 *Your Life 4*, pages 106–107

Aim: To review and record what you have learned from studying the units in *Your Life 4*.

Starter

Explain that the aim of the session is to help the students to reflect on what they have learned from doing the course. Remind them that the course was divided into four sections and explain that you want them to write a statement about each section. To give them an idea of the type of comment they might write, read and discuss what Jemma wrote about what she learned from the 'Keeping Healthy' section.

Suggested activities

- Split the class into four groups and ask each group to discuss the questions on one of the four sections. Encourage them to remind themselves of what they did in the units from that section by referring not only to the relevant pages of the student book, but also to any work based on those units that they have in their files. Suggest that during their discussions they make notes of any particularly important things they feel they learned. Then get them to appoint a reporter to feed back to the rest of the class.

- Ask individuals to begin to draft statements on one of the four sections of the course.

Plenary

Ask students to share some of their draft statements with the class.

Extension activity

Ask students to complete any unfinished statements on the section that they began in the lesson and then to draft statements on the other three sections.

UNIT 1 The UK and its relations with the rest of the world

Your Life 5/Year 11

Lesson 1 *Your Life 5*, pages 6–7
Citizenship 2.1a, 2.1b, 2.1c, 3m

Aim: To understand what the European Union is and how it is organised.

Preparation

Make a copy of copymaster 1 (European Union – fact-check) for each student.

Starter

Introduce the topic by asking students how much they know about the European Union. How many member states are there? Which countries are members? What are the aims of the EU? Then read the first paragraph of 'What is the EU?'

Suggested activities

- Explain what is meant by sovereignty (the supreme and unrestricted power of an independent state to make its own decisions). Then read the rest of the article 'What is the EU?' Discuss with the class what the article says the EU has achieved. Do they agree that the EU 'has achieved remarkable things'? Ask the students: How is the EU unique in the way that it is organised? How is it different from the United States and the United Nations?

- Students list all the ways they think the EU affects them, then read 'How does the EU affect us?'

- Study 'The main institutions of the EU'. Ask groups to discuss how decisions are made in the EU and which institution is the most powerful. Then remind the class how laws are made in the UK. Ask: What are the similarities and differences with how laws are made in the EU?

- Read 'European elections'. Discuss why turnout is lower than in national elections. Remind the students that EU law takes precedence over UK law and ask how they would try to convince people that it is important to vote in European elections.

Plenary

Recap the aims of the EU and its achievements.

Extension activities

- Test knowledge and understanding of the European Union by asking students to complete the multiple choice quiz on copymaster 1. The answers are: 1d, 2c, 3a, 4c, 5c, 6a, 7b, 8d, 9d, 10d

- Students use the Internet to find out which European Constituency they are in, who their MEPs are, and what political parties they represent.

- In pairs, students use the Internet to research the history of the European Union and to produce a time chart of key events in the development of the EU.

- Students visit the website of the European Parliament (www.europarl.org.uk) and find out what issues the EU has been debating, and why.

Further resources

Details of people willing to give talks in schools about the EU and factsheets and worksheets on the EU are available from www.civitas.org.uk

European union – fact-check

○ On your own

look at the following multiple-choice quiz. In 10 minutes, see how many of the questions you can answer. Then, in pairs, look at pages 6–7 of *Your Life 5* and check your answers.

1 How many countries are there in the European Union?

a) 12

b) 16

c) 20

d) 27

2 What was the name of the 1957 treaty which set up the European Economic Community?

a) The treaty of Maastricht

b) The treaty of Brussels

c) The treaty of Rome

d) The treaty of Lisbon

3 Which one of the following is the main decision-making body of the European Union?

a) The Council of the European Union

b) The European Commission

c) The European Parliament

d) The European Court of Justice

4 Which of the following is not one of the aims of the European Union?

a) To raise the quality of life for its citizens

b) To improve the economic position of its citizens

c) To introduce a national health service across the European Union

d) To promote common foreign and security policies

5 Where does your EU passport allow you to travel freely to?

a) Any country in Europe

b) Anywhere in the world except the USA

c) Any country in the European Union

d) Any country in the Commonwealth

6 Why was the European Economic Community originally formed?

a) To prevent war in Europe from occurring again

b) To build a single European government

c) To provide a trading block to counterbalance the power of the USA

d) To help rebuild Europe's economy after the Second World War

7 Which of these bodies scrutinises and develops policies within the European Union?

a) The European Court of Justice

b) The European Parliament

c) The European Court of Auditors

d) The European Commission

8 When are elections to the European Parliament held?

a) Annually   b) Every 3 years

c) Every 4 years   d) Every 5 years

9 What is the single market?

a) Governments are only allowed to provide support to one area of industry

b) Companies have one place where they can meet on line and trade goods

c) Towns in the European Union are only allowed one market per town

d) Goods and services can be freely traded across the European Union

10 Who are European Union Commissioners meant to be loyal to?

a) The political party to which they belong

b) Each other

c) The countries that they come from

d) The common interests of the people of the European Union

UNIT 1 The UK and its relations with the rest of the world

Your Life 5/Year 11

Lesson 2 *Your Life 5*, pages 8–9
Citizenship 2.1a, 2.1b, 2.1c, 3m

> **Aim:** To explore Britain's relationship with the EU and to discuss the issues of expansion of the EU and reform of its institutions.

Preparation

Make a copy of copymaster 2 (What do people think about the European Union?) for each pair.

Starter

Explain that the attitudes of British people towards the EU vary. Write the term 'Eurosceptic' on the board, explain what it means and read the paragraph on 'Britain and Europe'.

Suggested activities

- Read 'The expansion of the EU' and get groups to discuss the reasons why some people support the expansion and why others think that expansion has gone too far. Hold a class discussion on whether the EU should continue to expand.

- Study 'The development of the EU' and 'The Treaty of Lisbon'. Remind then what national sovereignty is and explain what the national veto is. Ask students to list areas in which they think the national veto should apply and discuss whether they are in favour of the idea of a federal Europe.

- Students study 'The UK Independence Party' and in groups of 3 invite them to role play a scene in which one of them chairs a TV discussion between a pro-European and a member of the UK Independence Party. One group could then present its discussion before the rest of the class, who could act as a studio audience.

Plenary

Ask students what their attitude is now towards Europe. Are they pro-European or Eurosceptic? Do they think Britain should withdraw from Europe? Get them to share their views in a class discussion.

Extension activities

- Students use copymaster 2 to carry out a survey of people's attitudes to the EU.

- Ask students to choose one political party and look at its website to find out what its policies are towards the EU, especially with regard to expansion and the national veto. Students write up a report, and present it to the rest of the class.

What do people think about the European Union?

Look at the following survey sheet. In pairs, each of you should speak to five people, and keep and record of your answers. At the end of the survey, add up your results. Compare your results with those of other groups. What do you learn?

1 How important do you think the
European Union is to you? Is it …

   a) important?

   b) not important?

   c) don't know

Person 1	Person 2	Person 3	Person 4	Person 5
☐	☐	☐	☐	☐
☐	☐	☐	☐	☐
☐	☐	☐	☐	☐

2 How much power do you think the
European Union has? Is it …

   a) too powerful?

   b) not powerful enough?

   c) about right?

3 What do you think of the UK's membership
of the EU? Should the UK …

   a) withdraw from the EU?

   b) stay in the EU but renegotiate its terms
of membership?

   c) remain a full member of the EU?

4 Can you name one of the members of the
European Parliament that represents you?

   a) yes (give name)

   b) no

5 The European Union has recently expanded
in size to 27 countries. Do you think the
European Union is now …

   a) too big, and should be smaller?

   b) about the right size?

   c) too small, and should carry on expanding?

6 Do you have any other comments about the European Union you would like to add?

Person 1 _____

Person 2 _____

Person 3 _____

Person 4 _____

Person 5 _____

Extension activity

Write up your results, and present them to the class.

UNIT 1 The UK and its relations with the rest of the world

Your Life 5/Year 11

Lesson 3 *Your Life 5*, pages 10–11
Citizenship 2.1a, 2.1b, 2.1c, 3m

Aim: To understand what the single currency is and to explore the arguments for and against the UK joining the euro.

Preparation

Make a copy of Copymaster 3 (Britain and the euro) for each student.

Starter

Introduce the concept of a single currency by asking students what money they take on holiday within the UK (pounds), and in Ireland (euros), France (euros) and the USA (dollars). Then read 'The single currency'.

Suggested activities

- Study what supporters and opponents of the euro argue and what the political parties say (see page 10). Discuss the different views with the class and ask: Should there have to be a referendum before Britain joins the euro?

- Invite students individually or in groups to design a campaign poster for a referendum on the single currency, either to get people to vote 'yes' or to vote 'no'.

- Read 'Joining the euro – what would it mean?' and discuss the effects of joining on homeowners, businesses and the high street.

- Organise a debate: 'This house believes that Britain should never join the euro.'

Plenary

Ask students in a single sentence to explain why they are for or against Britain joining the single currency. Invite some of them to share their views.

Extension activities

On their own, students complete Copymaster 3 – Britain and the euro. The answers are
1. False; 2. True; 3. False; 4. True; 5. False; 6. False; 7. False; 8. True; 9. True; 10. True.

Your Life 5/Year 11

3 | Britain and the euro: true or false

Look at the following statements about Britain joining the euro and decide whether they are true or false. Then compare your answers in groups.

		True	False
1.	Britain can only join the euro if the people of Britain vote 'yes' in a referendum.	☐	☐
2.	The price of certain expensive items, such as cars, would come down if Britain joined the euro.	☐	☐
3.	Britain will be forced to withdraw from the EU if we do not join the euro by 2015.	☐	☐
4.	Interest rates in Britain will be set by the Central European Bank rather than the Bank of England, if the UK joins the euro.	☐	☐
5.	The Labour Party is the only major political party in favour of joining the euro.	☐	☐
6.	The pound would not be abolished if we joined the euro. You could still use it if you wanted.	☐	☐
7.	The EU would set Britain's taxes if Britain joined the euro.	☐	☐
8.	If we joined the euro, trading with other EU countries would be simpler, because there would be no currency exchange involved.	☐	☐
9.	Only countries which belong to the EU can choose to have the euro as their currency.	☐	☐
10.	Surveys show that a majority of British people are against joining the euro.	☐	☐

UNIT 1 The UK and its relations with the rest of the world

Your Life 5/Year 11

Lesson 4 *Your Life 5*, pages 12–13
Citizenship 2.1a, 2.1b, 2.1c, 3m

Aim: To explore the UK's relationship with the Commonwealth, and how the Commonwealth works.

Preparation

Make a copy of copymaster 4 (The Commonwealth – true or false?) for each student.

Starter

Explain what the British Empire was and how, at the time of becoming independent, many countries chose to remain associated with Britain as part of the Commonwealth.

Suggested activities

- Read 'What is the Commonwealth?', 'The aims of the Commonwealth', and 'How the Commonwealth works'. In groups, students discuss what they learn from the articles about the origins and composition of the Commonwealth, its aims and how it works to achieve those aims.

- Explain that nations belonging to the Commonwealth have to abide by its rules, and then read 'Enforcing the aims of the Commonwealth'. Discuss the case of Zimbabwe and how the Commonwealth tries to put pressure on countries that break its rules, through suspension.

Plenary

Hold a class discussion on whether the Commonwealth serves a useful purpose. Do students think we need the Commonwealth today? Or does its role overlap too much with that of other international institutions like the EU and the UN? If we do need the Commonwealth, do they think its power should be stronger, to achieve its aims?

Extension activities

- Test knowledge and understanding of the Commonwealth by asking students to complete the true or false quiz on copymaster 4. The answers are: 1 true, 2 false, 3 false, 4 true, 5 true, 6 true, 7 false, 8 false, 9 true, 10 true, 11 true, 12 false.

- Find out more about the Commonwealth by visiting the Commonwealth's website (www.thecommonwealth.org). Choose one of the less economically developed countries that is a member of the Commonwealth and ask students to research this country on the Internet, finding out what problems it has and compiling a list of the ways they think the Commonwealth could help this country.

- Students can then look at a more economically developed country within the Commonwealth. How do they think this country benefits from membership of the Commonwealth?

- Ask students to write an essay comparing the aims and objectives of the Commonwealth with those of the UN and the EU. Do they think these aims overlap? If so, do they think it is important that we still have the Commonwealth? Does it still provide a useful role in international relations?

4 The commonwealth – true or false?

○ On your own

Look at the following statements about the Commonwealth. Decide whether they are true or false. Then compare your answers with a partner. When you have finished, check whether you were both correct by looking for the answers on pages 12–13 of *Your Life 5*.

❶ There are 54 countries in the Commonwealth.

❷ The United States of America is a member of the Commonwealth.

❸ The role of the Commonwealth is to create a world government.

❹ The head of the Commonwealth is the Queen.

❺ The headquarters of the Commonwealth is in London.

❻ The Commonwealth sends observers to elections in its member countries, to check that the elections are being carried out properly.

❼ The Commonwealth can sack the head of a government when they fail to follow the rules of the Commonwealth.

❽ The Commonwealth has a single market like the European Union.

❾ The Commonwealth provides technical help to its members to help their economies grow.

❿ The Commonwealth holds conferences on issues of importance to its members.

⓫ Zimbabwe was suspended from the Commonwealth for breaking the rules on free and fair elections.

⓬ There is a Commonwealth Parliament, made up of directly elected members from Commonwealth countries.

Extension activity

Write up your results, and present them to the class.

UNIT 1 The UK and its relations with the rest of the world

Aim: To understand what the United Nations is and what its aims are, and to examine its role in the world.

Preparation

Make a copy of copymaster 5 (The United Nations – Reform of the UN) for each pair.

Starter

Ask the students what they know about the United Nations and what it does. Explain that it was set up after the Second World War in the hope that it would enable countries to work together to prevent wars in the future.

Suggested activities

- Read 'The UN Charter' and discuss with the class what the UN is and what it does. What are the UN's aims?

- Study 'The UN General Assembly' and 'The UN Security Council'. Discuss with the class how UN policy is decided. What is the Security Council and what are its responsibilities? Why is the UK important on the Security Council? Ask groups to discuss whether membership of the Security Council should be changed to reflect changes in the world since 1945. See 'What do you think?'

- Read 'The UN Secretariat' and 'The UN – helping to solve the world's problems'. Then get groups to discuss what the page tells them about how the UN works to help to solve some of the world's problems.

- Invite students in pairs to compile a quiz consisting of true and false statements about the UN, then to exchange their quiz with another pair and to complete each other's quizzes.

- Ask students to draw up a factsheet of key facts about the UN, entitled 'Ten things you need to know about the UN'.

Plenary

Discuss the view that despite its failures in settling disputes and preventing conflicts, the UN has achieved a great deal. Ask them whether they agree or disagree with this verdict on the UN.

Extension activities

- Ask them to choose one of the UN's agencies or commissions such as the UN High Commission on Refugees or the UN Commission for Human Rights. In groups, students should research this body, write up a report, and present it to the class.

- Give out copies of copymaster 5. Ask pairs to study the two diagrams and to discuss the arguments for and against each of the suggestions for the reform of the UN. Prompt them to decide which reforms they think should be made, then to share their ideas in a group or class discussion.

Further resources

Information about the membership, structure and work of the United Nations can be found at www.un.org

The United Nations – reform of the UN

⚬ In pairs

Look at the two diagrams of the United Nations. One diagram shows how the UN is structured now, the other how it could be reformed in the future. Do you think the United Nations should be reformed? Give reasons for your views.

The United Nations now	**How the United Nations could be reformed**
Head of the United Nations elected by the UN assembly with limited powers.	New head could become a directly elected president as head of a world government.
One chamber – the UN Assembly, with each country having one representative.	Two chambers. Keep the UN Assembly, but add a House of Representatives, elected by population. This would mean less developed countries would be fairly represented in the United Nations.
The UN Security Council, with five permanent members who have the right of veto.	Reform so that the Security Council is elected by countries according to different regions. All decisions to be made by majority voting with no veto.
Authority of the United Nations means that it is not allowed to invade countries, and that its peacekeeping troops can monitor situations and defend themselves, but cannot attack anyone, even when human rights abuses are occurring.	Authority should be extended, so that the United Nations has the authority to enter countries to prevent human rights abuses, and remove governments from power if necessary.
No direct link to a world court, to enforce UN decisions.	Direct link to a world court, where dictators can be put on trial for human rights abuses and war crimes.

Extension activity

If there were one change you had to make to the United Nations, what would be your top priority? Compare your answer with that of other pairs.

UNIT 2 Human rights

Your Life 5/Year 11

Lesson 1 *Your Life 5*, pages 16–17
Citizenship 1.2a, 1.2b, 1.2c, 2.2a, 2.2b, 2.2c, 3a, 3n, 4g, 4h

> **Aim:** To explore human rights issues, focusing on cases of human rights abuses and looking at how human rights can be protected and enforced.

Preparation

Make a copy of copymaster 6 (Human rights – what do you think?) for each student.

Starter

Ask the students what they think could be done to protect and enforce human rights. Explain or elicit the following points: educating people, raising awareness, putting people on trial, stronger laws, writing letters, peacekeeping troops, and regime change.

Suggested activities

- Read 'Protecting human rights', 'Raising awareness' and 'Strengthening the law'. In pairs, students make notes summarising ways in which human rights can be protected. What is the most effective way of protecting human rights?

- Study 'Enforcing human rights internationally'. (Make sure the students understand the meanings of ethnic cleansing and genocide.) Ask students if they can remember any particular examples of war crimes they have heard about in the news over the last year.

- Read 'The International Criminal Court'. Ask students in groups whether they agree or disagree with the statement on whether the USA should co-operate with the court.

- Read 'Military intervention and regime change'. Ask the students in pairs whether they agree or disagree with the statements. Students should then share their ideas in a group discussion.

Plenary

Ask the students to discuss whether they agreed or disagreed with the invasions of Afghanistan and Iraq, and whether it has helped or hindered human rights, and for whom.

Extension activities

- Invite students to become involved in campaigns run by Amnesty International (www.amnesty.org.uk) or Liberty (www.liberty-human-rights.org.uk) see 'Take action' page 16.

- Ask students to write their views about Britain's involvement in the war in Afghanistan (see 'For your file' page 17).

- Use copymaster 6 to conduct a survey on human rights. Compare your results and discuss what they tell you about people's attitudes to human rights.

- In a group, imagine you have to write a leaflet educating students in a Less Economically Developed Country about their human rights. Write and design your leaflet, and compare it to other leaflets that other people in the class have produced.

- Look at the international news on the TV, the Internet, and the newspapers. Are there any cases where governments or the UN are acting to protect human rights? What are they doing? How effective is this protection?

Human rights – what do you think?

Use copies of this sheet to conduct a survey on human rights. Compare your results and discuss what they tell you about people's attitudes to human rights.

Student name: _____ **Class:** _____

Date survey was carried out: _____

1 Do you think human rights are important?   Yes ☐ No ☐ Don't know ☐

2 Do you think we should do more to protect human rights locally?

Yes ☐ No ☐ Don't know ☐

3 If yes, what do you think we ought to be doing?

_____

_____

4 What human rights do you have that you can remember? (List below)

_____

_____

5 Do you think more should be done to protect human rights internationally?

Yes ☐ No ☐ Don't know ☐

6 Do you think the Government was right to send troops to achieve regime change in Afghanistan?

Yes ☐ No ☐ Don't know ☐

7 Do you think the Government was right to send troops to Iraq to remove the dictator Saddam Hussein from power?

Yes ☐ No ☐ Don't know ☐

8 Do you think the invasions of Afghanistan and Iraq have strengthened or weakened human rights in those countries?

Strengthened ☐ Weakened ☐ Don't know ☐

9 Do you think that UK troops should have been withdrawn from Afghanistan and Iraq once regime change had been achieved?

Yes ☐ No ☐ Don't know ☐

10 Are there any other comments you would like to add?

_____

_____

_____

_____

UNIT 2 Human rights

Your Life 5/Year 11

Lesson 2 *Your Life 5*, pages 18–19
Citizenship 1.2a, 1.2b, 1.2c, 2.2a, 2.2b, 2.2c, 3a, 3n, 4g, 4h

Aim: To explore human rights issues, and to examine cases of human rights abuses.

Preparation

Make a copy of copymaster 7 (Human rights – fact check) for each student.

Starter

Ask students to think about their local area. Are there any homeless people or beggars? Do the students think that the basic necessities are being met in their area, for everyone?

Suggested activities

- Read 'Basic survival needs'. Look at the photo. Which rights and necessities do you think are not being met?

- Study 'Human rights abuses'. In groups, look at the list of different human rights. Rank them in order of importance. Then compare your list with those of other groups in a class discussion. Give reasons for your choices. Then discuss the statements in groups.

- Study 'China's human rights record' then ask groups to discuss the four statements, before sharing their views in a class discussion.

- Read 'India – the caste system'. Students use the Internet to find out more about the Dalits, then in pairs role play an interview with a Dalit.

Plenary

Focus on the list in 'Human rights abuses'. Hold a class discussion with students, in which they imagine they are experiencing some of these human rights abuses. How do they think a violation of their human rights would affect their lives?

Extension activities

- Test knowledge and understanding of human rights by asking students to complete the quiz on copymaster 6. The answers are: 1 The Hague in the Netherlands, 2 Amnesty International, 3 genocide, 4 United Nations, 5 regime change, 6 ethnic cleansing, 7 peacekeepers, 8 USA, 9 The European Charter of Fundamental Rights, 10 a large-scale set of human rights abuses that occurs in a conflict.

- In groups, look at the newspapers, the Internet, and TV programmes over the next week. Which particular human rights can they see being violated? Are any rights violations more common than others? Ask them to record their findings for their file.

- Ask students to use the Internet to find out about minority ethnic or religious groups which are the victims of human rights abuses, then to focus on one group and to draft a report about their treatment to present to the class. Information about minorities around the world can be found at the Minority Rights Group International website www.minorityrights.org

Human rights – fact-check

Complete the following quiz on your own. When you have finished, compare your answers with a partner, and then check them by looking at pages 16–21 of *Your Life 5*.

❶ Where is the International Criminal Court located?

_____

❷ What is the name of the pressure group that campaigns for human rights, and on behalf of prisoners of conscience?

_____

❸ What is the act of killing an entire race of people known as?

_____

❹ Which organisation created the Universal Declaration of Human Rights?

_____

❺ What is the act of invading a country and changing its Government known as?

_____

❻ What is the act of killing or forcing a particular group of people to move, so that there are none of them left in the area?

_____

❼ What are the United Nation troops who are sent into combat zones to protect human rights known as?

_____

❽ Which major country is not signed up to the International Criminal Court?

_____

❾ What is the European Union's new list of human rights called?

_____

❿ What is a war crime?

_____

Extension activity

Imagine you had to draw up a list of new human rights. What rights would you include? Would you have different rights for people of different ages? Give reasons for your views.

UNIT 2 Human rights

Your Life 5/Year 11

Lesson 3 *Your Life 5*, pages 20–21
Citizenship 1.2a, 1.2b, 1.2c, 2.1a, 2.2a, 2.2b, 2.2c, 3a, 3l, 4g, 4h

Aim: To understand why people become refugees and asylum seekers and to explore issues concerning their human rights.

Preparation

Make a copy of Copymaster 8 ('Refugees and asylum seekers – true or false?') for each student.

Starter

Write the terms 'refugee' and 'asylum seeker' on the board and ask students to write definitions of them. Share their definitions and make sure they understand what the terms mean.

Suggested activities

- Read 'Refugees and asylum seekers'. Discuss whether they agree or disagree with Nick Clegg's view.

- Invite groups to discuss what item they would take with them if forced to flee their home (see 'In groups') before sharing their views in a class discussion.

- Read 'How many refugees are there?' and study the table. Ask: Do any of the statistics surprise you? Then get groups to discuss how their lives would be different if they lived in a refugee camp.

- Examine 'Asylum seekers or economic migrants?' Ask students what the difference is between an asylum seeker and an economic migrant? Discuss the arguments for and against deporting asylum seekers immediately after their application has been turned down.

- Study 'Human trafficking'. In groups, ask the students to discuss which of the statements they agree with, and why. Ask them to share their views in a class discussion.

- In pairs, ask the students to imagine they are genuine asylum seekers. How would they expect to be treated when they arrived in a foreign country? What do they think could be done to make things easier for them?

Plenary

Share their views of the difficulties an asylum seeker faces in a foreign country. Ask: What are their human rights? and draw up a list.

Extension activities

- Read out the statements on Copymaster 8 in turn and ask the students to write down whether the statement is true or false, before reading out the answer. When they have completed the quiz, give them each a copy of the copymaster and discuss what are facts about refugees and asylum seekers and what are myths, before putting the sheets into their files.

- Invite students to write a short encyclopedia article on economic migration (see 'For your file' page 21).

Further resources

Information about refugees and asylum seekers can be found at the following websites:

www.unhcr.org.uk (the website of the United Nations High Commission for Refugees)

www.refugeecouncil.org.uk

www.star-network.org.uk

8 Refugees and asylum seekers – true or false?

Which of these statements are true and which are false?

❶ Most asylum seekers come from countries at war.

True. 74% of refugee claims are made by people from countries where there is ongoing conflict. Most others come from countries that are apparently at peace, but that are guilty of human rights abuses, such as China.

❷ Refugees bring crime to this country.

False. Asylum seekers are no more likely to commit crimes than anyone else, despite their very low incomes. In fact, refugees are more likely to be the victims of crime and often suffer from race-related violence.

❸ Britain's population is growing because of refugees.

False. At best, it is being balanced out. There are more people who leave the country every year than who come here. Very few of the people who leave Britain do so because they fear for their lives.

❹ Everyone in the world has the right to claim asylum.

True. The right to asylum is enshrined in international law. Countries have an obligation to investigate the claims of every person who applies for asylum. However, to be granted asylum, you must fulfil certain strict criteria.

❺ Refugees are mostly skilled and well qualified.

True. Most people who arrive in the UK have had to pay to make their journey, which would be impossible for most poor people in developing countries. Refugees contribute a lot to this country in taxes and service once they are allowed to work. 23% of doctors and 47% of nurses in this country were born outside the UK, many of whom are asylum seekers.

❻ Britain takes more refugees than any other country.

False. Britain takes less than 3% of the world's refugees. 38% of refugees are in Asia, 32% are in Africa and 80% of refugees flee to the often poor country next door. Pakistan takes the most, and even within Europe Germany takes four times as many as the UK.

❼ Most refugees want to go home.

True. Refugees have to leave their homes and loved ones behind, often to live in refugee camps, or to come to cold countries where they are often treated badly. Many families are separated. Most refugees intend to return home when their country becomes safe.

UNIT 3 Media matters

Aim: To explain how news is spread by the mass media.

Preparation

Make a copy of copymaster 9 (The TV licence fee) for each student.

Starter

Ask the students to consider where we get our news. Read 'The development of the mass media'. In pairs, students discuss how the way we receive information and news has changed with the development of broadcasting.

Suggested activities

- Read 'The broadcast media'. Discuss the effects of the development of satellite TV and cable TV.

- Study 'Pay-per-view and subscription channels' then ask groups to discuss the question of whether it is fair for so much live football only to be available on subscription channels. Ask them to list which key sports events (e.g. the Grand National, the university boat race) they think should be available free on BBC and/or ITV.

- Read 'The British Broadcasting Corporation or BBC' and ask groups to discuss the three statements and to share their views in a class discussion.

Plenary

Explain that while people now rely mainly on TV or the Internet for news, many people still read a daily newspaper. Discuss why they think newspapers remain popular e.g. because they give more detailed reports and contain articles commenting on issues and events.

Extension activities

- Students can conduct a survey on how people get their news (see 'For your file' page 23), write a report and share their findings in a class discussion.

- Give out copies of Copymaster 9 'The TV licence fee' and ask groups to discuss the three statements

Further resources

A useful source of information on the development of the mass media and other features of the media industry is http:/ketupa.net

9 The TV licence fee

THE LICENCE FEE COULD GO, ADMITS BBC BOSS:
Cost of watching TV might be put on countil tax bill

The BBC's director general has conceded that the licence fee could be scrapped and replaced with funding via council or income taxes – or even a levy on electricity bills. Mark Thompson's comments have been taken as an admission that the growing use of new technology to watch programmes will make the licence fee obsolete.

At present, anyone who owns a TV set is forced to pay for the BBC through the compulsory annual charge which is purchased online, over the phone or in shops. But increasing numbers are switching to computers and other devices to watch shows via websites such as BBC iPlayer – for which they do not need a licence. This has sparked fears that fewer and fewer people will actually bother to pay the £142.50 charge. Now the BBC's most senior executive has admitted

that 'you might define the licence fee in a different way'. He said 'perhaps' you could 'bung it in' with taxes or impose it via electricity bills – though he personally did not think this was a good idea.

Critics pointed out that this would be unfair for those who choose not to watch television shows at all ... and that those who claim benefits are exempt from income tax or council tax – meaning that those who do pay them would have to pick up the shortfall.

There are further concerns that the BBC's independence could be compromised if it becomes part of the overall general taxation regime.

In the interview, Mr Thompson admits that, in future, the Internet may be the main way the BBC broadcasts its content to all of its audiences.

Source: www.dailymail.co.uk

'The licence fee should be scrapped and the BBC should be funded by other means.'

'The licence fee is the fairest way offunding the BBC.'

'The BBC should have to generate its own revenue in the way that its commercial rivals do, through advertising or subscription.'

○ On your own

Read the article and discuss these views, then write your own comment on the article saying how you think the BBC should be funded.

Your Life 5/Year 11

Lesson 2 *Your Life 5*, pages 24–25
Citizenship 2.1a, 2.1b, 2.1c, 2.1d, 2.2a, 2.2b, 2.2c, 3g, 4a, 4i

Aim: To examine how the news agenda is created and to explore the power of the media in shaping people's opinions.

Preparation

Collect copies of different national newspapers for the same day. Make a copy of Copymaster 10 ('How stories are presented') for each student.

Starter

Explain what is meant by the news agenda. Who do they think sets the news agenda? Is it news editors? Individual journalists? Owners of newspapers and TV companies? Government advisers? Pressure groups? Public relations consultants?

Suggested activities

- Ask students how much influence they think the press has. Read 'How powerful is the media?' and discuss which they think shapes people's opinions more – TV or newspapers. Ask: How neutral do they think the BBC is?

- Read 'Gatekeepers – people who control the news'. Then discuss, in groups, what a gatekeeper is and how they make decisions that affect the news we receive. Invite groups to do the activity involving the selection of news stories to be included in a school newspaper (see 'In groups' page 24).

- Study 'Spin doctors' and get pairs to discuss what spin doctors do and to say what their views of spin doctoring are, then to share their opinions in a group discussion.

- Read 'Twitters and blogging'. Discuss how they allow people to comment at once on a breaking news story, then invite students to write a short comment on a current news story for a blogging site.

Plenary

Hold a class discussion on who controls the news agenda. Focus on the power of large media corporations and discuss whether it is right that they should have so much influence.

Extension activities

- Give out copies of copymaster 10. Ask the students in pairs to discuss the questions on the photographs, then to compare their answers in groups.

- Give each group copies of two newspapers for the same day and get them to compare the news stories they contain. Do they all have the same lead story? Do they give different amounts of space to particular stories? Do they report stories from the same viewpoint? Conclude the activity by asking what they have learned from studying these two newspapers about how gatekeepers control the news.

- Invite students to write two versions of the same story about a competitor in a Strictly Student Dancing event, one giving the story a positive spin, the other giving the story a negative spin (see 'For your file' page 25).

- Make recordings of TV news bulletins from two different stations on the same evening. Ask students to compare which stories were covered and how they were covered. What do they learn from this activity about how editorial decisions influence the news we receive on TV?

- Ask students to check the website www.projectcensored.org to see what stories did not make the news. Why did these stories not make the news? Which stories do they think should have been covered? Ask students to give reasons for their views.

10 How stories are presented

Working in pairs, look at the photos above, which are connected to the war in Afghanistan. Then answer the following questions:

❶ Which of the photos would you describe as positive? Which would you describe as negative?

❷ What do you think each photo tells us about the war in Afghanistan?

❸ If you were the UK Government, which photo(s) would you prefer to see in a newspaper? Why?

❹ Look at the following headlines, presenting the photos from a British viewpoint. Discuss how the pictures could have headlines presenting them from a different point of view and suggest examples of such headlines.

Taliban rebels continue their insurgency

Afghans show support for UK troops

Latest casualties return to the UK

UNIT 3 Media matters

Your Life 5/Year 11

Lesson 3 *Your Life 5*, pages 26–27
Citizenship 2.1a, 2.1b, 2.1c, 2.1d, 2.2a, 2.2b, 2.2c, 3a, 3g, 4a, 4i

---

Aim: To discuss freedom of speech in the media.

Preparation

Make a copy of copymaster 11 (Control of the Internet) for each student.

Starter

Ask the students if they can think of any situations where the freedom of the media should be limited. Use prompts if necessary, such as wartime, in a court case where the defendant is a minor etc.

Suggested activities

- Read 'A free media?' In groups students then discuss the question of whether we should have complete freedom of speech, as in the USA, or limited freedom of speech, as in the UK.

- Study 'Should the media ever be controlled?' Ask groups to identify circumstances in which the government would be right, in the interests of national security, to control information reported by the media.

- Examine 'The Internet in the world – a case of inequality?' In groups, students discuss what measures could be taken to prevent an information underclass occurring. Invite students to imagine what life would be like without the Internet. How would it affect them? How would it affect someone in a less developed country?

- Ask students to look at the case study on China. In groups, get them to discuss whether or not there should be any censorship of content and access to the Internet.

Plenary

Discuss the effect it would have on their use of the Internet if they could only access sites approved by the government, as happens in China.

Extension activities

- Give out copies of copymaster 10. Ask students in groups to read the information about the Internet in the USA and in the UK and to discuss whether or not there should be total freedom to post any material on the Internet. Then ask them to decide which sites they would stop children of certain ages accessing.

- Research the Campaign for the Freedom of Press Information at www.cfoi.org.uk Search the Internet for other pressure groups who campaign for media freedom, and freedom of information. Write a summary of the information you find, and present your results to the class.

Your Life 5/Year 11

Control of the internet

In groups

Read the following about the Internet in the USA. Do you think the USA is right to allow total freedom on the Internet? Or should there be some restrictions, such as controls on children's web browsers? Give reasons for your views.

Control of the Internet in the USA

In the USA, the country with the largest number of Internet users, there is total freedom of speech. This means that anyone can set up an Internet site, and publish any material they like. Supporters of free speech argue that this is key to a democracy. They also argue that such freedom promotes debate, and educates and informs people. However, in the USA, there are sites that promote racist and fascist ideas which critics argue ought to be banned because they encourage racist violence.

However, some limits can exist in the home. Many US families have controls on their web browsers for their children. This means that children's sites can be accessed, but many adult sites are banned. These controls allow parents to monitor and control what sites their young children may be accessing whilst they are on the Internet.

In the UK, the Government exerts more control over the internet. The main cases in which the UK Government has limited the content of internet sites has been:

● to prevent pornographic images of children from being displayed

● to protect the national interest (e.g. by limiting the amount of information available about the UK's nuclear industry to prevent terrorists from using it for wrongful purposes)

● to protect individuals from harm. When the police give a person a new identity, it is an offence under UK law to publish details of their identity. However, it is impossible to stop someone from doing so in another country, where there are no such media controls.

Extension activity

Imagine you are in control of the internet in your house. What sites would you let a 5-year-old, a 10-year-old and a 15-year-old visit? Why? Give reasons for your views.

Further resources

Information on issues connected with press freedom can be found at the Campaign for Press and Broadcasting Freedom's website www.cpbf.org.uk

UNIT 4 Global challenges – wars, weapons and terrorism

Your Life 5/Year 11

Lesson 1 *Your Life 5*, pages 28–29
Citizenship 2.1a, 2.1b, 2.1c, 2.1d, 3n, 4a, 4g

Aim: To understand the arms trade, what weapons of mass destruction are, and how they affect the world.

Preparation

Make a copy of copymaster 12 (Unilateral or multilateral?) for each student.

Starter

Introduce the concept of the arms trade. Ask the students why countries produce arms. Explain that they do so not just to supply their own armies but also to sell to other countries. Read 'What is the arms trade?' and discuss the three reasons why critics say the arms trade is damaging.

Suggested activities

- Students in groups study 'Arms races', and discuss why arms races occur. Then invite students to imagine they are the government of a less developed country. What would they do if their neighbour started developing arms? This activity could be expanded into a role-play, with each group of students role-playing the government of a different neighbouring country.

- Read 'An ethical arms trade'. In groups, students discuss the three statements and the principles on which they think an ethical foreign policy should be based.

- Study 'Weapons of mass destruction' and have a class discussion on which type of weapons pose the greatest threat to humanity.

- Students write an article expressing their views on the dangers of weapons of mass destruction (see 'For your file' page 29).

Plenary

Recap by drawing two columns on the board and asking students to list the positive and negative effects of the arms trade.

Extension activities

- Copymaster 12 presents the arguments used by supporters of unilateral disarmament and those used by supporters of multilateral disarmament. Ask students in pairs to rank the arguments according to which are the strongest and weakest, then to discuss in groups whether they are in favour of unilateral or multilateral disarmament.

- Organise a debate on the motion: 'This house believes that the UK should unilaterally give up its nuclear weapons'.

- Students use the Internet to find out more about the arms trade by visiting the website of CAAT (Campaign Against the Arms Trade) www.caat.org.uk.

- Ask students in pairs to imagine they have to produce a poster campaigning against the arms trade. What would their main message be? Ask them to design their poster, and then compare it to that of other pairs.

Further resources

The WMD Awareness Programme website includes lesson plans and up-to-date information about weapons of mass destruction – www.wmdawareness.org.uk

Your Life 5/Year 11

12   Unilateral or multilateral?

Look at the following arguments for and against unilateral and multilateral disarmament. Rank the arguments in each column, starting with the arguments you think are the strongest, down to the arguments that are the weakest. Then decide whether you are in favour of unilateral disarmament or multilateral disarmament.

Unilateral disarmament – giving up your nuclear weapons, regardless of what others do	**Multilateral disarmament – giving up your nuclear weapons when others agree to do so**
There is a guarantee that the number of nuclear weapons in the world will be reduced.	There is no guarantee that other countries will follow you, if you disarm unilaterally.
The cost of maintaining nuclear weapons is high, in the medium- to long-term.	The cost of disarming weapons is high in the short-term.
There is always the danger of a nuclear accident or theft of nuclear materials whilst these weapons remain.	Nuclear weapons have helped keep world peace over the last fifty years.
If we disarm first, that will encourage others to disarm.	More nuclear weapons will be destroyed if we use ours as a tool to negotiate with other countries and to encourage them to destroy theirs.
We're never going to use nuclear weapons, so why keep them?	Unilateral disarmament would be a sign of weakness.
Technological research can concentrate on areas that benefit all of us, rather than on building even more nuclear weapons.	Research into nuclear weapons can be used productively in other areas.
It is hypocritical of us to keep nuclear weapons but to tell other countries they can't have them.	Nuclear weapons give us a way of using nuclear waste from our nuclear power stations.

Hold a debate on the motion, 'This house believes that multilateral disarmament is the only sensible way of gradually reducing the number of nuclear weapons in the world today.'

UNIT 4 Global challenges – wars, weapons and terrorism

Your Life 5/Year 11

Lesson 2 *Your Life 5*, pages 30–31
Citizenship 2.1a, 2.1b, 2.1c, 2.1d, 3n, 4a, 4g

> **Aim:** To discuss what terrorism is, what causes and maintains it, and how terrorism can be fought.

Preparation

Make a copy of copymaster 13 (Reducing terrorism) for each pair.

Starter

Ask the students to name any terrorist groups they have heard of (e.g. Al Qaeda, the Real IRA. ETA, PLO). What is each fighting for? Draw two columns on the board and make a list of terrorist groups and their aims.

Suggested activities

● Read and discuss with the class 'What is terrorism and how is it caused?'

● Study 'What keeps terrorism going and how to stop it'. Discuss with the class each of the five things that fuels terrorism and what can be done to stop terrorism. Ask groups to list, in order of importance, what they think the causes of terrorism are and to share their views in a class discussion.

● Students examine the case studies 'New York 11 September 2001' and 'London 7 July 2005' and read 'The war on terror'. Invite groups to discuss whether the USA and UK were right to respond to September 11th by taking military action. Ask them to decide whether they agree or disagree with the two statements, and then to share their opinions with the rest of the class.

Plenary

Write these statements on the board: 'Even if we sympathise with the cause that terrorists are fighting for, there can be no justification for terrorism.' 'We must always take a hard line against terrorism.' Hold a class discussion of these views.

Extension activities

● Ask students to write a short statement of their views on whether terrorism can ever be justified (see 'For your file' page)

● Give out copies of copymaster 13. Ask pairs to rank the different suggestions for reducing terrorism in order according to which they consider would be the most effective. Then, in groups, invite them to compare their views and to discuss any other methods they think would be effective.

● Students use the Internet to research the situations in Afghanistan and Iraq. Have the US/UK's invasions made terrorism more likely? Or have they made the areas safer now in the long run?

● Ask students to imagine they have £100 million to spend on the fight against terrorism. What would they spend it on – resolving conflicts before they got out of hand, increasing security in more developed countries to prevent terrorist strikes, or increasing police resources to track down the terrorists? Ask them to give reasons for their views.

13 Reducing terrorism

Look at the following ways of reducing terrorism. In pairs, rank the following suggestions in order, from what you think are the most effective to the least effective. Then compare your ideas with other pairs in your class. Give reasons for your views.

1 Spending as much money in the UK on conflict solution as we do on the arms trade.

2 Creating amnesties, like the Good Friday Agreement, in which terrorists agree to cease violent activities in return for immunity against being charged for their crimes and sent to jail.

3 Gun amnesties, in which terrorists can hand in their weapons, with no questions asked.

4 Better education in schools around the world, to fight racism and religious hatred, which are the causes behind many terrorist acts.

5 Regime change backed by the UN, so that those that fight terrorists will replace governments supporting terrorists.

6 A stronger role for UN peacekeepers so that they can detain human rights abusers, and thus prevent a new generation of terrorists from growing up to avenge themselves.

7 A dialogue with terrorists so that their problems can be discussed and negotiated, thus removing the need for further violent activity.

8 A no tolerance policy, with no negotiation, in which terrorists are hunted down and killed, even if that means the occasional civilian casualty.

9 Stronger laws against terrorists, including the right to detain suspected terrorists without trial.

10 The freedom to use any interrogation method on terrorists that results in future terrorist acts being stopped, and lives being saved.

Extension activity

In pairs, list any other suggestions you can think of that would help fight terrorism. Are there any of the suggestions above that you think would be counter-productive? Give reasons for your views.

_____

_____

_____

_____

_____

_____

UNIT 5 Global challenges – environmental issues

Lesson 1 *Your Life 5*, pages 32–33
Citizenship 2.1a, 2.1b, 2.1c, 2.1d, 3i, 3n, 4a, 4g

Aim: To explain what sustainable development is, and the main ways it could be applied around the world.

Preparation

Make a copy of copymaster 14 (Sustainable or unsustainable?) for each pair.

Starter

Ask the students what they think are the main environmental problems facing the world today. List their suggestions on the board. Then read 'The economy and the environment', and discuss which of these problems is the most dangerous to the UK.

Suggested activities

- Introduce the concept of sustainability by reading 'Sustainable development'. Ask students to imagine that they are the passengers and crew of a liner shipwrecked on a desert island. There's plenty of food in the form of fish and fruit, but only a limited amount of water and trees. Talk about how they would need to ration their use of water and wood in order to achieve sustainability.

- Read 'Sustainable solutions around the world'. Ask pairs to discuss whether they would support or oppose the building of a wind farm or the planting of GM crops on land near their home.

- Study 'Sustainable development in developed and less economically developed countries', then ask groups to discuss the statements, before sharing their views in a class discussion, then writing a statement of their own views.

Plenary

Ask the students to imagine they are designing a town from scratch in a developing country. What features would they include to make it a sustainable development? The activity can be extended by asking students to think about the following: the materials it would be built of, energy consumption, food consumption, transport, and the protection of natural resources.

Extension activities

- Give out copies of copymaster 14. Ask students in pairs to decide which of the activities are sustainable and which are unsustainable, then to compare their views in groups before checking the answers which are: 1. sustainable, 2. unsustainable, 3. sustainable, 4. sustainable, 5. unsustainable, 6. sustainable, 7. unsustainable, 8. sustainable, 9. unsustainable, 10. unsustainable.

- Invite students to contact a charity such as Oxfam or Village Aid, and to find out what it does to help sustainable development in less developed countries.

- Ask students to research one of the following on the Internet or at the local library: global warming, species extinction, deforestation or acid rain. Invite them to write a report on how this issue is effecting the global environment, and to present their findings to the class.

- Ask students to draw a map of the town designed in the plenary, showing the main features that make it a sustainable development.

Further resources

The Sustainable Development Commission's website www.s-dcommission.org.uk has a comprehensive list of sites offering information and advice about sustainable development.

Sustainable or unsustainable?

 **In pairs**

Look at the following list. Decide whether each activity is sustainable or not sustainable in the long term. Compare your answers with other pairs, and then check with your teacher, to see if you are correct.

1 Composting kitchen scraps to be used as compost in the local allotments.

2 Driving by private car to do the recycling once a week.

3 Using solar panels to provide hot water showers where you live.

4 Using a clockwork radio to listen to the news.

5 Catching a bus to work rather than using a car.

6 Switching energy supplies to a company that only produces green electricity.

7 Having a wood or coal fire in the house to reduce your gas central heating bill.

8 Riding a bike to school rather than getting a lift with your parents.

9 Buying goods with lots of packing online, rather than from your local supermarket.

10 Buying a motorbike rather than a car because it uses less petrol.

Once you have checked the answers with your teacher, decide which of the sustainable activities above you could incorporate into your life, to make your life greener. Is there anything else you could do to help the environment?

UNIT 5 Global challenges – environmental issues

Lesson 2 *Your Life 5*, pages 34–35
Citizenship 2.1a, 2.1b, 2.1c, 2.1d, 2.3a, 3i, 3n, 4a, 4g

Aim: To understand what your water footprint is and to explore ways of taking action to reduce your consumption of natural resources.

Preparation

Make a copy of copymaster 15 (Changes for a greener town) for each group.

Starter

Ask the students to brainstorm things we can do to reduce our consumption of natural resources.

Suggested activities

- Explain that consumption of water is increasing and that water shortages are predicted in the future. Study 'Reducing your water footprint'. Ask groups to discuss whether products should carry water information and to list suggestions for how they might reduce their water footprint, prior to writing an article 'Why your water footprint matters'.

- Discuss how environmental problems affecting their local area could be sorted out using local solutions. Read 'Reducing rubbish' Discuss the recycling facilities that exist in your area. Ask the students, in pairs, to discuss whether it should be illegal not to recycle your rubbish and whether households should pay for the amount of waste that they produce.

- Read 'Reducing energy consumption' then invite groups to imagine they had to design a building e.g. a new school or office block and to list features they would include to make it environmentally friendly.

Plenary

Ask: If you had to choose one thing to do in order to cut down the consumption of natural resources, what would you choose to do? Share their views in a class discussion. See if the class can agree on what they would do, if necessary hold a vote.

Extension activities

- Use copymaster 15 to get groups of six or more to look at the list of suggestions for making a town greener. Each proposal has a cost and groups are given a budget and have to decide how they would spend it. Ask them to present their proposals in a class discussion, then to vote as a class to decide which proposals they would implement.

- Students research further ideas for dealing with rubbish or reducing energy consumption, using the library and Internet, then share what they have found out in a class discussion.

- Students search their local council's website to find out what it is already doing to make sure that rubbish is recycled, then write an e-mail to their local councillor suggesting what else the council might do.

Further resources

Useful sites for information about world water scarcity include:

www.waterfootprint.org

www.wwf.org.uk

www.wateraid.org.uk

15 Changes for a greener town

You represent the town council of Littledown. Here are 10 suggestions, with costings, of things that you could do to make the town greener. In groups, discuss which of these 10 things you would do. Any final decision has to be made with a two-thirds majority in the group.

Your total budget for Littledown is £5 million.

1 Introduce regular bus services from the north, south, east and west of the town. This will significantly reduce pollution, but will cost £3 million.

2 Incorporate solar panels into every new building that is built in the town. This will reduce heating and electricity bills, but will cost £0.5 million.

3 Introduce a green-box recycling scheme to every household in the town. This will increase the amount of material recycled by 75%, but will cost £2 million.

4 Introduce cycle lanes across the town. This will mean everyone can cycle safely from home to school or work, but will cost £1 million.

5 Introduce a congestion charge into the town, thus reducing the number of traffic jams by 50%. This will cost £1 million to set up, but will raise money in the future so that next year you will have more money to spend.

6 Introduce a composting scheme and more bottle banks, so that people can recycle more of their household waste. This will increase recycling by 25% in the town and will cost £0.5 million.

7 Introduce a tram system across all parts of the town. Cars will not be required in the town centre and will thus reduce congestion by 95%, but it will cost £5 million.

8 Introduce a park and ride scheme, so that people can leave their cars on the edge of town. This will reduce congestion by 25% and will cost £0.5 million.

9 Provide better education in schools and a public awareness campaign, so that people are aware of current schemes to make the town greener. This will cost £1 million.

10 Change all the council vehicles to battery-powered vehicles. This will reduce CO_2 emissions in the town by 10% and will cost £1 million.

What other suggestions can you think of to make a town greener? Which of the above suggestions are currently present in your town?

UNIT 6 Global challenges: poverty, health and education

Your Life 5/Year 11

Lesson 1 *Your Life 5*, pages 36–37
Citizenship 2.1a, 2.1b, 3n, 4a, 4e, 4g, 4h

Aim: To define poverty and to examine how it can be eradicated.

Preparation

Make a copy of Copymaster 16 (What is important?) for each student.

Starter

Ask each of them to write down their definition of poverty. Then read 'What is poverty?' and discuss what real poverty is. Introduce the concept of relative poverty and read 'Poverty in more economically developed countries'.

Suggested activities

- Study 'Poverty in less economically developed countries'. Invite pairs to imagine they lived without items such as a fridge and a washing machine. Ask: How would your life be different? What if you had no electricity supply or no water supply?

- Invite them to imagine having only £5 a day to live on and to decide how they would spend it. Share their ideas in a class discussion.

- Read 'Eradicating poverty' and the case study. Ask individuals to rank the six actions in order of importance, then to discuss their views in groups.

- Ask groups to plan a 30-second TV advert for a charity campaign End Poverty Now!

Plenary

Invite groups to share their plans for a TV advert and to decide which one would be the most effective and why.

Extension activities

- Students carry out the writing task suggested in 'For your file' (page 37), stating why they agree or disagree with the statement.

- On their own, students complete Copymaster 16, before comparing their two sets of answers in groups and sharing in a class discussion what the answers reveal about life in a rich country and life in a poor country.

Further resources

Useful websites include:

www.oxfam.org.uk

www.waronwant.org

www.actionaid.org.uk

16 | What is important?

○ On your own

Rate how important each of these things is to you on a scale of 1–10 (with 10 being very important and 1 being not important). Use a pencil.

	10	9	8	7	6	5	4	3	2	1
Having a vegetable patch										
Going to school										
Having your own bedroom										
Access to free healthcare										
Living in a country with a high rainfall										
Having a computer										
Access to clean water										
Having enough to eat										
Living in a democratic country										
Having a mobile phone										
Having fashionable clothes										
Access to public transport										
Having an electricity supply										
Having your own livestock										
Having a family car										
Being able to buy soap										
Living in a country where there is no armed conflict										
Being able to practise your religion										
Having cooking facilities										
Having seeds and agricultural tools										
Having a fridge										
Having access to leisure facilitie										

Now imagine you are a teenager living in a village in Africa. What things are important to you. Now using a pen, rate how important each of the things is to you. Compare your two sets of answers. Then in groups discuss the similarities and differences between them.

UNIT 6 Global challenges: poverty, health and education

Your Life 5/Year 11

Lesson 2 *Your Life 5*, pages 38–39
Citizenship 2.1a, 2.1b, 3n, 4a, 4e, 4g, 4h

Aim: To understand what life expectancy is and the causes of ill health in the world.

Preparation

Make a copy of Copymaster 17 (Word health problems) for each pair.

Starter

Explain what 'life expectancy is' and that it has increased by almost 20 years worldwide since 1950. There are three main reasons. Invite students to suggest what they are, then read 'Life expectancy', and ask pairs to list what they think are the reasons why so many African countries have a lower life expectancy than the UK.

Suggested activities

- Students read and discuss 'The causes of ill-health' and 'Sanitation – the facts'. Invite them to draft an e-mail expressing their concern about the global sanitation crisis (see 'For your file' page 39).

- Explain what 'immunisation' means. Read 'Preventing diseases' and discuss why immunisation plays such an important part in improving world health. Ask students in pairs to role play a scene in which a health worker tries to persuade a local village leader to allow all the children in their village to be immunised.

- Read 'Pandemics'. Discuss why they occur and why a new virus is able to travel so quickly around the world. Invite students to use the Internet to research pandemics, such as swine flu, and to report the key facts they discover about them in a class discussion.

- Study 'The overuse of antibiotics' then invite students, in groups, to discuss their views on the two statements (see 'In groups' page 39).

Plenary

Recap the causes of ill-health in the world. Ask: If you were the health minister in a country with a lower-than-average life expectancy what would be your top priority?

Extension activities

Ask students, in pairs, to choose a project to support from those described on Copymaster 17 and prepare a statement explaining the reasons for their choice to present in a class discussion. The class can then vote to choose the project most of the class would support.

Further resources

Information on world health issues can be found at the World Health Organisation's website www.who.int

A useful site on sanitation and health is www.endwaterpoverty.org

17 World health problems

Work in pairs. Imagine a group of multi-millionaires has asked you to recommend how they should spend £500 million on the world's health problems. Study the information on this page and choose one project on which to spend the money. Prepare a statement explaining why you chose this project rather than the others and share your views in a class discussion, before holding a vote to decide which project the class would choose, having heard all the statements.

Project 1 Providing immunisation against infectious diseases

- Every hour more than 300 children die because they do not have access to the vaccines which would save them.
- Each year more than 30 million children are not immunised against common childhood diseases.

Project 2 Providing clean water and sanitation

- Diseases which thrive in contaminated water include dysentery, cholera and typhoid.
- Lack of proper sanitation is responsible for the death of 6,000 children every day.
- Half of all the hospital beds in the world are occupied by people who have water-borne diseases.

Project 3 Controlling tobacco use

- Smoking is predicted to be the biggest killer of the 21st century.
  More than 15 billion cigarettes are smoked daily in the world.
- Smokers are 25 times more likely to get lung cancer and up to three times more likely to have a heart attack than non-smokers.
- Half of all smokers die prematurely – 4 million a year worldwide.
- Controlling tobacco use by increasing taxes, enforcing smoke-free workplaces and raising public awareness would prevent 14 million deaths over 10 years in developing and transitional countries.

Project 4 Prevention and treatment of HIV/AIDS

- There were 2.7 million new HIV infections in 2007. Half of these were people aged under 25.
- Almost 95% of people with HIV live in poorer countries. Access to antiretroviral treatment, which prolongs the lives of people with HIV, was just 43% in 2008.
- Providing young people with basic AIDS education enables them to protect themselves against infection.

Project 5 Educating people to lead healthy lifestyles

- The World Health Organisation (WHO) predicts that by 2030 three-quarters of all deaths in the world will be from chronic non-communicable diseases, such as heart attacks, strokes and some cancers.
- People who eat a diet that includes a lot of fried, fatty foods have a 35% greater risk of having a heart attack than those who eat little or no fried foods and meat.
- 30–40% of cancers are directly linked to the foods we eat, the amount of exercise we take and whether we watch our weight.

Project 6 Educating people about alcohol abuse

- Alcohol accounts for 4% of the global burden of disease and is a factor in about 60 diseases including cancers of the mouth, liver and breast, heart disease and stroke and cirrhosis of the liver.
- In developed countries alcohol is the third leading cause of disease and injury. For example, alcohol abuse is responsible for 195,000 deaths a year in the EU.

Project 7 Providing treatment for people with mental health disorders

- WHO predicts that in the next 20 years more people will be affected by depression than any other cause of ill-health worldwide.
- 450 million people are estimated to have a mental health or behavioural disorder.
- 1 in 4 people around the world will suffer from a mental health problem at some point.
- There is a large treatment gap in developing countries between the number of people with a mental disorder and the number who receive treatment.

UNIT 6 Global challenges: poverty, health and education

Your Life 5/Year 11

Lesson 3 *Your Life 5*, pages 40–41
Citizenship 2.1a, 2.1b, 3n, 4a, 4e, 4g, 4h

Aim: To understand the different levels of education around the world, and the barriers to education that exist.

Preparation

Make a copy of Copymaster 18 (Education for all) for each pair.

Starter

Invite students to list the difference it would make to their lives now and in the future if they had a) only a primary education b) only one year at school. Share their views in a class discussion, then read 'Levels of education' and discuss what they learn about the levels of education in different countries.

Suggested activities

- Read 'Education and poverty – a vicious circle'. Discuss the link between poverty and education and why it is described as a vicious circle.

- Study 'Less economically developed countries – the barriers to education' and the case study. Ask groups: What barriers to education exist in Jonas's life? What other barriers are there in less economically developed countries?

- Students, in groups, read 'More developed countries – unequal access', then discuss their views on whether the government should pay university tuition fees.

Plenary

Make a list of the main problems facing the world, e.g. poverty, famine, wars, terrorism, climate change, refugees, water supply, sanitation, AIDS, pollution, deaths in early childhood. On a scale of 1 to 10 (1 none at all, 10 an enormous amount) ask them to rate how much impact global education for all would have.

Extension activities

- Give each pair a copy of Copymaster 18 and ask them to draw up a true or false quiz consisting of statements about global education. They can then swap quizzes with another pair and do each other's quizzes. Prompt them to check their answers by looking at the facts given on the copymaster.

- Ask students to use the Internet to research what charities e.g. Oxfam and pressure groups e.g. the Global Campaign for Education are doing to help LEDCs to develop their education systems. How could your school get involved in the next Global Action Week? (see www.campaignforeducation.org)

Further resources

www.results-uk.org has information on the need for basic education to improve health and end poverty.

Your Life 5/Year 11

18 Education for all

The scale of the problem

❶ Over 72 million children in the world are out of school.

❶ One-in-five adults in the world are illiterate.

❶ Over 70% of the out-of-school children are in Sub-Saharan Africa and South and West Asia.

❶ Over 15% of children in developing countries do not complete a course of primary education.

❶ In Sub-Saharan Africa, less than 60% of children complete a course of primary education.

Why education is important

Education has been described as a 'silver bullet' in the fight to end poverty. Studies show that basic education – especially for girls and women – is one of the best development investments that can be made.

Education plays a pivotal role in the fight against poverty, maternal and infant mortality, ill-health and HIV/AIDS. According to UNICEF, one out of every six children born to women without an education dies before the age of five. That rate is reduced by half if a woman receives primary school education.

Primary education for all

In 2000, the World Education Forum in Dakar, Senegal, attended by representatives from 180 countries, promised to provide free and compulsory primary education for every child in the world.

Much has been achieved. Between 2000 and 2007, 41 million more children were brought into the schooling system and, since 1998, 47 out of 163 low-income countries have achieved universal primary education, with 20 more on course to achieve it by 2015.

However, there are at least 75 countries that will not achieve universal primary education by 2015.

Barriers to education

First, there is the cost. It would cost $11 billion per year to ensure that every child was able to go to school. That's an enormous amount but it's less than one-eightieth of the annual global military spending.

Another barrier is that many developing countries charge user fees for basic education, which include tuition fees as well as supplementary costs such as uniforms and textbooks. These fees put the cost of education out of reach of huge numbers of families.

Other barriers occur due to the social and political environment in which children live. About half of the world's out-of-school children live in countries where there is conflict.

Additionally, it is estimated that a third of out-of-school children have a disability, while more than 90% of children with disabilities in Africa do not go to school.

Source: adapted from pages on 'Basic education' www.results-uk.org

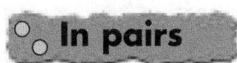 **In pairs**

Study the information on this page, then draw up a quiz consisting of true and false statements about the provision of education for all the world's children. For example: 'Universal primary education will be achieved throughout the world by 2015.' True or False?

When you have drafted your quiz, swop quizzes with another pair and complete each other's quizes.

UNIT 7 Working for change

Lesson 1 *Your Life 5*, pages 42–43
Citizenship 2.1a, 2.3a, 3g

> **Aim:** To explain what international pressure groups are, what issues they campaign on, and what campaign methods they use.

Preparation

Make a copy of copymaster 19 (International issues: past, present and future) for each pair.

Starter

Ask students to list international issues that pressure groups could campaign on (e.g. human rights, the arms trade, global warming). Read 'What are international pressure groups?'. Discuss with the class what their objectives are: to influence governments' policies, and the decisions made by international institutions and big businesses.

Suggested activities

- Study 'The anti-globalisation movement'. Ask what sort of tactics the group uses when campaigning. What effect have these tactics had? In pairs, role play a scene in which one of you tries to persuade the other to take part in an anti-globalisation protest.

- Read 'International pressure group issues' and ask groups to rank the issues in order of importance, then to share their ideas in a class discussion.

- Choose one of the 12 international pressure groups and design a poster to be used in one of their campaigns.

Plenary

Ask the students to complete the 'For your file' activity, saying which pressure group they would donate £100 to and why. Invite some of them to share their decisions with the rest of the class.

Extension activities

- Students work in pairs to complete Copymaster 19 and to decide which they think will be the three most important issues facing the world in ten years' time.

- Invite students to search the Internet for pressure groups that campaign on a particular type of issues (e.g. social issues). Write up a report on this group, and present it to the class.

- Contact the local MP, or local councillors. Ask them if they are in contact with any international pressure groups, and if so, in what way.

International issues: past, present and future

In pairs

Look at the following list of issues. Rank the issues according to which you think were important 50 years ago, which are important now, and which will be important in 50 years time.

	50 years ago	**Now**	**In 50 years' time**
Global warming			
International terrorism			
World peace			
Population growth			
Third World debt			
World poverty			
Access to clean water			
Dealing with natural disasters			
AIDS			
The spread of nuclear weapons			

Extension activity

Compare your answers with other groups. Then list any additional issues for the past, present or future that you think are important. Give reasons for your views.

UNIT 7 Working for change

Aim: To understand how international pressure groups campaign and to explore ways of getting involved.

Preparation

Make a copy of copymaster 20 (Slogans and issues) for each pair.

Starter

Ask students if they can list any examples in which international pressure groups have successfully campaigned on an issue (e.g. anti-globalisation marches, Comic Relief, Campaign against Landmines).

Suggested activities

- Read 'Getting the message across'. Ask pairs to discuss the different methods pressure groups use to get their message across.

- In the same pairs, students then choose an international issue about which they are concerned. Ask them to imagine that they are working for a pressure group and to draft a letter asking people for their support.

- Invite the students to imagine they are trying to lobby an international conference on the environment. What campaign methods would they use? Who would they target? Ask groups to draw up their campaign, showing how they would make it effective.

- Ask groups to discuss whether the end ever justifies the means. Should international pressure groups always work within the law? Can civil disobedience and/or violence ever be justified?

- Study 'Getting involved'. In pairs, students recap on which international issue concerns them most. Ask them each to decide which international pressure group(s) would be their first choice to support, and to write a statement similar to those of Mel and Harid.

Plenary

Look at 'Volunteering'. As a class students discuss why Laura considered her voluntary experience to be so rewarding, and whether they would ever do voluntary work abroad.

Extension activities

- Give out copies of copymaster 20 and ask the students individually to complete the matching activity, then to write their own slogans for issues that concern them.

- Ask students to use the Internet to look at the pressure groups Friends of the Earth (www.foe.co.uk) and Greenpeace (www.greenpeace.org.uk). What global issues are they campaigning on? Do they ever co-ordinate their campaigns? Ask groups to write up a report on one of these pressure groups and present their findings to the class.

- Students hold a survey asking people what they think are the most important issues affecting the world today. Are these the same issues that pressure groups are campaigning on in the media? Is there a gap? Students write up their results, and present them to the class.

Further resources

Details of opportunities for voluntary work overseas are available at the Voluntary Service Overseas (VSO) website www.vso.org.uk

20 Slogans and issues

In pairs

Look at the following list of slogans and issues. Match each slogan with an issue. Then decide which slogan you think is the most effective, and why. Compare your answers with other pairs.

Drop the Debt!

Not in my name!

Ban the ban!

A hand up, not a hand out

Ban the bomb!

Don't give up giving up

Free the rivers!

Remember the Big Issue

Keep the Pound!

Bring our boys home NOW.

'No' to the invasion of Iraq.

Stop our water from being polluted.

UK troops from Afghanistan.

Reduce Third World debt.

Stop the ban on foxhunting.

'No' to the Euro and the single currency.

Keep campaigning for homeless people.

Reform the welfare payments system.

Keep on trying to stop smoking.

'No' to nuclear weapons.

Look at some of the issues covered in *Your Life 5*. Write a slogan for one of the issues that you most care about. Compare your slogan with those of other pairs in your class.

UNIT 8 Co-operating on a community project

Your Life 5/Year 11

Lesson 1 *Your Life 5*, pages 46–47
Citizenship 2.3a, 2.3b, 2.3c, 2.3d, 2.3e, 3h, 4c, 4d, 4e, 4f; Economic wellbeing and financial capability 3a / Personal wellbeing 1.4b

Aim: To examine what volunteering involves and how it can benefit you and your local community.

Preparation

Make a copy of copymaster 21 (Getting involved in voluntary work) for each student.

Starter

Read 'What is volunteering?' Talk about the different reasons people can benefit from volunteering. Get them in groups to discuss if they know anyone who has done some voluntary work, what their reasons for doing this might have been, and why they might want to do voluntary work themselves in the future.

Suggested activities

- Study 'Getting involved'. In pairs, students discuss the four examples and what the benefits are to the community and to the individuals.

- Read 'Case study: Make a Difference Day'. Invite groups to discuss ideas for a MADD event, using the suggestions in the section 'How to identify your project' to help guide them.

- Share their ideas for a MADD event in a class discussion.

Plenary

Choose a MADD event from their ideas for the class to organise and draw up a plan listing what they would need to do in order to make it happen.

Extension activities

- Organise an afternoon for the whole class to take part in a MADD event. Afterwards, each class member can write up what he or she thought of the experience, and what he or she learnt from it.

- Find out what projects CSV is currently organising by visiting their website (www.csv.org.uk) and draft a statement to present to the school council arguing that the whole school should participate in this year's MADD scheme (see 'For your file' page 47).

- Ask students individually to complete Copymaster 21, then, in pairs, to discuss the type of voluntary work they would like to get involved in and how it would help them.

- Invite students to scan the local paper and the Internet to find out what voluntary positions exist so that people can get involved. Ask students in groups to discuss what they think the best voluntary positions are, and why.

Further resources

http://vinspired.com connects 16–25 year olds with volunteering opportunities in England

21 Getting involved in voluntary work

Look at the following sheet. Think about what sort of voluntary work you would like to do. How will this benefit you AND the person you work for? Fill in all of the questions where possible.

Job title: _____

Job description: _____

Number of hours you would like to work per week: _____

Days you would like to work: weekdays ☐   weekends ☐   either ☐

What will be the main benefit of you doing this voluntary work? _____

_____

What transferable skills will you be able to get from this voluntary work?

_____

_____

Office skills:

●   Answering the phone   ☐

●   Typing/word processing   ☐

●   Using spreadsheets and databases   ☐

●   Filing   ☐

●   Other _____

Are there any manual skills you will be able to gain from this voluntary work?

1. _____

2. _____

3. _____

What personal skills will you be able to improve through this voluntary work?

●   Dealing with a range of people   ☐

●   Meeting tight deadlines   ☐

●   Managing your own workload   ☐

●   Being punctual and reliable   ☐

●   Other _____

Will this work be temporary or permanent? If it's temporary, how long will it last?

_____

_____

_____

Will you be able to get a reference from this voluntary work?

_____

_____

_____

UNIT 8 Co-operating on a community project

Your Life 5/Year 11

Lesson 2 *Your Life 5*, pages 48–49
Citizenship 2.3a, 2.3b, 2.3c, 2.3d, 2.3e, 3h, 4c, 4d, 4e, 4f; Economic wellbeing and financial capability 3a; Personal wellbeing 4a

Aim: To explore how to choose, get involved in and complete a community volunteer project.

Preparation

Make a copy of copymaster 22 (Running a community voluntary project) for each student.

Starter

Ask the students if there is anything they would choose as a voluntary project to work on to help their local area, and why. Draw up a list of projects.

Suggested activities

- Read 'Meeting the needs of the local community' and 'Getting involved'. Ask the students in pairs to study the list of voluntary projects carried out by schools elsewhere, and to decide which one would most benefit their local area, and why.

- Study 'Resources needed'. In groups, students pick a project from those suggested in the starter activity, and decide what resources they would need to make the project successful. Compare the ideas as a class.

- Examine 'Planning a voluntary project' and the case study (page 49). In groups, students either decide on a project or draft a questionnaire to survey what local people see as the community's needs before deciding on a project. They then decide what the aim of their project is and how the project could be broken down into manageable stages with a clear timetable.

Plenary

Emphasise the importance of developing a project in manageable stages and having a clear timetable.

Extension activities

- Give out copies of Copymaster 22 and invite the students, in groups,to draw up a plan for a community voluntary project. Then ask them in turn to present their ideas to the rest of the class.

- Students could research what resources are available from the local council, charities, the school, and local businesses. They could then compile a report for use when voluntary projects are planned in future.

- Pick one project as a class project, to be completed over a term. Ask the students to keep a diary, so that progress on the project can be recorded.

- Organise a role-play afternoon, in which students have to choose, plan, and execute a project. Remember to include a few problems and dilemmas for them to consider.

22 Running a community voluntary project

 **In groups**

Look at the following 10 stages necessary for managing a successful community project. Pick a project and plan out stages 1–6.

Stage 1 – Identifying the needs of the local community:

    a) walk around the area to see what needs doing, OR

    b) conduct a survey of people's opinions to see what needs to be done.

Stage 2 – Choose the project you are going to work on.

Stage 3 – Check that you have the resources you need to carry out your project:

    a) human resources

    b) financial resources

    c) raw materials.

Stage 4 – Decide how you will break your project into manageable stages:

    a) Who will do what?

    b) Who will manage the entire project to make sure it stays on track?

    c) Who will help out when people run into problems or difficulties?

Stage 5 – Decide how you will measure the success of your project.

Stage 6 – Develop a clear timetable for completing your project.

Stage 7 – Get started!

Stage 8 – Review the progress of your project at regular intervals. Make notes on what is going well, and where you are having problems as you overcome them.

Stage 9 – Completion of the project.

Stage 10 – Review how the project went after it has finished. Write up a report on how your project went, using the notes from stage 8.

Extension activity

Pick a project that has been recently completed. Talk to the people involved, to see how they tackled the project. What did they learn? What would they have done differently?

UNIT 9 Developing your own values

> **Aim:** To consider different opinions on social and moral issues, and to explore your own views and opinions.

Preparation

Make a copy of copymaster 23 (What do you think about …?) for each student; gather a selection of recent news headlines from newspapers.

Starter

Write headings for two lists on the board: 'Liberal/permissive views' and 'Conservative/ traditional views'. Brainstorm any views on any subjects (they don't have to be held by the students) and ask the students under which column each view should go. Give one or two examples to start them off, e.g. "There should be stricter penalties for drug dealing". This activity gets students thinking in very general terms about the kinds of issues there are and how to categorise them.

Suggested activities

- Ask pairs of students to read the two articles 'Teenagers react against "anything goes" society' and 'Katie believes in God and marriage. Her mother doesn't', and to list the issues as bullet points. There is no need to discuss the issues at this stage. Lower ability students should focus on just one article.

- Pairs join to form small groups, and discuss what they have learnt. The questions given act as the focus of their discussion. A spokesperson from each group then reports their views in a class discussion.

- Alternatively, individual students could be given copies of copymaster 23, which asks them to rank their views on a series of the issues mentioned. This can be used in pairs or groups as a basis for further discussion.

Plenary

Ask students to write a) if they now have a clearer idea about what kind of values they hold, and b) if they have changed any of their views as a result of this lesson. Ask three or four students to share and explain what they have written.

Extension activities

- Students attempt the 'Research' activity, designing a questionnaire to determine the views of different generations on a series of the issues discussed. Alternatively, the class could work together designing a single questionnaire, so that the results of all the students' individual questionnaires can be collated and compared in a future lesson.

- Bring in some recent news headlines from a series of newspapers. Students, in pairs, choose a headline and research the issue further, using newspapers and the Internet. They analyse the issue, stating the main views held, and then add a short statement about their own views.

23 What do you think about ...?

Think carefully about the questions below, and mark how strongly you feel about each issue by circling one of the numbers on the right. (1 = strongly disagree, 3 = don't know/don't mind, 5 = strongly agree)

❶ It is a woman's right to have an abortion.

    1   2   3   4   5

❷ ID cards should be introduced to help prevent terrorist attacks.

    1   2   3   4   5

❸ Couples should marry before they have children.

    1   2   3   4   5

❹ Cannabis should be legalised.

    1   2   3   4   5

❺ I am proud to be British.

    1   2   3   4   5

❻ The Monarchy should be abolished.

    1   2   3   4   5

❼ Britain should be a positive member of the European Union.

    1   2   3   4   5

❽ There should be tougher penalties to discourage underage sex.

    1   2   3   4   5

❾ The death penalty should be brought back for certain crimes.

    1   2   3   4   5

❿ Teenage drinking has got out of hand.

    1   2   3   4   5

UNIT 9 Developing your own values

Aim: To examine two social and moral dilemmas, and explore your own views and opinions.

Preparation

Make a copy of copymaster 24 (What do you think about human cloning?) for each student.

Starter

Explain the meaning of the term 'euthanasia'. Ask students to read the article 'Assisted suicide' and discuss the issue in pairs or small groups, having first listed the key points in the article. Then hold a class discussion of their views on whether the law should be changed.

Suggested activities

- Students read the article 'The Pros and Cons of Human Cloning' and list the key points and the main points of view. Ensure that students understand the difference between therapeutic cloning (the use of material from human embryos to research and cure diseases) and reproductive cloning (creating human clones for reproduction). Students then discuss the questions in small groups and prepare a presentation on human cloning. (NB In August 2004 Britain granted the first licence to clone human embryos to a group of scientists hoping to find cures for diseases including diabetes and Alzheimer's.)

- After reading 'The Pros and Cons of Human Cloning' students can use copymaster 24 to help clarify their own views before contributing to the discussion. Note that the questionnaire focuses on the pros and cons of reproductive cloning, rather than therapeutic cloning, although some issues relate to both.

Plenary

Ask groups to present their presentations on human cloning.

Extension activities

- Organise a debate on human cloning: 'This house believes that all forms of human cloning should be banned'.

- Students write their response to Alexander Chancellor's statement about assisted suicide (see 'In groups' page 52)

Further resources

More arguments for a change in the law on assisted suicide can be found at www.dignityindying.org.uk

More facts and arguments about human cloning are available at www.abpischools.org.uk

What do you think about human cloning?

Discuss each statement with a partner and put a tick in the box that represents your own view.
(Note that this questionnaire relates mainly to reproductive cloning.)

	Yes, definitely	Yes, I think so	I don't know	No, I don't think so	Definitely not
1 Cloning is wrong because it involves murdering embryos.	☐	☐	☐	☐	☐
2 It lets parents do the best for their children.	☐	☐	☐	☐	☐
3 It is playing God.	☐	☐	☐	☐	☐
4 Cloning is going to happen anyway – you can't stand in the way of progress.	☐	☐	☐	☐	☐
5 It reduces a person's uniqueness and individuality.	☐	☐	☐	☐	☐
6 It would help infertile people, or those who have lost a child.	☐	☐	☐	☐	☐
7 Cloning could be misused to create a master race – or a race of slaves.	☐	☐	☐	☐	☐
8 People should be allowed to reproduce in the way they choose.	☐	☐	☐	☐	☐
9 Cloning does not respect human dignity.	☐	☐	☐	☐	☐
10 You shouldn't ban anything – including cloning – if it doesn't hurt anyone.	☐	☐	☐	☐	☐

Now write a paragraph explaining your own views on human cloning. You need to say whether your views relate to reproductive cloning, therapeutic cloning, or both.

_____

_____

_____

_____

_____

_____

UNIT 10 Managing your time and studies

Aim: To improve your study skills, especially when revising for exams.

Preparation

Make a copy of copymaster 25 (How not to study) for each pair.

Starter

Get students in groups to discuss their feelings and approaches to revision. Do they have any mental or practical strategies that help them? Or are they at sea when it comes to revision? Get a spokesperson to report back to the class with a summary of what has been expressed.

Suggested activities

- Pairs read the article 'Planning ahead' and discuss each other's study planners in the light of the advice given.

- Pairs or small groups read the article 'Learn actively' and discuss the differences between passive revision and active revision (see page 55). Each group should come up with three key points to feed back to a whole class discussion.

- Give pairs copymaster 25. The students discuss the article and prepare a rewritten version giving 'straight' advice.

Plenary

Ask students to read out their rewritten versions, 'How to study effectively'. Ask for class feedback.

Extension activities

Students in groups role-play a radio phone-in on study skills and coping with exams. Groups prepare various questions and each plans an answer. After completing the role-play, the rest of the class becomes the studio audience and can ask the panel questions.

Further resources

More advice on revision and skills can be found at
www.bbc.co.uk/schools/studentlife/revisionandskills/

How **NOT** to study

Do you want to make the **worst use** of your time when you get down to work? *Nigel Roonie* has some advice...

✪ **Don't get into a study routine.** If you find you are developing a routine, for example getting down to work at a particular time in the evening, or as soon as you get home from school, then cut it out. Routines only make it easier to start work, as they get you into the habit of studying at a particular time. So make sure you are as haphazard as possible in your working habits.

✪ **Never prioritise.** Don't think about which pieces of work need to be done first, or list them in order of priority. That will help you plan your time really well. Instead, simply sit down to do 'a couple of hours' work' – you'll be amazed at how the time just whizzes by without you achieving what you really need to do.

✪ **Make your studying really dull.** On no account should you build variety into your work. If you find that you are doing different things, such as reading, writing, thinking and research, and studying different subjects in a session, that's bad news. You will be able to concentrate for longer periods and get more done.

✪ **Work non-stop.** Regular breaks actually increase your output of work because you return to work refreshed and with your concentration levels high. So cut them out. If, however, you don't lift your nose from your desk for a good three hours or so, you'll be able to work really ineffectively. You may even achieve your goal of going into a complete daze and falling asleep.

✪ **Make each task impossibly big.** Resist the temptation to break down your work into small manageable tasks. Keep it big – preferably mountainous – and it will wear you out in body, mind and spirit. And never tick off each task as you complete it. It is far better not to have any idea of how much studying you are doing, and what there is left to do. Ticking off tasks can give you a horrible sense of achievement.

✪ **Seek out distractions and interruptions.** Study in a place where there are lots of distractions, such as people talking or watching TV. The bus journey home is a good one. If there's a phone call, don't say that you are busy and will ring them back later – it's a good opportunity to waste half an hour and get out of your train of thought.

✪ **Be disorganised.** It's an excellent waste of time to start a piece of work only to find that you've left your notes behind, or that you haven't got a vital book, journal or piece of equipment. Make sure you leave all your resources at home (if you're at school) or at school (if you're at home). Being organised is the kiss of death to someone who really wants to study inefficiently.

✪ **Finally, AVOID STARTING.** There are lots of ways you can do this, such as getting distracted onto an unimportant task, or counting the number of minutes you have in which to study. Daydreaming is a no brainer. Your work won't go away, and your stress and guilt will increase. Anything to prevent you actually getting down to your studies is worth trying.

Working in pairs, read the above article. What is the real message that Nigel Roonie is trying to get across? Summarise each of his points in a single sentence, and turn them into a positive list. Call your list: 'How to study effectively'.

UNIT 10 Managing your time and studies

Aim: To explore strategies to use when preparing for and taking exams.

Preparation

Make a copy of copymaster 26 (Answer the question!) for each student.

Starter

Put students in groups to discuss how they feel as they approach an exam. Do they have any mental or practical strategies that help them? Do they know what the physical and mental signs of stress are? Invite a spokesperson to report back to the class with a summary of the group's range of feelings.

Suggested activities

- Groups read the article 'Beat pre-exam stress' and share any other stress-busting techniques that they may have.

- Pairs read and discuss the articles 'Exams – your strategy for success' and 'Exam survival'. They should draw up a list of the six most useful pieces of advice from both the articles and share their lists in a whole class discussion.

- Ask students to write an answer to Gus (see 'For your file' page 57).

Plenary

Ask students to read out their responses to Gus, and get the class to comment.

Extension activity

Students read 'Answer the question!' in pairs and answer the questions beneath the article. Give students copymaster 26, which asks them to match ten exam question terms with their correct meanings. The answers are: 1D, 2H, 3F, 4A, 5G, 6J, 7I, 8B, 9E, 10C.

Further resources

Further help with exam stress can be found on these websites: www.examaid.co.uk, www.childline.org.uk/Examstress.asp, and www.pupiline.net

26 Answer the question!

The precise instruction word that an exam question uses will tell you what kind of answer the examiner is expecting.

Think about each of the exam terms on the left. What is the instruction asking you to do? Draw a line to connect each term with one of the descriptions on the right. One has been done to start you off.

❶ Discuss, e.g. Discuss the value of weight training to footballers.

❷ Illustrate, e.g. Illustrate how you might gather information about the rainfall.

❸ Define, e.g. Define the term 'metaphor'.

❹ Comment on, e.g. Comment on the arguments for and against abortion.

❺ Evaluate, e.g. Evaluate the practical work you have completed.

❻ Prove, e.g. Prove that the triangle has a right angle by using Pythagoras' theorem.

❼ Trace, e.g. Trace the course of the Second World War in the Far East.

❽ Summarise, e.g. Summarise Hitler's foreign policy before the Second World War.

❾ Compare, e.g. Compare the way in which each poem engages the reader.

❿ Analyse, e.g. Analyse the results of your survey.

A Give your own opinion on something.

B Mention the key points of a subject.

C Make a careful and thorough investigation of all aspects of a subject.

D Look at the arguments on both sides and come to your own opinion about the subject.

E Look at the similarities and differences between two things.

F Give a clear meaning of something.

G Write about the strengths and weaknesses of a subject.

H Explain by giving examples.

I Give an account of the development of something.

J Establish the truth of a statement through a chain of reasoning.

UNIT 11 Marriage and commitment

Your Life 5/Year 11

Lesson 1 *Your Life 5*, pages 58–59
Personal wellbeing 3f

Aim: To discuss attitudes to marriage and long-term commitment, and explore their implications.

Preparation

Make a copy of copymaster 27 ('More than just a piece of paper') for each student.

Starter

Invite groups to discuss the question 'Why marry?', focusing on the reasons given in the quotations by the young people, and feed back to a whole class discussion.

Suggested activities

- Students read the article 'Attitudes to marriage and cohabitation' and discuss their view on cohabitation as an alternative to marriage. Copymaster 27 presents two extended viewpoints on the issue, with some focusing questions to help develop the debate.
- Students read the article 'New rights for unmarried fathers' and discuss the questions in groups.
- Pairs analyse the statistics about marriage and divorce and answer the questions.
- Students write a reply to Jill Curtis's statement (see 'For your file' page 59).

Plenary

Ask students to write down the three most important facts they have learned during this lesson. Ask some students to share their lists and discuss as a class.

Extension activities

Students use the Internet to research the rights which cohabiting couples have.

Further resources

- www.oneplusone.org.uk, the relationship and marriage research organisation, has information, statistics and a huge media archive.
- The Institute for the Study of Civil Society has produced a free pamphlet 'Does marriage matter?' and a factsheet and lesson notes on cohabitation, which are available from www.civitas.org.uk

 **More than just a piece of paper**

Traditionally, marriage has had a special status in British law and society. Marriage developed as a way to provide stability for families and for all of society. Marriage is a declaration of commitment which has public as well as private consequences. It is an institution that offers benefits not only to the couples themselves but to society as a whole.

When people marry, they commit themselves not only to being emotional and sexual partners, but also to taking care of each other – for richer or for poorer, in sickness and in health. They promise to stick by each other through the ups and downs that occur in everyone's lives. This promise and the trust it builds encourage partners to make sacrifices for the good of the family.

Traditionally, British government and society have supported the institution of marriage by giving it certain privileges and responsibilities, and by enforcing consequences for breaking marriage vows.

Civitas

What is important in a relationship is the level of commitment of the two people, not whether they have performed a ceremony called 'marriage' or signed a piece of paper. There are countless examples of unmarried couples who are just as committed and loving and responsible as married couples. And you only have to look at the high divorce rate to see that marriage on its own is not enough to keep a relationship – and a family – together.

Yes – people who cohabit have fewer rights than married couples. But the way to deal with that is to campaign for the law to be changed, not sell out to a system that you don't believe in. As Mae West said, 'Marriage is an institution, and who wants to live in an institution?'

Let's face it, marriage is a relic from a time when everyone was religious. It's now time for us to grow up and make commitments to each other in private, rather than in front of a God we don't believe in, or a magistrate who doesn't know us.

Paula, Reading

In groups

Read the two statements on marriage above. The first is by the organisation Civitas, which believes marriage is important for stable families and a stable society. The second is a contribution to an online forum on relationship issues. Now discuss these questions:

1 How important is marriage as a statement of commitment?

2 Is marriage good for the family, and for society, as Civitas believes?

3 Should the government continue to support marriage by giving married couples more rights than cohabiting couples?

4 Is the form that a relationship takes a purely private matter, as Paula believes?

UNIT 11 Marriage and commitment

Lesson 2 *Your Life 5*, pages 60–61
Personal wellbeing 1.4a, 3f

Aim: To explore what it means to make a long-term relationship work.

Preparation

Make a copy of copymaster 28 (To have and to hold…) for each pair.

Starter

Brainstorm key words and ideas that contribute to making a long-term relationship work. Write these words on the board.

Suggested activities

- Students read the article 'Be a perfect partner' in pairs and discuss what it says. Then ask them to draw up a list of key skills, also using the Starter activity to inform their thinking.

- Students read 'The wedding planners' in small groups and discuss what they learn, focusing on the specific questions asked. Ask a spokesperson from each group to report back their ideas in a class discussion. (It is important to make a clear distinction between arranged marriages that are consensual and 'forced marriages' that are arranged without the consent of the individuals involved. These are against the law in this country.)

- Ask students to write a personal statement about arranged marriages.

Plenary

On the basis of the work done this lesson, students vote for the three most important qualities required for maintaining a long-term relationship. Ask for a show of hands as you read out each word on the board from the starter activity and count the votes.

Extension activities

- Give pairs of students copymaster 28. They complete the activity, then join up with another pair and share what they have written.

- Explain that the vows made in a civil (non-religious) marriage ceremony are very different from those made at a religious ceremony. Often the couple only declare that they 'know of no legal impediment' to their marrying each other. Do the students think this would make a difference to a couple's commitment to each other in marriage? Which set of vows – religious or civil – are more appropriate for a modern marriage? Then, in groups or as a class, invite students to share their views.

To have and to hold...

What does marriage mean? Relationship therapist Paula Hall gets you thinking …

When you are first thinking about marriage, you are bound to be caught up in the romance and glamour of it all. But marriage is for life – not just for Christmas. What does the commitment of marriage really mean?

In the Church of England marriage service, the bride and groom make solemn promises to each other. These are on the left, below. Think about each one in turn, focusing on the questions on the right. Write down a few notes on your thoughts.

To have and to hold...

What does it actually mean to be a couple?
How much control and how much independence would you want?

_____

_____

From this day forward...

How do you feel about commitment?
Is marriage 'for ever' in your view?

_____

_____

For better for worse...

How should couples manage their differences?
Will there always be romance and intimacy? If not, what then?

_____

_____

For richer for poorer...

What does marriage mean financially?
Should a couple's attitudes towards employment change?

_____

_____

In sickness and in health...

How should couples support each other during ill health?
What about in times of sadness and difficulty?

_____

_____

To love and to cherish...

How should love be shown in a marriage?
How important should sex be in a relationship?

_____

_____

Source: www.bbc.co.uk

UNIT 12 Parenthood and parenting

Your Life 5/Year 11

Lesson 1 *Your Life 5*, pages 62–63
Personal wellbeing 3d, 3g, 3h

> **Aim:** To explore the effect that becoming a parent has on a person's life, particularly in relation to teenage pregnancy.

Preparation

Make a copy of copymaster 29 (When are women becoming mothers?) for each pair of students.

Starter

Ask students in pairs to make lists of the positive and negative aspects of starting a family, under the headings 'The pleasures' and 'The problems'. Pairs then join up and share what they have written. A spokesperson reports back the group's ideas to the class.

Suggested activities

- Read 'Big Daddy' with the class. Get pairs to list the changes that early parenthood made to Darren and Natalie's lives, e.g. restricting their social life, exhaustion, pressure on their relationship, interference with their careers. Ask them to report back to the class, bringing out the positive elements in the discussion too. Allow a free discussion in the whole class on whether their age and non-marital status made their situation more difficult. Ask the class what would have happened if Natalie had got pregnant at 15 or 16.

- Prompt pairs to discuss the reasons given by teenage girls for having a baby, and to make and then share notes on two of the replies.

- Small groups discuss the opposed views on sex education and report back their responses to the class. Check that students understand what the two main views are actually saying before they start their discussion.

Plenary

Ask students to write down one key fact or feeling that they have taken away from this lesson. Ask volunteers to share theirs and explain why it is important for them.

Extension activities

Give pairs Copymaster 29 and invite them to discuss what they learn from the statistics about when women become mothers. Various reasons could be presented for why women are having children later, including the increase in second relationships and the desire to start a career first (along with the greater willingness among employers to allow breaks in a career).

Then ask them to discuss why they think the UK has such a high rate of births to teenage mothers. They can use the Internet to research what steps the government is taking to try to reduce the rate, before discussing in groups what measures they think would be most effective.

29 When are women becoming mothers?

Average age of mother at childbirth (mean age in years) in England and Wales

Year	1971	1981	1991	2000
All births				
All live births	26.2	26.8	27.7	29.1
All first births	–	–	25.7	27.1
Births inside marriage				
All births inside marriage	26.4	27.3	28.9	30.8
First births inside marriage	24.0	25.4	27.5	29.6
Births outside marriage				
All births outside marriage	23.8	23.5	24.8	26.5

Source: Office for National Statistics

Despite the high rate of teenage pregnancies in the UK, there is an overall trend towards later childbearing. In England and Wales the average age of mothers at childbirth increased by three years between 1971 and 2000.

Births outside marriage tend to take place at a younger age than those inside marriage. In 2000 women giving birth outside marriage were more than four years younger than their married counterparts.

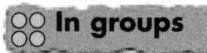 **In groups**

Why do you think there is a trend towards later childbearing?
List all the reasons you can suggest to explain the trend, then
share your views in a class discussion.

Teenage birth rates

The UK has the highest teenage birth and abortion rates in Western Europe. Rates of teenage births are seven times higher than those in the Netherlands, double those in France and more than twice those in Germany.

However, in 2008, the rate of births teenage mothers in the UK was actually at its lowest level since the mid 1950s.

Why are rates so high in the UK?

According to Brook, which provides young people with advice on sexual health, there are three main reasons why other countries have lower teenage pregnancy rates:

- Good comprehensive sex and relationship education.
- Better access to young people-friendly services.
- A more open attitude to sex.

Teenagers themselves say the sex education they receive in the UK is 'too late, too little and too biological.'

In groups

What do you think are the reasons why teenage pregnancy rates are
so high in the UK?

Use the Internet to research what the government is doing in order
to try to reduce the number of teenage pregnancies. Which measures
do you think are most likely to be effective? Suggest any other
measures you think might be effective.

UNIT 12 Parenthood and parenting

Your Life 5/Year 11

Lesson 2 *Your Life 5*, pages 64–65
Personal wellbeing 3d, 3g, 3h

Aim: To explore the roles and responsibilities of parents.

Preparation

Make a copy of copymaster 30 (How to avoid smacking). Have available images of children at different stages of development.

Starter

Show images of children at different stages of development, e.g. baby, toddler, primary school age, teenager, and brainstorm with the class what their needs are. Write these words on the board. As an overview at the end, consider what needs, if any, seem to be present across all age ranges.

Suggested activities

- Pairs or small groups read 'Being a parent' and 'How to be … a good enough parent' and discuss the questions. Split each group up so that one part is thinking about the children's needs (this reinforces and deepens the work done in the Starter) and one is thinking of the adults' skills and qualities, then bring them back together and discuss. Ask one or two groups to present their findings and get other groups to comment.

- Ask the class if this activity has made them see parenting in a different light. Do the students have the skills and qualities needed to be parents?

- Individuals write a paragraph explaining why they should aim to be merely 'good enough parents'. Ask a few students to read out their paragraphs and get the class to comment.

- Pairs read and discuss 'What is a father?' and 'What is a mother?' Be aware of the feelings this may stir up in students who are suffering from family difficulties or bereavement.

Plenary

Ask students to jot down three key things that children need, and three key qualities that parents need to show, and get individuals to read out their lists.

Extension activities

- When discussing the qualities and skills of parents, students could further differentiate between mothers and fathers. What roles does each gender have at each of the different stages?

- Hand out copymaster 30 to individuals. Read through the article with the class, and then ask groups to discuss the questions. Ask students if they think the government should leave the smacking law as it is (which allows 'reasonable chastisement' – smacking for a good purpose); or reform it (as proposed by the House of Lords, July 2004) to make only a 'minor slap' legal; or ban smacking completely.

Further resources

Useful materials can be found at the website of the National Family and Parenting Institute www.nfpi.org.uk, and at www.parentlineplus.org.uk, www.bbc.co.uk/parenting, and www.fathersdirect.com

30 How to avoid smacking

Most parents don't think hitting children is right, yet in times of stress, anger or frustration find themselves lashing out. But many feel guilty afterwards and want to find better ways of handling difficult behaviour.

Positive parenting and positive discipline

The following techniques work with any child, regardless of temperament, background, culture or tradition. They build on a childish natural wish to please you, and will ensure a happier child and less stressed parents.

- **Babies:** behave as they do to get their needs met. When they cry or don't sleep, they're not doing this to be 'naughty' or to wind you up. 'Baby-proof' your home so your baby can enjoy challenges without battles. Use distraction with older babies, e.g. point out something happening out of the window when they head for the video, or swap your keys for a toy if they try to grab them.

- **Toddlers:** Most naughty behaviour in toddlers is part of normal development. All toddlers test limits, try to be independent, get into everything, get mad and have tantrums. Praise good behaviour that you want to encourage. If you ignore behaviour you don't like, it is less likely to be repeated. Keep 'No' to a minimum. Acknowledge your child's feelings, e.g. "I know you're cross". Remain calm and reasonable yourself.

- **School-age children:** Being 'cheeky' or disobedient may show a natural desire in your child to assert independence and show he or she has a mind of their own. Listen to your child about friends, their day, and any worries that may make behaviour worse. Keep criticisms to a minimum and only criticise a behaviour, not your child. A 'broken record' approach can work well, calmly repeating what you expect your child to do.

- **Teenagers:** It is normal for young people to challenge you more. Their friends start to exert a greater influence and they just can't go along with everything parents want. Don't take bad behaviour personally. Keep communicating. Try not to use threats or orders. Talk and negotiate solutions when there is a disagreement.

Why smacking is never a good idea

Parents may believe there are occasions when only a smack will do. For example, when your child is really cheeky and disobedient; when your toddler runs into the road; when one of your children bites a playmate. It can be tempting to think a smack sorts out these incidents quickly, but it does nothing to teach your child how you want him or her to behave. Instead, it

- ○ gives a bad example of how to handle strong emotions
- ○ may lead children to hit or bully others
- ○ may make them lie, or hide feelings to avoid smacking
- ○ can make defiant, uncooperative behaviour worse, so discipline gets even harder
- ○ can make children feel resentful and angry, which can spoil family relationships if it goes on for a long time.

Source: www.nspcc.org.uk

⫴ In groups

Read the article above and discuss what you learn. Is 'positive disciplining' a better way of dealing with difficult behaviour than smacking? Which do you think are the best pieces of advice on disciplining children without resorting to smacking?

Draw up a list of 'Top Ten ways to be a great parent without smacking', and present it to the class.

UNIT 13 Challenging offensive behaviour

Your Life 5/Year 11

Lesson 1 *Your Life 5*, pages 66–67
Personal wellbeing 1.5a, 1.5b, 2.1a, 2.3d, 3a, 3j, 4d; Citizenship 2.1a, 4a

> **Aim:** To examine what sexism and sexual harassment are, and to explore how to challenge them.

Preparation

Make a copy of copymaster 31 (Pornography) for each student.

Starter

Ask the students what they understand by the term 'sexism'? before reading 'What is sexism?' Ask the students in groups to think about examples of sexism that they have encountered, to make a list of sexist attitudes and to compare their lists in a class discussion.

Suggested activities

- Ask the students: Why do you think sexism is damaging? Then invite them to read 'Why is sexism damaging?' Ask groups to study the statements, and decide which ones they agree with, and why.

- Study 'Sexual harassment'. In groups, students then decide which of the examples are sexual harassment. The answers are: wolf whistling, putting your arm around someone, saying somebody looks nice repeatedly, and refusing to take 'No' for an answer. Point out that asking somebody out could be sexual harassment – it depends on how it is done (e.g. asking someone out publicly in front of a group of people could be sexual harassment). Discuss other types of behaviour that they suggest are examples of sexual harassment.

- Read the article 'Case study: street harassment'. In groups, ask students what they learn about men shouting at women. Why do men do this? Do they agree that when a man shouts at a woman it is an act of hostility? How do they think this makes the woman feel? Then get them to design a poster as part of a campaign against sexual harassment.

- Introduce the question of sexism in the workplace. Prompt groups to discuss what they should do in each of the work situations (see 'In groups' page 67), and then to share their views in a class discussion.

Plenary

Recap on the types of behaviour that they consider to be sexual harassment. Talk about ways of dealing with sexual harassment assertively and what you should do if the harassment persists.

Extension activities

- Ask students to study Copymaster 31 and invite them to share their views on pornography in a class discussion

- Ask individuals or pairs to research any examples of sexism and sexual harassment, such as prominent court cases, in which a woman has sued for sexual harassment or constructive dismissal.

- Ask students to contact a local trade union to invite someone to come and give a talk on how they are fighting sexual harassment in the workplace.

31 Pornography

Pornography is the publication of sexually explicit photographs and films. Usually these are of women, designed to be desirable to men. Pornography comes in two forms: soft porn, which often involves topless girls such as on page 3 of some newspapers, magazines and calendars; hard porn involves detailed naked pictures or videos of people involved in sex acts.

Many people argue that pornography is sexist, because it promotes women as sex objects, to be used and discarded. The Campaign Against Pornography aims to have pornography banned, as it 'degrades, damages, and disadvantages women'. It aims to do this by publishing the ways women are damaged by pornography, mobilising support, and by getting women to write to their MPs to have the law changed.

" Pornography distorts the relationships between men and women. And this can lead to men using them, knocking them about, an ultimately, raping them. **"**
Clare Short MP, who tried to have pornography banned in 1998

" Pornography is designed to turn you on. A page 3 photograph is harmless, and it's a good way to earn some money. Why shouldn't I be allowed to be photographed if I want to pose topless? **"**
Sally, page 3 girl

" Soft porn is OK. But hardcore porn should be banned. It's one thing to have a photo of a page 3 girl on a calendar, it's another thing to have her being used as a sex object by a man in a video. **"**
Melanie, film critic

" We've always had our pin-ups. David Beckham and Wayne Rooney feature in many posters in teenage girls bedrooms. So why shouldn't newspapers be allowed to published photos of topless women? Both are examples of sex symbols. **"**
Tom, footballer.

" All pornography should be banned. Any photos, which portray anyone as a sex object, are harmful, to both women and men. All people are real people with feelings. Society should stop exploiting young women, and start providing them with better job opportunities outside of the sex industry. **"**
Sasha, feminist

 **In groups**

Discuss the different opinions of pornography. Which ones do you agree with? Why? Give reasons for your views.

UNIT 13 Challenging offensive behaviour

Your Life 5/Year 11

Lesson 2 *Your Life 5*, pages 68–69
Personal wellbeing 1.5a, 1.5b, 2.1a, 2.3d, 3a, 3j, 4d

Aim: To understand what homosexuality and homophobia are, and to be aware of the different attitudes towards homosexuality that exist.

Preparation

Make copies of copymaster 32 (Homosexuality) for each student.

Starter

This topic needs sensitive handling. Be aware that there may be teenagers who are homosexual in the group, so introduce the topic by setting guidelines for the discussion. Explain that under no circumstances will personal remarks be tolerated. Then go on to explain what the terms 'homosexual', 'gay', 'lesbian', 'bi-sexual' and 'heterosexual' mean.

Suggested activities

- Read 'What is homosexuality?' Ask the students in groups to discuss what they have found out about the different myths surrounding homosexuality, and whether they can think of any other myths. Draw their thoughts together in a class discussion.

- Study 'How society discriminates against homosexuals'. Ask: Do you think homosexuals are discriminated against in the UK?

- Look at 'Different attitudes towards homosexuality'. In groups, students discuss which statements they agree with, and why.

- Read 'Why is homophobia damaging?' In groups, students discuss where homophobia comes from, why it is damaging, and what to do to challenge homophobic behaviour in each of the situations (see 'In groups' page 69).

Plenary

Sum up what the students have learnt from the lesson about what homophobia is, where it comes from and the damage and hurt it causes. Ask them to imagine they have to e-mail a letter to a local newspaper condemning homophobic behaviour. What points would they make in their letter?

Extension activities

- Ask students to read and discuss the article on homophobic bullying on Copymaster 32, then to design a poster against homophobia for display in the school.

- Invite groups to imagine they are members of the government in a new state. Discuss what laws they would introduce in order to ensure fair treatment for homosexuals in their society. Then share their ideas in a class discussion.

- Ask the students to research groups like Stonewall (www.stonewall.org.uk) and OutRage! (www.outraged.org.uk), then to write up a report on what they have learnt, and present it to the class.

Further resources

Details of an ATL briefing paper on challenging homophobia and sexist bullying can be found at www.atl.org.uk

www.eachaction.org.uk, the website of Educational Action Challenging Homophobia has useful materials.

Holly Anderson was coming out of the girls' toilet when the shouting began, as it always did. "You dirty lesbian! We don't want you in this school!" But this time, a girl punched Holly and her lip began to bleed. After suffering almost three years of bullying for being gay, Holly, now 16, told her school.

Some 85% of lesbian and gay children say they've been bullied at school, from being stared at to being called names; 68% have been hit or kicked. Even though most schools have an anti-bullying policy, only 6% refer specifically to homophobic bullying.

Holly tried to ignore and put up with the rumours and teasing for years before telling a member of staff. "I didn't really feel comfortable reporting it, until I was punched in the face," she says. "I didn't really want anyone else involved in my personal life. I didn't want to be judged by my teachers."

Homophobic taunts may be directed at anyone, gay or not. Laura Dunstan, an educational psychologist, believes teachers don't take the taunts seriously. "They say, 'The boy isn't gay – so the others don't really mean it.'" But that's not the point. There could be a child next to them who is gay. It's offensive language. It's unacceptable.

The effect can be profound. Homophobic bullying leads to high levels of absenteeism and truancy among gay and lesbian pupils. They are also far more likely to leave school at 16 than their straight counterparts, however good their GCSE grades. Holly says: "I didn't want to be in school. I'd do anything to get out. I pretended to be ill so I could stay at home." After briefly going to college, Holly has dropped out of education. "I don't want to go through the whole coming out thing again." She now works as a sales assistant in a clothing store.

HOMOPHOBIC BULLYING

Source: *Education Guardian*

In groups

1 Discuss what you learn from Holly's story about what it feels like to be the victim of homophobic bullying.

2 Do you think teachers take homophobic taunts seriously enough?

3 Look at your school's anti-bullying policy. Does it specifically mention homophobic bullying? If it doesn't, draft a paragraph stating how homophobic bullying should be dealt with whenever it occurs in your school.

4 Design a poster against homophobia, which could be displayed in your school. What will your main message be?

Advice and support

The freephone helpline for young people affected by homophobia is 0808 1000 143 and www.eachaction.org.uk

UNIT 14 Managing stress and dealing with depression

Your Life 5/Year 11

Lesson 1 *Your Life 5*, pages 70–71
Personal wellbeing 1.2b, 2.1d, 3c

> **Aim:** To understand what stress is and what causes it and to explore ways of dealing with stress.

Preparation

Make a copy of copymaster 33 (What causes teenage stress?) for each student.

Starter

Ask the class: What is stress? Collect their ideas on the board. Explain that it's natural to feel stress at times, and that it is important to learn how to handle stress.

Suggested activities

- Read 'What is stress?' and discuss with the class what Erica Stewart says about why the teenage years are often stressful. Why does she say that a certain amount of stress is good for you?

- Working in groups prompt students to read 'What stresses you out?' Ask them to discuss the different reasons the teenagers give for feeling stressed and to make a list of what they consider to be the top five causes of stress for teenagers. Suggest the students share their views in a class discussion.

- Read 'Signs of stress', 'Dealing with stress' and 'Advice for beating the blues'. Ask pairs to identify the different pieces of advice given in the articles and the reasons for that advice. Then encourage them to draft an e-mail to someone who is feeling stressed, offering advice on what to do to relieve their stress.

Plenary

Ask students to read out their e-mails and summarise what they have learned from the lesson on how best to deal with stress.

Extension activities

Ask individuals to study copymaster 33 and to rank the list of causes according to which they consider to be the most significant. Encourage them to share their views in either a group or class discussion.

33 What causes teenage stress?

○ On your own

Study the list of possible causes of stress. Which do you think are the most significant causes of stress among teenagers? Rank them in order of significance from 1–15, starting with what you think is the most significant. Then form groups and compare your lists.

Conflicts with brothers/sisters

Having to move house and/or school

Arguments with parents

Parents separating or divorcing

Getting into trouble with the law

Money problems

Pressure to do well in exams

Concern about appearance

Concern about sexuality

Feeling lonely and having no friends

Being teased or bullied

Dealing with pressure from friends

Learning how to handle sexual relationships

Splitting up with boyfriend/girlfriend

Choosing a career

UNIT 14 Managing stress and dealing with depression

Your Life 5/Year 11

Lesson 2 *Your Life 5*, pages 72–73
Personal wellbeing 1.2b, 2.1d, 3c

> **Aim:** To explore what depression is and different types of depression and to examine ways of coping with depression.

Preparation

Make a copy of copymaster 34 (Understanding depression) for each student.

Starter

Recap on what stress is and explain that whereas stress can lead to depression, not everyone who suffers stress has depression. Talk about how depression is a mental illness that many people will suffer in their lives, and explain that like a physical illness it can be treated. Then read and discuss 'What is depression?'

Suggested activities

- Read 'Types of depression' and discuss the information given in the article with the class. Then invite groups to do the discussion activity.

- Explain that doctors may treat a person with depression by giving them medication, but there are also things that a depressed person can do to help him or herself. Read 'Coping with depression' and 'Talk to someone', then prompt pairs to discuss the advice given on the page and to decide who they think is the best person to talk to, if you are depressed.

Plenary

Ask pairs to decide on three key things they have learned about depression from the lesson. Get some to report back to the rest of the class and make a list on the board of key facts about depression.

Extension activities

- Ask individuals to complete Copymaster 34, then to discuss their answers in groups, followed by a class discussion.

- Invite individuals or pairs to use the Internet to research further information about depression among young people and how to deal with it. Useful websites include: www.depressionalliance.org and www.youngminds.org.uk

- Invite students to design a poster for people of their own age, giving key information about depression.

 Understanding depression

Study each of these statements and decide whether you agree with it, disagree with it or are not sure. Then compare your answers in a group discussion.

	Agree	Disagree	Not sure
❶ Depression is a very common illness.			
❷ There's no shame in admitting you're depressed. You shouldn't feel embarrassed about it.			
❸ Depression is always triggered by an upsetting or stressful event.			
❹ Depression can be hard to recognise because it affects different people in different ways.			
❺ Everyone feels low at times, but a person with depression has persistent feelings of helplessness and hopelessness.			
❻ Depression is a mental illness that can be treated, and it does not develop into insanity.			
❼ Sharing your thoughts and feelings when you're depressed is much better than bottling them up.			
❽ The best person to talk to if you're depressed is your doctor.			
❾ You can help yourself if you're depressed by eating healthily and taking exercise.			
❿ If a friend is depressed, it's best to leave them alone.			

UNIT 15 Safer sex

Your Life 5/Year 11

Lesson 1 *Your Life 5*, pages 74–75
Personal wellbeing 1.2a, 1.2b, 1.3a, 2.2a, 2.2c, 3d

Aim: To understand what sexually transmitted infections are and how to protect yourself against them.

Preparation

Make a copy of copymaster 35 (Sex diseases soaring) for each group.

Starter

Remind the students that there is no such thing as completely safe sex, which is why people talk about safer sex. Ask them for their definitions of safer sex.

Suggested activities

- Read 'Be smart, be protected'. Discuss with the class what they learn from it about how STIs are caught, how you can avoid catching STIs, how you can tell if you have an STI and what to do if you think you may have one. Discuss Becky's experience (see 'Case study' page 75). Ask the class if she was just unlucky. What does she say she has learned from her experience?

- Read 'Before you do it, talk about it'. Discuss with the class what Erica Stewart says. Ask if they agree with her. Are there any other questions you should ask your partner? Then ask groups to discuss the four statements (see 'In pairs'), before sharing their views in a class discussion.

- Ask pairs to imagine that they have been asked by the Health Protection Agency to design a poster to warn young people about the risks of STIs. Ask them what messages they would want to put across. Encourage them to do a rough design and draft the text for the poster.

Plenary

Invite students to share their ideas for the posters and draw up a list of the main points they would try to put across.

Extension activities

Ask students to read the information on copymaster 35. Groups discuss whether they think 16–19 year olds are too casual in their attitudes towards sex, why they think sex disease cases are soaring and whether screening for STIs should be made available in places other than clinics.

Further resources

Useful articles on sex issues including STIs and safer sex can be found at www.teenissues.co.uk

35 Sex diseases soaring

Health Protection Agency figures show that 121,986 people sought treatment for chlamydia in 2007 compared to less than 49,000 in 1998.

Cases of gonorrhoea now stand at 18,700 annually – a 42% increase since 1998.

Cases of syphilis are rapidly rising after the disease was almost eradicated a few years ago. There were 2,680 cases in 2007, compared to just 139 in 1998.

Chlamydia is a leading cause of pelvic inflammatory disease which can damage the fallopian tubes and leave women infertile. The National Chlamydia Screening Programme, which offers free screening to under 25s, has found that 1 in 10 under 25s, who have been tested, have the infection. Do-it-yourself chlamydia tests are now available in colleges and pharmacists.

Some people blame the increase in STIs partly on 'sex in the sun' reality TV shows which depict promiscuity as the norm. Others say teenage magazines put too much emphasis on sex, which encourages casual sex.

A scheme introduced in six Oxfordshire schools allows girls to request the morning-after pill by text message. Some people think that making the morning-after pill so easily available may cut the number of teenage pregnancies, but lead to an increase in casual sex and the number of cases of STIs.

In groups

Discuss the following. Why do you think sex disease cases are soaring? Is it because too many 16–19 year olds are too casual in their attitudes towards having sex? Are reality 'sex in the sun' TV shows partly to blame? Do teenage magazines put too much emphasis on sex, which encourages promiscuity? Do you think the availability of the morning-after pill has led to an increase in the amount of unsafe sex?

Should screening for STIs be made available in places other than clinics? If so, where should test centres be set up? What are the arguments for and against having test centres in schools?

If you think you have an STI...

- Stop having sex with anyone until you've had a medical check.

- Go to your doctor, a family planning clinic or a sexual health clinic – called a GUM (genito-urinary medicine) clinic. All of these places offer confidential advice, so please don't be worried about anyone finding out.

- If you have got an STI, the doctor will give you treatment to cure it. Tell whoever you had sex with so that they, too, can be treated. (The only STI that cannot be cured is HIV/AIDS see pages 76–77.)

- Avoid high-risk sex activities and unprotected sex in the future.

- Phone Sexwise on 0800 282 930 for advice or check out www.ruthinking.co.uk

UNIT 15 Safer sex

Your Life 5/Year 11

Lesson 2 *Your Life 5*, pages 76–77
Personal wellbeing 1.2a, 1.2b, 1.3a, 2.2a, 2.2c, 3d

> **Aim:** To explore what the facts are about HIV/AIDS and to examine attitudes to AIDS.

Preparation

Make a copy of copymaster 36 (Anxious about AIDS) for each group.

Starter

Explain what HIV and AIDS stand for (see the first paragraph of 'HIV and AIDS – Your questions answered'). Talk about how the AIDS epidemic affects the whole world, and how it is most widespread in the countries of sub-Saharan Africa. It is estimated that nearly 50,000 people in the UK are infected and the number of infections is rising annually.

Suggested activities

- Read the rest of 'HIV/AIDS – Your questions answered' and read 'Myths about HIV infection'. Discuss the information with the class, and then get pairs to draw up a test-yourself quiz consisting of true and false statements about HIV/AIDS. Ask the students to join up with another pair and to do each other's quizzes.

- Read 'Ellen's story'. Discuss what they learn from the article about what life is like for a young person who is HIV positive. Then get groups to imagine they are part of a government body responsible for drawing up a campaign to warn young people of the dangers of unsafe sex, to draft a proposal for such a campaign, then to share their ideas with the rest of the class.

- Study 'People with HIV living longer'. Discuss why HIV is now described as a chronic condition rather than a fatal disease.

- Prompt groups to read and discuss the statements in the section 'Attitudes to AIDS'.

Plenary

Ask the students to share their views of attitudes towards HIV and AIDS in a class discussion.

Extension activities

Ask pairs to study the letters on copymaster 36 and to draft replies to the letters, then to share their replies in a group or class discussion.

Further resources

Avert, an international AIDS charity, has information about HIV, AIDS and safer sex on its website www.avert.org

COPYMASTER

36 Anxious about AIDS

Working in pairs, study these letters, then draft Erica's reply to them.

Dear Erica
A couple of months ago, my boyfriend and I had unprotected sex. Since then we've always used a condom, but I've been worrying about AIDS. My boyfriend tells me not to be silly, he's only had one partner before me. I haven't got any signs or symptoms. How can I be sure he hasn't infected me? Am I right to be worried? – J

Dear Erica
Recently I got a tattoo on my shoulder. My friend was horrified when I told her. She says I could have caught the HIV virus. Is that true? – K

Dear Erica
My boyfriend is pressurising me to experiment when we have sex. I keep putting him off because I think some of the things he's suggesting are too risky. Please tell me what's safe and unsafe. I don't want to risk catching the HIV virus. – L

Dear Erica
My brother's got this friend who's HIV-positive. He often comes round our house for meals and once or twice he's stayed the night. I'm worried about having him around in case one of our family gets infected. – M

UNIT 16 Drugs and drugtaking

Your Life 5/Year 11

Lesson 1 *Your Life 5*, pages 78–79
Personal wellbeing 1.2a, 1.3a, 2.2a, 2.2c, 3d

Aim: To explore the reasons why young people take drugs, to examine the risks and to provide information about ecstasy, ketamine and anabolic steroids.

Preparation

Make a copy of copymaster 37 (What do you know about anabolic steroids?) for each pair.

Starter

Introduce the topic by asking students individually to write down what they see as the risks from taking illegal drugs and how dangerous they think drugtaking is. Share some of their views in a class discussion.

Suggested activities

- Read 'Why do young people take drugs?' Invite groups to discuss their views, then to share them in a class discussion.

- Read 'So what's the deal?' Prompt groups to look again at what they wrote at the start of the lesson, and to add any risks mentioned in the article that they didn't think of. Encourage them to share their views of dealers in a class discussion.

- Discuss how dangerous they think ecstasy is, then read 'Ecstasy factfile'. Ask: Why do people take ecstasy? What are the risks? Invite pairs to draft a reply to Treena's letter (see 'For your file').

- Study 'Ketamine factfile'. Ask groups to discuss which they think is the more dangerous drug – ecstasy or ketamine.

Plenary

Focus on the risks involved in taking ecstasy by getting some of the students to read out their replies to Treena's letter and discussing what they say.

Extension activities

- Give students copymaster 37 and ask pairs to study the information before listing three reasons why people take anabolic steroids.

- Ask students to use the Internet to get further advice and information about different drugs (www.talktofrank.com and www.drugfreeworld.org are useful websites). They could produce their own fact files on different drugs, e.g. 'Ten things you need to know about heroin'.

37 What do you know about anabolic steroids?

Anabolic steroids are synthetic derivatives of the male hormone, testosterone. They are performance-enchancing drugs, which can be taken to build up muscles and strength. Because they give people who take them an unfair advantage, their use in sports is banned and professional sportspeople are regularly tested to check that they have not been taking them.

Some teenagers are tempted to take them in order to develop their bodies, but they can have nasty side effects.

Doctors sometimes prescribe steroids for various medical conditions, and it's not illegal to possess them. But the Misuse of Drugs Act classifies them as Class C drugs and it is an offence to supply them.

Wanting to be stronger

Dear Dr Ann

Are there some drugs I can take to make me stronger without anyone knowing?

Boy, age 15

Dear 'Wanting to be stronger'

The answer to this is NO. People do it all the time and they get caught doing it all the time. The best way to make your muscles stronger is to do regular exercise – running, swimming and other sports will all help. You may see pictures of 'strong men' lifting weights, whose bodies look totally weird. Some of these men and women will have taken anabolic steroids to develop their muscles, but it is against sporting rules to use almost any drugs and take part in competitive sports. Even if you just want to take them to be stronger, they are dangerous. As well as increasing muscle strength, they can damage the liver, make you very moody, increase the risk of cancer, cause acne, make men have breasts, give women hair on their face, make you bald and cause men to have difficulty getting erections…Best stick to exercise and give these drugs a miss.

In groups

Working in pairs, study the information above, then discuss and write at least thee reasons why people take anabolic steroids. What are their effects? Exchange and compare your list with another group's.

UNIT 16 Drugs and drugtaking

Lesson 2 *Your Life 5*, pages 80–81
Personal wellbeing 3d, 4b, 4e

Aim: To discuss the drugs laws and to debate whether they should be changed.

Preparation

Make a copy of copymaster 38 (Drugs and the law: what's your attitude?) for each group.

Starter

Introduce the topic by explaining how the manufacture and supply of drugs for medical use is controlled by the Medicines Act 1968. It divides drugs into three categories. The most restricted drugs can only be obtained on prescription. Explain that the non-medical use of drugs, which are considered to be dangerous, is controlled by the Misuse of Drugs Act 1971.

Suggested activities

- Read 'Drug laws – time for a change?'. Discuss how the laws have been altered recently with the reclassification of cannabis as a Class B instead of a Class C drug. Explain how any proposed changes to the drugs laws in Britain would have an impact on the other member states of the European Union and how any changes would have to be in accordance with EU law.

- Prompt groups to study the results of the Telegraph YouGov survey and to discuss what they learn from it about people's attitudes to the drugs laws and what effect they think changing them would have.

- Invite groups to discuss the drugs laws, why we have them and whether they should be changed, by sharing their views on the opinions expressed in the section 'In my opinion'.

Plenary

Conclude the lesson by getting representatives from the groups to share their views on why they would either keep the drugs laws as they are or make changes to them.

Extension activities

- Ask groups to discuss the views expressed on copymaster 38, and to then share their views in a class discussion.

- Organise a formal debate on the motion: 'This house believes that decriminalising the use of illegal drugs would do more harm than good'.

Further resources

Drugscope is a source of up-to-date information on drugs issues including drugs and the law (www.drugscope.org.uk).

Drugs and the law: what's your attitude?

⣿ In groups

Discuss each of these pairs of viewpoints in turn, then share your views in a class discussion.

1 "Drugs are a serious problem for the whole of society."

"The drugs problem is exaggerated by the media."

2 "It was right to reclassify cannabis as a Class B drug."

"Cannabis should be a Class C drug."

3 "Drugs like heroin should be legalised and sold in licensed premises in the way that alcohol is."

"Drugs like heroin are so dangerous and potentially damaging that it would be wrong to legalise them."

4 "If drugs were legalised or decriminalised, drug use would increase considerably."

"Only a few more people would use drugs if they were legalised or decriminalised."

5 "The legalisation or decriminalisation of drugs would cut crime."

"Crime would not drop if drugs were made legal, because you'd still have addicts desperate for money to buy drugs."

6 "Prohibition clearly isn't working, as drugs are readily available and so many people use them."

"Just because people flout the law isn't a good reason to change the law: drugs are dangerous and people need to be protected by the drugs laws."

7 "Legalising drugs wouldn't cut the number of addicts: there would still be a drugs problem."

"Legalising drugs would mean that money could be spent on rehabilitation of addicts rather than on fighting a losing battle against the drug traffickers."

8 "Drugs are here to stay, so we need to adopt a different approach to them."

"You can't get away from the fact that drugs ruin lives, therefore it would be wrong to adopt a different approach to them."

UNIT 17 Emergency first aid

Your Life 5/Year 11

Lesson 1 *Your Life 5*, pages 82–83
Personal wellbeing 3e

Aim: To understand how to deal with an emergency and how to treat a casualty who is unconscious.

Preparation

Make a copy of copymaster 39 (First aid for unconsciousness) for each student.

Starter

Ask the students whether they would know what to do if they were first on the scene in an emergency and someone was badly injured. Invite students to share any experiences they have had in dealing with emergencies and of accidents in which they were given first aid.

Suggested activities

- Read 'Coping with a crisis'. Discuss with the class the advice about what to do when an attack has occurred. Then invite pairs to draw up lists of Do's and Don'ts about giving first aid in a crisis, then share their lists.

- Read 'Dealing with unconsciousness' and discuss what the priorities are when dealing with an unconscious person. Invite two students to demonstrate how to put someone into the recovery position.

Plenary

Remind students that in a crisis your own safety must come first, and explain that the golden rule of first aid is not to do anything that will cause the casualty further harm. Recap how their first priorities in an emergency must always be the ABC of first aid.

Extension activities

- Test students' understanding of how to deal with an unconscious casualty by asking them to complete copymaster 39, and then get them to compare and check their answers.

- Ask students to use the Internet to research what first aid to give in other situations, e.g. for cuts and severe bleeding, for a fracture, for burns and scalds. They could prepare presentations to give to the rest of the class, perhaps inviting a question-and-answer session.

- Ask students to find out which groups offer first aid courses in your area. Suggest they invite someone, e.g. from St John Ambulance (www.sja.org.uk) or the Red Cross (www.redcross.org.uk) to give a first aid talk to the class. Alternatively get them to investigate the setting up of an after-school 'First aid club'.

39 First aid for unconsciousness

Answer these questions on your own. Then join up with a partner, compare your answers and check them against the information on page 75 of *Your Life 5*.

1 List three common causes of unconsciousness.

_____

_____

_____

2 What are your three priorities in dealing with an unconscious person?

_____

_____

_____

3 Why is an unconscious person in danger of choking to death?

_____

_____

_____

4 When is it dangerous to move an unconscious person?

_____

_____

_____

5 Draw diagrams and write instructions explaining how to put someone in the recovery position.

UNIT 17 Emergency first aid

Your Life 5/Year 11

Lesson 2 *Your Life 5*, pages 84–85
Personal wellbeing 3e

Aim: To understand how to treat someone for shock and to know how to give artificial respiration to someone who has stopped breathing.

Preparation

Make a copy of copymaster 40 (Cardio-pulmonary resuscitation) for each student.

Starter

- The information and activities in this lesson will be most effective if included as a follow-up to a talk and demonstration by a first aid trainer, e.g. someone from the local St John Ambulance, whom you have invited in to speak to the class.

- Write the terms 'shock', 'artificial ventilation' and 'resuscitation' on the board and discuss their meanings, explaining that shock is a medical condition which people may develop in certain circumstances (e.g. after a severe accident), and that anyone suffering from severe shock needs urgent medical attention.

Suggested activities

- Read and discuss the information on shock, then get the students to make notes for their files under the headings: 'What shock is'; 'What causes shock'; 'The symptoms of shock'; 'How to treat shock'.

- Study and discuss the explanation of mouth-to-mouth resuscitation, and then ask the students, in pairs, to take it in turns, without referring to the book, to explain to each other how to give mouth-to-mouth resuscitation.

- Read the information on 'Cardio-pulmonary resuscitation (CPR)', then ask students to complete the 'For your file' activity.

Plenary

Recap what you should and should not do when treating someone for shock. You could do this by drawing two columns on the board and listing the actions to take and not to take as 'Dos' and 'Don'ts'.

Extension activities

Give out copymaster 40 and read it to the class. Stress how important it is to be trained in the use of this technique and the dangers of using it if someone's heartbeat is very weak. It is included to make students aware of this life-saving technique as a way of resuscitating someone, so that some of them may be encouraged to sign up for a first aid course in order to learn it.

Further resources

A leaflet 'Basic Advice on First Aid at Work' is available from the Health and Safety Executive website www.hse.gov.uk

40 Cardio-pulmonary resuscitation (CPR)

If a person's heart has stopped beating, it may be possible to get it working again by external cardiac massage, using the technique known as cardio-pulmonary resuscitation. Only a trained first aider should do this, as there are dangers involved if you start to use it on someone whose heartbeat is very weak. It can cause their heart to beat very irregularly and it may stop completely.

How to tell if someone's heart has stopped beating

- Check for a pulse. The best place to find if they have a pulse is in the neck, because the neck pulse is stronger than the wrist pulse. If there is no pulse, the heart has stopped.
- Look at the colour of their face. Very pale skin and blueness round their lips are signs that the heart has stopped beating.
- Look at their pupils, which will be very enlarged if their heart has stopped.

A person whose heart has stopped will also have stopped breathing. So providing external cardiac massage by giving chest compressions to restart the heart must always be combined with artificial respiration to restart the casualty's breathing.

Note: The technique described below is for giving cardio-pulmonary resuscitation (CPR) to an adult. The guidelines for giving it to babies and children under the age of 8 are different.

Giving CPR to an adult

1. ASSESS CASUALTY FOR CIRCULATION
- ➤ Check the pulse for up to 10 seconds, and look for other signs of recovery, such as return of skin colour or any movement.
- ➤ **IF you cannot find the pulse,** or there are no other signs of recovery, begin CPR immediately.

2. POSITION HANDS FOR CHEST COMPRESSIONS
- ➤ Place the middle finger of your lower hand over the point where the lowermost ribs meet the breastbone.
- ➤ Place your index finger above it on the breastbone.
- ➤ Place the heel of your other hand on the breastbone, slide it down to meet your index finger.
- ➤ Place the heel of your first hand on top of the other hand, and interlock your fingers.

3. GIVE CHEST COMPRESSIONS AND MOUTH-TO-MOUTH
- ➤ Lean well over the casualty with your arms straight.
- ➤ Press down vertically on the breastbone and depress it by approximately 4–5cm.
- ➤ Complete 15 chest compressions, aiming for about 100 per minute.
- ➤ Give two breaths of mouth-to-mouth ventilation.
- ➤ Continue alternating 15 chest compressions with two breaths of mouth-to-mouth ventilation.

UNIT 18 Thinking ahead – planning your future

Lesson 1 *Your Life 5*, pages 86–87
Economic wellbeing and financial capability 1.1a, 1.1b, 1.1c, 1.2c, 2.1c, 2.1d, 2.2a, 2.3c, 2.3d, 4e, 4j

> **Aim:** To examine choices in education, work or training available after the end of Year 11.

Preparation

Make a copy of copymaster 41 (Choosing the way ahead) for each student.

Starter

Get students in groups to discuss how they feel about their future after Year 11. Do they have clear ideas, or are they confused? Get a spokesperson to report back to the class with a summary of the group's range of feelings, and a list of the key things that they need to know.

Suggested activities

- Students read 'What are your options at 16?' and the case studies and, in small groups, discuss what they have learnt. The groups should draw up a full list of the pros and cons of each of the three main options, and report back in a whole class discussion.

- On their own, students write a personal statement about their choices after Year 11. The quiz on copymaster 25 may help them to organise their ideas first.

Plenary

Ask students to write a sentence saying if they are clearer about their options at the end of the lesson than at the beginning, and why. Get them to write another sentence, if necessary, outlining what they still need to know. Ask students to read out their sentences. Tell the class that they will be exploring further education and training in more detail next lesson, and that this may answer some of their specific questions.

Extension activities

Students write a reply to Jennifer.

Further resources

- The DfES booklet for choices at 16+, *It's your Choice* is available at www.connexions-direct.com/itsyourchoice

- Interactive careers guidance can be found at www.fasttomato.com

41 Choosing the way ahead

Which track would suit you best? Circle all the statements you agree with, then add up the number of shapes.

I want to....

⭐ **1** Achieve more qualifications after GCSEs.

🔺 **2** Start work, but I would like to get qualifications at the same time.

✚ **3** Take more qualifications, but I am not sure which ones would be best for me.

⭐ **4** Study subjects I am good at and interest me.

🔺 **5** Gain a qualification that will help me do my job.

✚ **6** Get some advice about the best type of qualification for me to take.

⭐ **7** Take a full-time course at school or college.

🔺 **8** Work and study part time.

✚ **9** Find out more about the job that suits me and then work out the best track to take.

⭐ **10** Earn more money in the long term by getting lots of qualifications.

🔺 **11** Work and earn a wage now.

✚ **12** Get some advice about how I could get help to pay for the course I want to do.

⭐ **13** Get higher level qualifications that will help me to get the job I want.

🔺 **14** Just get started at work.

✚ **15** Get some help, as I'm confused!

How many did you agree with?

3–5 ⭐ Staying on at school, or going to college full-time, seems to be the way you are thinking at the moment. Think about the subjects you're going to take, and find out more about the types of courses on offer. Look into NVQs and Vocational A levels, e.g. in business or health. There are loads available, and they can lead to university and/or employment. It will help you to find out if there is any financial help available to you and how much higher education will cost.

3–5 🔺 Starting work, maybe on an apprenticeship or other training programme, looks like the most suitable route for you. As an apprentice you will be able to earn a wage or training allowance and study for qualifications at the same time. Find out more about the different types of apprentice. Focus on building the skills you need to succeed in getting a job.

3–5 ✚ **(or a mix)** You seem to be unsure at the moment about what to do and should ask for some advice from your careers teacher or Connexions personal adviser. They will be able to help you decide what to do next. It might be that you need help to resolve a problem before you can make a decision, or you might feel there are too many choices on offer. Whatever the reason, do ask for help. You're not on your own.

Source: www.connexions-direct.com

UNIT 18 Thinking ahead – planning your future

Your Life 5/Year 11

Lesson 2 *Your Life 5*, pages 88–89
Economic wellbeing and financial capability 1.1a, 1.1b, 1.1c, 1.2c, 2.1c, 2.1d, 2.2a, 2.3c, 2.3d, 4e, 4j

Aim: To explore the options of further education and training.

Preparation

Make a copy of copymaster 42 (Apprenticeships: your questions answered) for each group; gather a selection of job adverts.

Starter

Recap the previous lesson and invite the students to remind themselves of any further things they needed to know by looking again at what they wrote during the Plenary session of Lesson 1.

Suggested activities

● Divide the class into small groups according to whether students are thinking about staying in full-time education or training/employment and get groups to discuss the questions that relate to their chosen path on page 88. Groups of students who are unsure should look at both boxes if possible. Students will need to read 'Looking at qualifications in depth' and refer to the 'Qualifications at a glance' table to inform themselves and the discussion. Give copymaster 26 to those who may be considering apprenticeships.

● Ask students to chart two possible routes for their future, on their own (see 'For your file'). Explain to the students that the table and notes on qualifications tend to simplify a complex and changing area. Courses are increasingly flexible, so that they can mix vocational and general courses, even at different levels, and combine NVQs with other qualifications.

Plenary

Ask students to read out their routes for the future. Ask for comments from the class.

Extension activities

Students look at a selection of job adverts and note down the basic facts about four jobs, one at each level of qualifications. They can conclude with a personal statement about what they have learnt from the exercise about their own future qualifications and career.

Further resources

www.apprenticeships.org.uk has information on apprenticeships.

www.dius.gov.uk has a downloadable booklet 'Your Future, Your Choice'

Your Life 5/Year 11

Apprenticeships: your questions answered

Apprenticeships: your questions answered

Q **Are there different types of apprenticeship?**

A There are over 190 types of apprenticeship available across many sectors of industry. Which apprenticeship is right for you will depend on your experience and the opportunities in your area. However, all apprenticeships include the following basic elements:

- an appropriate National Vocational Qualification (NVQ) at either Level 2 or Level 3;
- Key Skills qualifications (Application of Number; Communication, ICT), e.g. working in teams, problem-solving, communication and using new technology;
- a technical qualification such as a BTEC or City & Guilds (relevant to the specific apprenticeship)
- other qualifications or requirements as specified by the particular occupation.

Q **How long does an apprenticeship take?**

A There is no set time to complete an apprenticeship as they vary widely in content and size. The length of time taken will depend on the ability of the individual apprentice and the employer's requirements. An apprenticeship will typically take anything from 1 to 4 years.

Q **How do apprenticeships work?**

A Your employer pays your wages and gives you on-the-job training which allows you to achieve National Vocational Qualifications (NVQs). You will also spend time with a learning provider, gaining key skills that'll be useful in the job market, such as working in teams, problem-solving, communication and using new technology. In addition, you will study for a technical certificate, which will give you further knowledge and understanding of your job.

Q **How much do I get paid?**

A Most apprentices are employed by business and are paid a salary that reflects their skills, experience, age and ability.

Q **Do I get holidays?**

A You will receive at least twenty days holiday per year (including bank holidays). Your individual entitlement will be detailed in your terms of employment or training agreement.

Q **What qualifications do I get when I've finished my apprenticeship?**

A You will get a package of qualifications when you finish your apprenticeship: a National Vocational Qualification (NVQ), a technical certificate such as a BTEC National Diploma or a City & Guilds Progression Award, and Key Skills qualifications. Apprenticeships lead to either an NVQ Level 2 or an NVQ Level 3. Apprenticeships can also help you to enter higher education.

Q **How do NVQs relate to other qualifications?**

A There are five levels of NVQ:

- Level 1 = 5 GCSEs at grades D–G
- Level 2 = 5 GCSEs at grades A–C
- Level 3 = 2 A levels/1 vocational A level
- Level 4/5 = HNC, HND and degree level

Source: www.apprenticeships.org.uk

UNIT 18 Thinking ahead – planning your future

Your Life 5/Year 11

Lesson 3 *Your Life 5*, pages 90–91
Economic wellbeing and financial capability 1.1c, 2.1c, 2.1d, 3f

> **Aim:** To understand what makes a good application form and CV, and how to prepare for an interview.

Preparation

Make a copy of copymaster 43 (A letter of application) for each student; gather a selection job adverts; prepare examples of traditional and skills-based CVs, if possible.

Starter

Put these statements on the board: 'It's not what you know – it's who you know', 'If you're bad at interviews you won't get a good job' and 'It's how you look on paper that really counts'. Get small groups to discuss how these statements may or may not relate to applying for jobs. What are the students most concerned about?

Suggested activities

- Pairs of students read sections 1 and 2 of 'Job applications'. They then draft a letter of application for a job advertised in the paper.

- Go through the skills-based example on page 91, and show students an example of a traditional CV, if possible. Discuss the advantages and disadvantages of each. Students then write their own CV.

- Pairs read the article on preparing for interviews and list the three best pieces of advice.

Plenary

Ask pairs of students for their lists of top tips for preparing for interviews. Does the rest of the class agree?

Extension activities

- Give pairs copymaster 43, which consists of a badly written letter of application. Students should comment on: the untidiness; the missing date and address/phone number of the applicant; the inappropriate start (Keith should state that he is applying for the job at the start); the bad spelling and grammar; more details of work experience and details of relevant experience in general needed; inappropriate chatty tone; an evaluation of his character and why he'd be good at the job are missing; full contact details of two referees are missing.

- Students role-play interviewing each other for a job or college course that they are interested in.

- Get students to write an advice leaflet on how to write a job application letter or CV, or on how to prepare for an interview.

Further resources

www.whatwilltheyask.co.uk has advice on writing a CV and tips on job interviews.

43 A letter of application

Keith has applied for the trainee sales assistant job advertised in the local paper (right).

Read his letter of application (below) and annotate it to suggest how it could be improved.

Is it:

- appropriate and relevant
- well organised
- in good English
- set out like a letter
- neat and tidy?

> **Wanted**
> B&B JEWELLERS
> Trainee sales assistant required to work in busy jewellers.
> You need to be:
> - good with customers
> - keen on sales
> - willing to train.

Mrs J Butler
B&B Jewellers
High Street

Dear Mrs Butler

You may remember that I came in with a folty watch the other week and was very interested in what you did as a jewler. Well, I'm still very interested!

I've just finished (hurrah!) at Wye Valley High School. My results arent out yet though, I am hoping to pass English, Art and ICT GCSEs and a BTEC Business coarse. So I want to start work while training, ideally in a shop. Yours!

While at school, I did a 2 weeks work experience placement. I've also had a job washing up in the Britannia for a year or so which was really dull, I'm obviously meant for better things!!

So I hope you'll give me the job of 'trainee sales assistant'. It was advertised in the Jobs and Career's newspaper yesterday.

The head at Wye Valley High School will give you a reference if you write to her.

Yours sincerely

Keith Paterson

Your Life KS4 Co-ordinator's File © *HarperCollinsPublishers.* This page may be photocopied for use in the classroom.

UNIT 19 Managing your money

Your Life 5/Year 11

Lesson 1 *Your Life 5*, pages 92–93
Economic wellbeing and financial capability 1.2b, 1.3b, 2.2a, 2.4a, 2.4b, 2.4c, 3h, 4a

Aim: To explore the world of borrowing, credit and debt, so as to be able to make informed and prudent choices when thinking about borrowing money.

Preparation

Make copies of copymaster 44 (Forms of borrowing) for each student (or each pair).

Starter

Note that debt is an issue that requires sensitivity as some students may have personal experience of the hardships and stress that being in debt causes families. Put the terms 'borrowing/loan', 'credit', 'mortgage' and 'debt' on the board and ask the class what they mean. Make sure they understand that some borrowing is almost unavoidable in the real world, e.g. to buy a house, but also that getting into debt is an increasing problem. Ask for reasons for this, e.g. the ease of getting credit and credit cards; lack of financial management skills.

Suggested activities

- Read 'Borrowing money' with the class. Ensure students understand what interest is, and how it is worked out. Emphasise the importance of money management in not getting into debt. Pairs compose a quiz for each other.

- Allow time for questions about issues they don't understand, and then ask groups to plan and role-play a radio phone-in programme about borrowing money in which an expert answers young people's questions about the purpose and pros/cons of each main method of borrowing. They should plan the programme by making a list of questions for the young people to ask and discussing the answers that the expert is going to give. When groups have rehearsed their programmes, ask one or two groups to present their programmes to the rest of the class.

- Pairs discuss how to reply to Trefor's letter (see 'For your file'), and then individuals draft a reply.

Plenary

Ask students to read out their replies and invite comments from the rest of the class. Emphasise the danger of getting caught up in credit card debt, especially when you are not earning.

Extension activities

- For differentiation, as an alternative to the radio programme presentation, pairs should be given the cards on copymaster 28 and asked to group them into the four categories of borrowing, together with their description/purpose and the pros and cons of each.

- Students research two different credit cards and two store cards. How do they compare in terms of interest rates and other details?

Further resources

- The Citizenship Foundation's guide to basic finance, *Money money money*, includes material on credit cards and borrowing money in its guide 'Banks, building societies and plastic cards' (see www.citfou.org.uk/money).

- The RBS/Nat West MoneySense for schools programme includes a module on borrowing, debt and the importance of saving (see www.natwest.com/moneysenseforschools).

44 Forms of borrowing

Credit cards

Purpose/method: to buy things now and pay for them later. If you pay off the whole amount of the bill, you don't get charged any interest. But if you pay less than the full amount, you are charged interest on the whole lot.

Pros: convenient, and a good way of getting an interest-free loan if you pay off the outstanding balance each month.

Cons: an expensive way of borrowing in the long-term if you are only able to pay off a small amount of what you owe each month.

Overdraft

Purpose/method: to spend more money than you have in your bank account. It is best to arrange this in advance with your bank, to avoid paying huge fees and interest.

Pros: this can be a cheap flexible way to help with temporary cash flow problems – some accounts even allow you to go overdrawn a small amount each month without charges.

Cons: an expensive way of borrowing if it hasn't been arranged with the bank in advance. Not suitable for longer-term borrowing.

Bank loan

Purpose/method: to borrow a large amount over a period of time, say to pay for a car or music system. You agree to make a fixed payment each month for a set number of years.

Pros: a good way of paying for long-term borrowing, as it allows you to plan your finances. Often the person selling the goods can arrange the loan for you.

Cons: not very flexible, and watch out for the interest rates on the loan.

Hire purchase

Purpose/method: to pay for goods in instalments. You only become the legal owner of the goods when you have paid off the final instalment.

Pros: allows you to pay off a purchase over a long period of time, in a planned way.

Cons: an expensive way of borrowing money, and you don't own the goods until you have paid off the whole loan.

UNIT 19 Managing your money

Aim: To understand the financial aspects of starting work.

Preparation

Make a copy of copymaster 45 (What do you know about money in the real world?) for each student. Gather copies of the 'situations vacant' pages from local newspapers.

Starter

Ask if any students have part-time jobs (if not, their siblings may) and jot details on the board of job description, hours, rate of pay, age of student etc. Ask groups to study the information and discuss what they learn about money and work, and what questions they may have. Ask groups to report their findings and questions. Make it clear that all their questions cannot be answered in this lesson, but that the questions indicate the complexities of the world of work.

Suggested activities

- Read 'How do I get paid?' with the class and ensure they understand the basic terms.
- Get groups to read the articles 'The ins and outs of part-time jobs' and 'Minimum wage for young people is pathetic', and to discuss them, e.g. do they agree that 16–18 year olds should work no more than 48 hours per week? (NB this refers to school leavers). Do they agree with the views expressed in the article 'Minimum wage for young people is pathetic'?
- Read the article 'Your first payslip' with the class and ensure they understand the terminology and the purpose of each entry on the payslip. Invite brief discussion on the fairness of having so many deductions from the gross pay, and ensure they understand what the benefits are.
- Pairs read Christine's letter, discuss her questions and draft a reply. (see 'For your file')

Plenary

Ask students to read out their replies to Christine's letter and invite comments from the rest of the class.

Ask students to jot down three facts that they have learned about money and the world of work, and elicit feedback.

Extension activities

- Get pairs to research jobs advertised in the local paper and compare the rates of pay and hours offered. They can prepare their presentations to any degree of complexity, depending on the amount of time available.
- Hand out copymaster 45 to individuals (or pairs, for differentiation) to test their financial knowledge of this unit. The answers are: 1b, 2a, 3a, 4c, 5a, 6b, 7a, 8c, 9c, 10b.

Further resources

- The Citizenship Foundation's guide to basic finance, *Money money money*, includes guides to starting work and claiming benefits (see www.citfou.org.uk/money).
- www.thesite.org has information on workers' rights and what's on your payslip.

45 What do you know about money in the real world?

Complete this multiple-choice quiz to test how much you know about money in the real world of credit and jobs.

1 When do banks and other lenders start offering young people loans and credit cards?

   a) When you are 16

   b) When you are 18

   c) When you are 21

2 What is the interest on a loan?

   a) The extra amount that you have to pay, as the price for taking out the loan

   b) The amount that you have to pay back each month

   c) The amount that you get back if you pay off the loan early

3 Which is the better deal, a loan at 10% APR or one at 20% APR?

   a) The loan at 10% APR

   b) The loan at 20% APR

   c) They are both the same in the long run

4 What is an overdraft?

   a) The extra amount that you have to pay, in order to take out a loan

   b) The total amount that you owe a credit card company

   c) A form of borrowing from the bank, because you spend more money out of your account than you have in it

5 What is hire purchase?

   a) An agreement to pay for goods in instalments

   b) The additional price that you pay for borrowing money

   c) A short-term loan at a high rate of interest

6 If your salary is £12 000 per year, how much will your gross pay be each month?

   a) £12 000

   b) £1000

   c) Less than £1000

7 Your personal allowance is:

   a) the amount you are allowed to earn before tax is deducted

   b) what you are left with after all deductions from your pay

   c) the minimum that you must be paid by an employer

8 A commission of 5% on the sales you make each month means:

   a) you get paid an extra 5% salary each month

   b) you have to pay 5% National Insurance contributions each month

   c) you get paid 5% of the sales you make on top of your basic income

9 The national minimum wage of £5.80:

   a) applies to everyone over 16

   b) applies to everyone over 18

   c) applies to everyone over 22

10 What is net pay?

   a) Your total earnings before all deductions have been made for tax, NI and pension

   b) Your total earnings after all deductions have been made for tax, NI and pension

   c) The total amount of the deductions made for tax, NI and pension

UNIT 20 The UK economy

Your Life 5/Year 11

Lesson 1 *Your Life 5*, pages 96–97
Economic wellbeing and financial capability 1.4a; Citizenship 2.1a, 2.1b, 3j, 4a

Aim: To explore how the economy functions.

Preparation

Make a copy of copymaster 46 (The economy – true or false) for each student.

Starter

Ask individuals to make a list of all the goods and services that they have used so far during the day. Invite some of them to share their lists.

Suggested activities

- Read 'What is the economy?' Emphasise that the size of the manufacturing sector of the economy has decreased in recent years, while the size of the service sector has expanded. Focus on the paragraph on GNP and make sure the students understand it.

- Write the terms 'capitalism' and 'socialism' on the board and invite students to look them up in their dictionaries. Read 'Economic systems', then ask the students to discuss the questions that follow in groups, before sharing their views in a class discussion.

Plenary

On their own, ask students to write down three key facts about the UK economy that they have learned from the lesson. Invite some of them to share what they have written in a class discussion.

Extension activities

- Ask individuals to complete the True or False quiz on Copymaster 46, then in pairs to check their answers by looking at the information on pages 96–97. The answers are 1. False; 2. True; 3. False; 4. False; 5. True; 6. False; 7. True; 8. True; 9. False; 10. True.

- In groups, ask students to think about your town/local area. What are the most important parts of the local economy ? Are there any areas their town specialises in? Does any single industry/business dominate? If so, what effects do decisions made by the business have on the local economy? Share their ideas in a class discussion.

46 The economy – true or false

On your own

Study each statement and write down whether it is true or false. Then compare your answers with those of a partner and together check whether you are right or wrong by looking again at the information on pages 96–99.

	TRUE	FALSE
1 The number of manufacturing businesses has remained the same in the last 60 years.	☐	☐
2 A country's Gross National Product (GNP) is measured by adding up the value of all the goods and services it produces in a year.	☐	☐
3 A manufacturer's profit is calculated by deducting the cost of raw materials from the price paid by the consumer.	☐	☐
4 Specialisation drives costs up because businesses have to rely on buying in bulk.	☐	☐
5 A capitalist economy is one based on the private ownership of the means of production, distribution and exchange.	☐	☐
6 Small businesses prosper because they can achieve the same economies of scale as large businesses.	☐	☐
7 The Conservative Party has traditionally supported a free market.	☐	☐
8 One of the drawbacks of large firms is that they can monopolise markets.	☐	☐
9 In a socialist economy there is less public ownership of industries than in a capitalist economy.	☐	☐
10 Businesses may be more interested in keeping costs down than in the environmental wellbeing of a local area.	☐	☐

UNIT 20 The UK economy

Your Life 5/Year 11

Lesson 2 *Your Life 5*, pages 98–99
Economic wellbeing and financial capability 1.4a, 4i; Citizenship 2.1a, 2.1b, 3j, 4a

Aim: To understand how the government manages the economy and how it collects and spends money.

Preparation

Make a copy of copymaster 47 (The economy – word quiz) for each student.

Starter

Ask who the Chancellor of the Exchequer is and what he does. Explain what the budget is and that like every household in the country the government has to make sure that it balances its books and that expenditure doesn't exceed income.

Suggested activities

- Read 'Managing the economy'. Focus on each section in turn to make sure the students understand the reasons why the government tries to control inflation and unemployment, what a recession is and the different ways of managing a recession.

- Discuss what the effects of the 2008–10 recession had on the national economy and on the local economy, before inviting groups to share their views on whether the Labour government was right to spend so much public money to manage the economy during the recession.

- Students read 'Government taxation'. Ask groups to role play being members of the government and to decide whether they are going to reduce the debt by raising direct or indirect taxes.

- Students study 'Government expenditure'. Students, in groups, then imagine they are members of the government and consider how they would spend their budget. What areas would they prioritise? In which areas would they cut spending? Ask them to give reasons for their views. Draw a pie chart for how you would spend your revenue. Compare your pie chart with those of other groups in the class.

Plenary

Discuss the current state of the UK economy. What do the students think should be the main priority of the Chancellor of the Exchequer in their next budget – increasing public spending and/or raising taxes or cutting public spending and/or reducing taxes?

Extension activities

- Copymaster 47 provides a matching activity that can be used to test the students' knowledge of economic terms that are introduced in this unit. It can be completed by either individuals or pairs, who can then check their answers by looking at the text in the student's book.

- Research on the Internet what the current rate of inflation, interest rates and unemployment are, and how these have changed over the last year. Draw a graph showing the trend for the last year.

Further resources

www.bized.co.uk has a worksheet on taxation.

COPYMASTER

47 The economy – word quiz

○ On your own

Look at the following ten words, and their definitions which have been mixed up. Match the words with the correct definitions. Then compare your answers with a partner. When you have finished, you can check your answers on pages 96–99 of *Your Life 5*.

Recession	A tax which each household pays to help finance local government.
Inflation	Value added tax – the tax we pay on goods and services, which is set at 17.5%.
Unemployment	The amount you are charged to borrow money each year.
Interest rates	A period of time during which the economy contracts.
Deflation	Taxes that are placed on goods or services.
Direct taxation	Money which the government provides in benefits to help people who are sick, ill, etc.
Indirect taxation	Taxes that are deducted from the amount you earn, and depend on how much money you earn.
National Insurance	An increase in the general level of prices.
Council tax	A form of direct taxation, which provides insurance to us if we are injured or sick.
VAT	A fall in prices caused by a reduction in economic activity.
Social security	The number of people out of work, who don't have a job.

Extension activity

Name 5 major areas of Government expenditure.

❶ _____

❷ _____

❸ _____

❹ _____

❺ _____

UNIT 21 The global economy

Lesson 1 *Your Life 5*, pages 100–101
(Economic wellbeing and financial capability 1.4a; Citizenship 2.1a, 2.1b, 3j, 3n, 4a)

> **Aim:** To examine global economic development and how globalisation has brought both benefits and problems.

Preparation

Make a copy of Copymaster 48 (Banks and the Credit Crunch) for each student.

Starter

Ask students what goods or services come into their mind when they think of Japan. Record the answers, e.g. cars, electronic goods, computers.

Suggested activities

- Read 'How the global economy works'. Ask groups of students to think of three other countries and what they may specialise in.

- Examine 'Globalisation', 'Case Study – The Fashion Industry' and 'Problems in the global economy'. Invite groups to draw up lists of the benefits and drawbacks of globalisation and to discuss how globalisation has produced winners and losers.

- Read 'The credit crunch'. Discuss with the class what effect the credit crunch had in your local area before inviting individuals to write about it and its effects (see 'For your file' page 101).

Plenary

Pairs of students imagine that due to a natural disaster the supply of raw materials to the largest industry in an area is cut off and list what the effects would be. They then share their lists in a class discussion.

Extension activities

- Give pairs Copymaster 48 Banks and the Credit Crunch to study. Ask them to discuss the causes and effects of the credit crunch, then to use the internet to find out more about it.

- Students look at newspapers, the TV news, and on the internet to find events over the last month that will affect the global economy. Which countries do they think the events will affect? Ask students to write down their views, and compare them with others in the class.

Further resources

Key facts about the global economy can be found at news.bbc.co.uk/2/shared/spl/hi/guides/457000/457

48 Banks and the Credit Crunch

The credit crunch was caused by the collapse of the banking system in 2008, when banks around the world found that they had lent too much money to people who could not repay it.

How do banks work?

Banks obtain money from –
ordinary people depositing their savings
shareholders investing their money
businesses and ordinary people repaying loans
borrowing money from other banks.

Banks lend money to –
ordinary people (e.g. who take out mortgages to buy a house)
businesses (e.g. to build a new factory) other banks

Why do banks stop lending?

In difficult times, businesses may not be able to repay loans.

People may be unable to make their mortgage repayments.

The banks have less cash, so they stop lending money – to individuals, businesses and to other banks.

How does this cause a crisis?

Ordinary people fear that the banks are running out of money, so they withdraw their savings. People queue up outside banks to take their money out. At the same time, other banks try to withdraw their loans.

The banks become even more short of cash. They try to preserve what money they have. When the banks all reduce their lending at the same time, no one can borrow money easily. This is called a credit crunch.

What are the effects of a credit crunch?

Businesses suffer because they cannot borrow money either to help them in difficult times or to invest in new developments.

Homeowners suffer because mortgages are harder to arrange.

Retailers suffer because it is more difficult for consumers to get credit.

Unemployment rises as businesses try to save money by cutting jobs or stopping hiring new employees.

The whole economy suffers a downturn and the government is forced to step in to save banks from going bankrupt.

Adapted from 'The credit crunch' www.teachable.net C Teachable and Edward Upton

In pairs

Read the article and then answer the following questions:

1 How were banks responsible for the credit crunch?

2 What effects did the credit crunch have?

Use the internet to find out more about why the credit crunch happened and its effects on the world economy.

UNIT 21 The global economy

Your Life 5/Year 11

Lesson 2 *Your Life 5*, pages 102–103
(Economic wellbeing and financial capability 1.4a; Citizenship 2.1a, 2.1b, 3j, 3n, 4a)

Aim: To examine how free trade has created economic growth bringing prosperity to some countries but not others.

Preparation

Make a copy of Copymaster 49 (The Global Economy – True or False) for each student.

Starter

Ask: Why is it in a country's interests to trade with other countries? Elicit points such as to make money by selling the goods and services it produces; to obtain goods that it can't or doesn't make itself; the more trade a country does the more prosperous it will become.

Suggested activities

- Read 'Free trade'. Discuss what free trade means, what perfect competition is and why it does not exist in practice.

- Ask groups to read 'Free trade = Unequal trade', 'Subsidies and tariffs' and 'Free trade and the environment' and to discuss why free trade benefits rich countries rather than poor countries.

- Study 'Economic growth' and explain that countries fall into two categories – more economically developed countries and less economically developed countries. Discuss why some countries e.g. China and India do not fit into either category.

Plenary

Ask students to write down 2 or 3 key facts about free trade that they have learned during the lesson. Invite a number of them to share what they have written.

Extension activities

Give individuals a copy of Copymaster 49 – The Global Economy –True or False?' Ask them to complete the activity, then to join up with a partner to compare their answers. The correct answers are: 1 False 2 True 3 True 4 False 5 True 6 False 7 False 8 True 9 False 10 True.

The Global Economy – True or False?

◉ On your own

Decide whether each statement is true or false. Then join up with a partner and compare your answers.

	TRUE	FALSE

1 When the price of oil is high, goods become more competitive and the whole economy benefits.

2 Globalisation is the process whereby the countries of the world become economically interdependent.

3 Free trade is international trade which is not hampered by government interference.

4 A subsidy is a type of loan given to a company in danger of going bankrupt.

5 A tariff is a tax levied on imports or exports.

6 OPEC stands for the Organisation for the Protection of European Commerce.

7 Business failures and unemployment went down during the credit crunch.

8 Free trade benefits richer countries more than poorer ones.

9 India's rapid economic growth during recent decades has eradicated poverty throughout the country.

10 Economic slavery is the term used to describe a situation in which a worker receives little or no pay.

UNIT 21 The global economy

Your Life 5/Year 11

Lesson 3 *Your Life 5*, pages 104–105
(Economic wellbeing and financial capability 1.4a, 3k; Citizenship 2.1a, 2.1b, 3j, 3n, 4a)

Aim: To understand what multi-national corporations are, their benefits and drawbacks and how exploitation of workers can amount to economic slavery.

Preparation

Make a copy of copymaster 50 (Globalisation – A force for good?) for each student.

Starter

Write the term 'multi-national corporation' on the board and discuss what it means. Then encourage the students to suggest examples. Prompt them, as necessary, by suggesting that examples can be found among banks, oil companies, the technology industry and the car industry.

Suggested activities

- Read 'Multi-national corporations' and 'Do multinationals help or harm?'. Invite groups to list the advantages and disadvantages that the operations of multi-national corporations can bring to a country.

- Students, in pairs, draft a press release listing the advantages that an investment of £100 million by a multinational corporation MEGA will bring to an LEDC. (See 'In pairs' p. 104)

- Pairs design a poster as part of a campaign to point out the drawbacks of the ways that multinationals operate. (See 'In pairs' p. 104)

- Read 'Problems with multinational corporations', then invite groups to do the role play about a multinational corporation discussing whether it should relocate a factory (see p. 105)

- Discuss what the term 'economic slavery' means and read the case study. Then encourage individuals to research other examples of economic slavery on the internet, before writing an e-mail protesting about the exploitation of workers, particularly child workers.

Plenary

Ask students: Who believes that multinational corporations do more harm than good? Have a show of hands and invite some of them to explain why they voted as they did.

Extension activities

- Give students a copy of Copymaster 50 Globalisation – A force for good? Groups discuss the statements, then individuals write their views of globalisation.

- Students individually research examples of economic slavery on the internet, then draft an e-mail protesting about the exploitation of workers, especially child workers.

50 Globalisation – A force for good?

'Many multi-nationals bring great benefits to the countries in which they invest, providing additional capital, helping to transfer new technologies, increasing local skills and generating employment. And all the evidence suggests that multinationals do pay their workers significantly better than local employers and provide better protection.'

Mike O'Brien, MP

'Globalisation means that large multi-nationals have enormous power. Companies make decisions based on how much profit they can make and what is best for their shareholders. So they locate their factories where labour is cheap and they can keep wages low. Thus the rich get richer and the poor stay poor.'

Erica Stewart

'Some people say that globalisation is destroying local culture. But if it brings economic growth and lifts people out of poverty, then it's a price worth paying.'

John Scotby

'One problem of globalisation is that it has increased the use of non-renewable resources. It has also contributed to increased pollution and global warming. Firms can also outsource production to where environmental standards are less strict.'

from www.economicshelp.org

'In Bangladesh the growth of the garment industry has created over one million jobs – most of them for women. Each of these jobs supports children on schools, provides access to nutrition and pays for health care.'

Kevin Watkins, Oxfam

'Economic growth brought about by globalisation can have a positive effect not only raising living standards, but also bringing improvements to a country's infrastructure. In addition, as a country's wealth increases, more of the population have money left over to buy consumer goods, after they have bought the necessities.'

Suresh Patel

UNIT 21 The global economy

Your Life 5/Year 11

Lesson 4 *Your Life 5*, pages 106–107
(Economic wellbeing and financial capability 1.4a, 3k, 4a; Citizenship 2.1a, 2.1b, 3j, 3n, 4a)

Aim: To understand what fair trade is and how the Ethical Trading Initiative works to improve the working conditions of workers around the world.

Preparation

Make a copy of copymaster 51 (Fairtrade) for each student.

Starter

Ask students what they think fair trade and ethical trading are and to draft definitions of them for a dictionary. Compare some of them in a class discussion.

Suggested activities

- Read the information on fair trade and the case study. Ask students, in groups, to discuss what the fair trade system is. Then invite them to design a leaflet in order to try to persuade people to change their shopping habits by buying more Fairtrade products.

- Study the information on page 107 about ethical trading, the Ethical Trading Initiative and the ETI Base Code. In pairs, students discuss what ethical trading is and why it is difficult to put into practice. They then individually prepare two-minute talks about the Ethical Trading initiative which they give to each other in small groups.

Plenary

Explain the price of Fairtrade products is often higher, because the workers who produce them are getting paid more. Ask: Do you think most shoppers would be prepared to pay extra to ensure that they are buying only Fairtrade products? How would you try to persuade them to do so?

Extension activities

- Prompt individuals to write an e-mail protesting about the harsh treatment of a worker in a footwear factory (see 'For your file page 107).

- Ask pairs of students to investigate what fair trade products are on sale at their local supermarket. Are they the same price as other non-fair trade products of the same type? Invite them to compare their findings in a whole class discussion.

- Give individuals copies of copymaster 51 (Fairtrade). Prompt students to use the information on the copymaster as the basis for an article for a teenage magazine about fair trade and trade justice.

- Encourage students to research on the internet what groups are campaigning for more fair trade, including the Fairtrade Foundation (www.fairtrade.org.uk) and the Trade Justice Movement at www.tjm.org.uk, and to find out what the school can do to become a Fairtrade School.

Further resources

- Students can find out more about the Ethical Trading Initiative at (www.ethicaltrade.org)

- The World Development movement contains materials on trade justice (see www.wdm.org.uk)

51 Fairtrade

What is Fairtrade?

Fairtrade is about better prices, decent working conditions, local sustainability, and fair terms of trade for farmers and workers in the developing world. By requiring companies to pay sustainable prices (which must never fall lower than the market price), Fairtrade addresses the injustices of conventional trade, which traditionally discriminates against the poorest, weakest producers. It enables them to improve their position and have more control over their lives.

What is the FAIRTRADE mark?

The FAIRTRADE Mark is an independent consumer label which appears on UK products as a guarantee that they have been certified against internationally agreed Fairtrade standards. The Mark indicates that the product has been certified to give a better deal to the producers involved.

Is buying Fairtrade products a good idea?

By buying products that carry the FAIRTRADE Mark, shoppers can be assured that disadvantaged producers and workers in developing countries are getting a better deal: receiving a fair and stable price for their products which covers their costs of production; benefiting from longer-term trading relationships; and receiving the Fairtrade premium – money paid on top of the Fairtrade minimum price that is invested in social, environmental and economic developmental projects decided upon by the producers or workers themselves.

How much of the price paid for Fairtrade products goes to the producers?

Whatever the price paid by the shopper, the FAIRTRADE Mark ensures that the producers receive a fairer price, as well as the social premium to invest in their communities.

Adapted from FAQs on the Fairtrade website
www.fairtrade.org.uk

From www.tjm.org.uk

Use the information on this page to write an article for a teenage magazine about Fairtrade and trade justice.

UNIT 22 Reviewing and recording

Your Life 5/Year 11

Lesson 1 *Your Life 5*, pages 108–109

Aim: To review and record what you have learned from studying the units in *Your Life 5*.

Starter

Explain that the aim of the session is to help the students to reflect on what they have learned from doing the course. Remind them that the course was divided into four sections and explain that you want them to write a statement about each section. To give them an idea of the type of comment they might write, read and discuss what Corinne wrote about what she learned from Unit 11 on marriage and commitment in the 'Developing relationships' section (pages 58–61).

Suggested activities

- Split the class into four groups and ask each group to discuss the questions on one of the four sections. Encourage them to remind themselves of what they did in the units from that section by referring not only to the relevant pages of the student's book, but also to any work based on those units that they have in their files. Suggest that during their discussions they make notes of any particularly important things they feel they learned. Then get them to appoint a reporter to share what they felt they learned from that section of the course with the rest of the class.

- Ask individuals to begin to draft statements on one of the four sections of the course.

Plenary

Share some of their draft statements.

Extension activities

Ask students to finish drafting the statements on the section that they began in the lesson, and then to go on to draft statements on the other three sections.

Acknowledgements

'When being black and driving a Jaguar makes you a criminal' by Michael Eboda, *The Observer*, 23 February 2003, © Observer Newspapers. Used with permission; Extracts from 'Susan takes good care of us' and 'Erdington – What a difference a year makes', © Birmingham City Council; Information on Age UK's priorities reprinted from www.ageconcern.org.uk and www.helptheaged.org.uk; Extracts from 'Enough to make a grown man weep', from *The Independent*, 8 April 2004. Reprinted with permission; Extract from 'Women "suffer poor self-esteem due to airbrushing in advertising"', *The Daily Telegraph*, 27 November 2009, © Telegraph Group Limited 2009. Reprinted with permission; Extracts from *Sisters Unlimited* by Jessica Howie, published by Vermillion. Used by permission of The Random House Group Limited; Extract from *Relationships: What's at Issue?* by K Dunbar, published by Heinemann 2000; Extract from 'At last we can abandon that tosh about low self-esteem', by Polly Toynbee, *The Guardian*, 28 December 2001, © Guardian Newspapers Limited 2001; Extracts from *Adolescence, the survival guide* by E Fenwick and T Smith (Dorling Kindersley Revised Edition 1993) copyright © Dorling Kindersley 1998. Reproduced by permission of Penguin Books Ltd; Extract from 'Is a roof over your head a home?' adapted from www.housemate.org.uk; Extract from *Wise Guides: Eating* by Anita Naik, published by Hodder & Stoughton. Reprinted with permission of Hodder & Stoughton Ltd; Extracts from *The Health and Safety Textercise Book*, copyright Textercise Books. Reprinted with permission; Extract from 'The licence fee could go, admits BBC boss: Cost of watching TV might be put on council tax bill', Mail Online, by Paul Revoir, 5 July 2009. Reprinted with permission of Solo Syndications; 'To have and to hold … What does marriage mean?' by Paula Hall, www.bbc.co.uk; 'When are women becoming mothers?' from www.direct.gov.uk, © Crown Copyright; Extract 'Why smacking is never a good idea' from www.nspcc.org.uk; Homophobic bullying extract from 'Glad to be inclusive', *Education Guardian*, 23 November 2004 © Guardian Newspapers Limited 2004; Extracts from www.connexions-direct.com, © Crown Copyright; Information on Fairtrade and the Ethical Trading Initiative adapted from www.ethicaltrade.org; Extracts 'Young people and knife crime' and 'Focus on knife crime', from www.direct.gov.uk, © Crown Copyright; Know the facts: Carrying knives from Source: www.droptheweapons.org.

NOTES